THE CRIMINAL AREA

THE CRIMINAL AREA

A Study in
Social Ecology

by
TERENCE MORRIS

Foreword by
HERMANN MANNHEIM

GREENWOOD PRESS, PUBLISHERS
WESTPORT, CONNECTICUT

Library of Congress Cataloging in Publication Data

Morris, Terence.
   The criminal area.

   Reprint. Originally published: London :
Routledge & Kegan Paul ; New York : Humanitites
Press, 1958. (International library of sociology
and social reconstruction)
   Includes index.
   1. Criminal behavior, Prediction of. 2. Human
ecology. 3. Environmental psychology. 4. Crime
and criminals--England--London--Case studies.
5. Croydon (London, England)--Case studies. I. Title.
II. Series: International library of sociology and
social reconstruction (Routledge & Kegan Paul)
HV6150.M6 1985   364.2'5   85-8015
ISBN 0-313-24427-8 (lib. bdg. : alk. paper)

Reprinted in 1985 by Greenwood Press
A division of Congressional Information Service, Inc.
88 Post Road West, Westport, Connecticut 06881

Printed in the United States of America

10 9 8 7 6 5 4 3 2 1

CONTENTS

TABLES

LIST OF MAPS

FOREWORD
by Hermann Mannheim

'In Britain . . .', writes Dr. Morris, 'the study of criminology has never enjoyed more than a precarious foothold in the Universities from which the impetus of research must ultimately come'. How very true this is; and those who may ask for chapter and verse for this statement can now find at least part of the story in the recent UNESCO survey of *The Study of Criminology* in ten selected countries, including Great Britain. Still, as so often not only in military history but also in the history of scientific disciplines, even the most precarious foothold has occasionally led to important conquests extending far into the mainland of the opposing party. Among others, the various sections of this Library, with their diverse contributions to the study of crime and delinquency from the viewpoints of the sociologist, lawyer, psychologist, psychiatrist and penal administrator bear witness of such conquests in the field of Criminology. The present book with sub-title "A Study in Social Ecology" — it might perhaps just as well have been: "ecological Criminology" — is an important addition to the International Library, and it gives me much pleasure to introduce it to the reading public. Dr. Morris has produced what is perhaps the clearest exposition so far written of the merits as well as the limitations of the ecological interpretation of crime and juvenile delinquency and, more specifically, of the work of the so-called Chicago School. Moreover, his analysis of conditions in Croydon shows his ability not merely to criticize the work of others but also to apply ecological concepts and techniques in order to test the principal findings of Clifford Shaw and his fellow-workers. In the course of his historical researches he does full justice to the significant contributions to ecological Criminology made by such mid-nineteenth century writers as A. M. Guerry, R. W. Rawson, Joseph Fletcher, Henry Mayhew and others who, although still belonging to what might be described as the "semi-scientific" or, in the case of Mayhew, even "pre-scientific" stage of Criminology, were nevertheless in their different ways aware of the need for scientifically valid techniques of criminological investigation, whether such techniques were statistical and cartographic or, as in the case of Mayhew, consisted also of personal interviews and observations. When our author refers to Mayhew's "particular account of the area east of what is now Kingsway around Clare Market", we might perhaps note that ecological Criminology has now returned to one of its starting points, the Clare Market area. However, as Dr. Morris observes, the sociological approach of these writers was "almost totally eclipsed by Lombroso's theories" until, more than half a century later, the foundations of modern American Sociology were laid by Ross, R. E. Park, W. I. Thomas and the Chicago School. Naturally, substantial sections of the present book had to be devoted to a critical re-appraisal of the work of this School, a task which the author has performed with exemplary fairness. As others before him, he draws attention to their statistical weaknesses and to one of the basic omissions in the work of most ecologists, i.e. their failure to relate the study of delinquency "breeding areas" to an equally careful analysis of delinquency "attracting areas". It is indeed only by paying due attention to both sides of the problem that a complete picture of the situation can be obtained. On the other hand, as the author rightly stresses, it is sometimes overlooked that Clifford Shaw's work has to be understood as an attempt to combine a kind of factorial analysis of objective social data with a situational analysis of individual behaviour, in other words, his case studies such as *The Natural History of a Delinquent Career* and others are of equal importance as his statistics.

A discussion of the interesting work done in the post-war period in this country, notably in Liverpool by John B. Mays and in the Midlands ("Radby") under the direction of Professor Sprott, leads to the description of the author's own field work in Croydon which is, in some ways, the most important part of the book. While he was fortunate in having before him the models of the Chicago studies as well as of their English counterparts, he had to labour under the well-known handicaps and frustrations of the private research worker who, with no governmental authority behind him, has to do everything single-handed and within an all-too-short span of time. In the circumstances, the quantity and quality of the local material collected is greatly to his credit. In fact, his investigation has become something more than merely an ecological picture of crime and delinquency in Croydon: starting with a discussion of the "criminal area" he finds himself in his last two chapters discussing the wider issues of social class, local housing policies and social policy in general. Notwithstanding certain differences, his material tends to confirm the findings of the "Radby" study. More important than living in a certain area are the facts of belonging to a certain category of working-class families and the psychology of family relations. In similar, though not identical, terms as Professor Albert K. Cohen in his widely discussed *Delinquent Boys*, also published in this Library, he arrives at the conception of the delinquent sub-culture. In each occupational category, in each of the social classes, however, there is of course also a hard core of approximately one quarter of all cases which the author regards as "psychiatric delinquency", leaving the majority as "social delinquency" to be explained in terms of their cultural milieu. As already found in previous studies, it is the housing policy of local authorities which, largely without their fault, almost inevitably tends to aggravate the position by "segregating" most of the "social problem families" in one area. What is the answer? The "mixing" of different categories of families too, is likely to produce serious problems of adjustment. Various other specific recommendations have been made by social reformers, but only some of them, the author complains, have so far been implemented. One remarkable finding of the Croydon study is that the Probation Service, originally created only for very limited purposes, has in some areas more and more become the "Jack of all Trades" in social casework. Not surprisingly, the author does not profess to be able to offer any easy solutions as to how to change those deep-rooted negativistic attitudes which seem to be characteristic of some of his cases. Nor does his material, or that of his predecessors in this country, enable us to say with any certainty whether these attitudes are equally strong and widespread as would appear from Prof. Cohen's American study. He is right in criticizing, as the expression of an "old man's view", all those who see the problem in terms of a "lowering of moral standards", but granting that moral standards, much as they may change in matters of detail, have undergone no wholesale falling off, the question of how to deal with those negativistic attitudes still remains unanswered. It is here, when faced with such basic issues, that Criminology merges into general social policy and moral philosophy and the criminologist cannot claim to speak with any special authority.

London, February 1957.   Hermann Mannheim

PREFACE

The subject of this book was not suddenly conceived, but rather, like Topsy, 'just growed' partly out of interest in that field of sociological inquiry which may be termed social ecology and partly out of interest in the problem of crime and delinquency in the town in which I had spent a great deal of my life. The research which is described in the latter part of this book took place during the period 1953-55 but was in fact based upon a design which had evolved slowly over the preceding years.

Because of this gradual development of the research scheme many people contributed to it, both directly and indirectly. I am most deeply indebted to Dr. Hermann Mannheim whose guidance and help has been of the greatest value to me, and to the Home Office for granting access to many of the substantive records of data. Mr. T. S. Lodge of the Statistical Division rendered me invaluable assistance and Sir Ronald Howe at New Scotland Yard kindly allowed me to analyse certain Police Records. Through the assistance of the Children's Department and the Probation Division I was able to examine the case files of delinquent and refractory children which provided the data for much of my analysis.

In Croydon I am indebted to Superintendent Giles of 'Z' Division Metropolitan Police, to Mr. Chislett, Clerk to the Justices, to the Town Clerk for regularising my contacts with departments of the Local Authority, to Mr. Stephens the Youth Organiser and to Mr. Ronald Hyder, J. P., a member of the Juvenile Panel. To Mr. Frank Hepworth the Chief Probation Officer and his staff there is a special debt for they gave most generously of their time to assist in numerous ways.

The fieldwork was made possible by the award of a Research Studentship by the London School of Economics augmented by a grant from the University of London Research Fund.

Throughout I have been fortunate to have the untiring assistance of my wife, Pauline Morris, who like so many sociologists' wives performs the task of research assistant with exemplary efficiency.

Terence Morris

London School of Economics.
May, 1957.

xiii

I

THE CONCEPTS OF ECOLOGY

I

HUMAN or social ecology is concerned with the relationships which exist between people who share a common habitat or local territory and which are distinctly related to the character of the territory itself; it is a study of social structure in relation to the local environment. The history of human civilisation is in great part the account of man's efforts to free himself from the restrictions imposed by his natural environment; not only can he now live and work under practically all climatic conditions, but he can inhabit great conurbations which, though unable to support them selves, can exist by means of ingenious technology and efficient transport. In overcoming nature, however, he has created for himself new environmental settings, which in turn impose their restrictions upon him. The great city or suburbia may set limits upon human activity which, though of a different order, are no less real than those set in the past by mountains and rivers, deserts and oceans. To admit to the existence of an urban or rural way of life is to admit of the primal association between patterns of behaviour and the characteristics of the local community.

The term "ecology" which has been borrowed from the field of biology, seems first to have been used in the year 1878 by the German biologist and philosopher, Ernst Haeckel, but it was the Dane, Eugenius Warming who brought the term much nearer the social sciences in his book *"Plant Communities"* (1895). He drew attention to the fact that different kinds of plants tended to grow together, and like human communities, had a temporal beginning, experienced changes and finally entered into a decline being gradually superseded by other plants. It was this dynamic aspect of ecology which perhaps brought it closest to the field of sociology, for in the latter part of the last century sociologists were absorbed in the study of social development or the evolution of human institutions and freely incorporated concepts from the natural into the social sciences.

The adaptation of ecology as a sociological theory was accomplished in America by Robert Ezra Park and his followers at the University of Chicago, and the school of sociology which he founded owed much to his essentially un-academic approach to his subject. Park was born in Minnesota in 1864, into a community composed predominantly of Scandinavian immigrants. His interest in "marginal cultures" and awareness of the problems of their assimilation into American society derived in part from his membership of a youthful gang. After a university education he began work as a journalist, a calling for which he appeared to have a natural talent. In his own view, it was these years that gave him his first real insight into human ecology.

'While I was a newspaper reporter' he later wrote 'I used to do a good deal of writing for the Sunday papers. I found that (they were) willing to publish anything so long as it concerned the local community and was interesting. I wrote about all sorts of things, and in this way became intimately acquainted with many different aspects of city life. I expect that I have actually covered more ground tramping about cities in different parts of the world than any other living man. Out of all this I gained, among other things, a conception of the city, the community, and the region, not as a geographical phenomenon merely, but as a kind of social organism.'[1]

More important in some ways than his interest in such a conception of social structure was his concern with the effects of social change. From the 1860's onwards immigrants from all over Europe began to arrive in America in growing numbers, crossing the Appalachians and settling in the towns of the mid-west. Here the rapidity and magnitude of social change and the dramatic problems of culture conflict, were social facts which could scarcely be missed by even the most casual observer and were to

[1] '*Race and Culture*', p. viii. *Collected Papers of* R. E. Park. *Vol.* 1 ed. Hughes Glencoe Ill. 1950.

have a profound effect upon Park's later formulations in sociological theory. In 1914 he returned as a lecturer in sociology to the University of Chicago and a year later published an article which was to be a blueprint for studies in urban sociology at Chicago for two decades.[1]

He was perhaps above all a convinced empiricist, and a fervent advocate of the fieldwork methods later to be advocated so forcibly by Malinowski when the latter wrote " . . . information must come to (the fieldworker) full flavoured from his own observations . . . and not be squeezed out of reluctant informants as a trickle of talk."[2] Park's method was essentially the anthropological method of participant observation and it seemed to him that if Boas and Lowie could study the culture and social organisation of the American Indians by living among them, then the culture and social organisation of "Little Italy" on Chicago's North Side might be studied by similar methods and with at least equal profit. Accordingly his seminars discussed papers based not upon library research, but on the contents of the notebooks of his students whom he sent out into the city streets to collect the first hand material of direct observation. The proposals set out in his article of 1915 became the basis of a research programme for Park's graduate students, and notwithstanding the limitations of these techniques it must be admitted that there is scarcely a university department in the world which can claim to have produced such an outstanding series of monographs in urban sociology in a similar period of time. In 1923 appeared McKenzie's *"The Neighbourhood. A Study of Columbus Ohio"* and Nels Andersen's *"The Hobo. The Sociology of the Homeless Man"*. In 1927 came Thrasher's classic *"The Gang"*, in 1928 Louis Wirth's *"The Ghetto"*, and in 1929 Harvey Zorbaugh's *"Gold Coast and the Slum"* and Clifford Shaw's *"Delinquency Areas."* These were no more than the most important works, for a great variety of students both academic and non-academic were attracted to Chicago and produced works of lesser merit, and, as Alihan remarked in 1938 "the plethora of monographs and articles, each elaborating some specific application of the ecological approach, gains in volume year by year."[3]

[1] 'The City: Suggestions for the Investigation of Human Behaviour in the Urban Environment'. *Am. Journ. Sociology.* Vol. 20, 1915.
[2] *'Magic Science and Religion'*. London 1948, p. 123.
[3] M. A. Alihan. *'Social Ecology. A Critical Analysis'*. Columbia, 1938, p. 2.

The writings of the Chicago School were not confined to the descriptive; McKenzie's study of Columbus had put forward a conceptual scheme for the study of urban growth and in 1924 Park and Burgess published a textbook, the *"Introduction to the Science of Sociology"* A year later they edited a symposium, *"The City"* and in 1927 selected papers from the proceedings of the American Sociological Society were published under the title of *"The Urban Community."*

It may be questioned why the development of ecological theory should have taken place predominantly within the field of urban sociology and so particularly in relation to studies of the city of Chicago. There is nothing intrinsic in the nature of the ecological approach which brings it nearer to the study of urbanism rather than say rural sociology, indeed McKenzie's interests in particular extended later outside the confines of the city to the metropolitan region and beyond.[1] It was rather because human ecology is concerned essentially with social processes, and that cultural change and urban expansion in the mid-west were epitomised in the growth of Chicago, that Park and his followers concentrated their attention upon their own city and the problems which arose directly out of its changing character. In 1860 its population had been in the region of 110,000; by 1870 this had risen to 300,000. Between 1880 and 1890 the number rose from 500,000 to over one million, and by 1910 the population exceeded two millions. Into the city came wave after wave of immigrants, and descriptions of their conditions of life and employment bear striking parallels with accounts of the growth of industrial cities in Britain half a century before.[2]

This, then, is the background against which the development of human ecology by the Chicago School must be considered. Some critics have argued that by their excessive pre-occupation with the changing environment about them, the ecologists' theories tended to be subjectively biased.

'(they) undertook to explain the social complex by fastening attention on its salient manifestations such as the growth of cities, the spread of industry, the extensions of railways and highways, the mosaic of nationalities and races, the movements and distribution of people and utilities. The conditions of

[1] See *The Metropolitan Community;* Chicago, 1933 and 'The Concept of Dominance and World Organisation', *Am. Journ. Sociology.* Vol. 33, 1927.
[2] See espec. Edith Abbott, *'The Tenements of Chicago'*, Chicago, 1936.

social change became to them the *facts* of social change. Thus their universe of discourse became limited to extremities, and the interpretation of social life hinged upon its most concrete aspects.'[1]

Before attempting any evaluation of the validity of the ecological method, we must first consider its more important theoretical concepts, and to sift them from empirical data in the literature of the Chicago School is not always an easy matter. A general outline of these concepts can however be drawn from articles and prefaces by Park, Burgess and McKenzie who may be regarded as its most important theoreticians.

Symbiosis

Symbiosis may be defined as the habitual living together of organisms of different species within the same habitat. It is a concept taken directly from the study of plant ecology and entomology. The relationship between the ant and the greenfly is a common but nevertheless striking example of two distinct natural species living together to their mutual advantage. Warming noted similar associations between plants and cited as examples the meadow with its grasses and perennial herbs, or the deciduous forest in which plants grow under the shade and protection of other species. Within plant communities he noted that the different species might live in harmony, or sometimes in conflict. The *biotic balance* is the term used to describe such relationships when they exist in a state of equilibrium. Perhaps the most familiar example of biotic balance is the well-ordered domestic fish tank. In it, each different species has a part to play, the plants and molluscs keeping the water clean and fresh, enabling the fish to live healthily, the fish themselves living in harmony or conflict depending upon their kind.

Park argues that the aim of human or social ecology is to investigate:

(a) the processes by which the biotic balance and the social equilibrium are maintained once they are achieved, and
(b) the processes by which, when the biotic balance and the social equilibrium are disturbed, the transition is made from one relatively stable order to another.[2]

---

[1] Alihan, *op. cit. p.* 6.
[2] 'Human Ecology', *Am. Journ. Sociology,* Vol. 42, 1936.

McKenzie's definition is somewhat broader and distinguishes sharply between human and plant ecology. In his view human ecology

' . . . deals with the spatial aspects of the symbiotic relations of human beings and human institutions. It aims to discover the principles and factors involved in the changing patterns of spatial arrangement of population and institutions resulting from the interplay of human beings in a continuously changing culture. It has very little in common with plant and animal ecology, for while symbiotic processes are alike for all organisms, their mode of operation in the human community is hardly comparable with the food chains and environmental controls existing in plant and lower animal communities. . . . Knowledge of ecological processes . . . is basic to all social sciences, as social and political institutions have a spatial base, and arise and function in response to changing conditions of environment and competition. Institutional stability is largely dependent on the stability of space relations.'[1]

Community and Society

If human ecology is so different from plant ecology as McKenzie maintains, and yet symbiosis is common to all groups of organisms which share a common habitat, what is the nature of these differences? In the plant community, the processes of control and co-ordination which make a state of equilibrium possible are physical and external; in the human group, on the other hand, they restraints are " . . . internal and moral, based upon some kind of consensus."[2]

The character of restraints is the criterion used by Park to distinguish between community and society. The *community* exists only insofar as symbiotic competition has not been limited or transformed by social control. The evolution of *society* in contrast has been the " . . . progressive extension of control over nature and the substitution of a moral for a natural order."[3] In other words he claims that there is an essential distinction between symbiosis, on the one hand, and cultural or social processes on the other. Such a distinction would appear trivial if it

[1] 'Human Ecology', *Encyclopaedia of the Social Sciences*, 1942 ed.
[2] Park. *Human Ecology*, 1936.
[3] Park and Burgess. *Introduction to Science of Sociology*, Chicago, 1924. See espec. Ch. III.

were not for the fact that certain phenomena in human society provide parallels with plant and animal communities. Park goes on to argue that the economic theories of the French Physiocrats, and those of Adam Smith and Ricardo, were based upon analyses of symbiotic competition for resources.

Communication

Human beings do not constitute a society merely by living together in close proximity, nor in the modern world is social contact entirely limited by distance. The essential feature of cultural relationships is therefore communication, for without it the social or moral order, the "consensus" could not exist. Communication is also clearly necessary if the continuity of the social order is to be ensured just as it is an essential pre-requisite of social change. The assimilation of immigrants into America for example was not achieved simply by their entry into the symbiotic relationships of the economic system but by their adaptation and adoption of American culture through the communication of ideas.

"Axiate Growth" and the Zonal Hypothesis

Ecology is essentially an organismic social theory and it is hardly surprising that the ecologist should have examined the growth of urban settlement in those terms. C.M.Child[1] in his work on the physiological aspects of behaviour, noted that certain organs are the centres of activity and that other organs occur in a definite order of importance along the nervous axes radiating from the brain and the central nervous system. He further postulated increasing differentiation among the component parts of the total organism and increasing concentration of control at the point of dominance as a result of this evolutionary growth. From this followed the notion of a "gradient" of activity or organic importance from nervous centre to the periphery of the organism.

The ecologists' view of the growth of the mid-western city is a direct analogy of this; the business and administrative district being located at the centre and the less important residential districts being situated at the periphery. Along the lines of transportation satellite business and administrative centres arise to cater for the needs of the immediate locality. McKenzie speaks

[1] C.M. Child, 'Biological Foundations of Social Integration'. *Proc. Am. Sociological Assoc.*, 22, 1928.

of the dominant centre as the focus of organic activity, the means whereby the component parts are integrated into the whole.[1]

In his study of Columbus in 1923, McKenzie had formulated a scheme of dividing cities into concentric zones to illustrate the pattern of urban growth. Within such limitations as are imposed by topographical features, the city develops outwards through five successive zones which resemble the rings formed on the surface of still water when a stone has been dropped in. Chicago was analysed by Park and Burgess in "The City" as follows:

Zone 1   The "Loop" or central business district.
Zone 2   The zone of transition containing the rooming house district, the underworld dens, the brothels, China-town, the Ghetto, and "Little Sicily".
Zone 3   The zone of working men's homes.
Zone 4   The residential zone of apartment houses (flats), residential hotels, and, on the edge, single family dwellings.
Zone 5   The commuters' zone, i.e. respectable suburbia.

These zones are the outcome of the ecological processes of urban growth, of population movements and economic development. The zonal hypothesis owes much to the work of R. N. Hurd, a real estate agent who had published his *Principles of City Land Values* in 1911. As an economic analysis it is concerned with the symbiotic process whereby land as a resource which may be exploited is allocated by competition, just as the resources of the plant community are distributed. The ecologists viewed population movements and changes in land utilisation in terms of the sequence of "invasion", "dominance" and "succession", stages observable in the plant community when new species come in and oust existing ones. Originally, the population of the city lived around the central business district, but this area was the most obvious choice for the location of new commercial and industrial enterprise. As industry moved in, so the wealthier inhabitants moved out, and as the area's decline in terms of desirability of residence depressed rentals it became the obvious choice for newcomers to the city, usually poor immigrants in search of housing at lowest possible cost. The respectable artisans were as a result encouraged to move out, and they in

[1] McKenzie, *The Concept of Dominance and World Organisation*, 1927.

turn began to displace the well-to-do who moved out further still.

Natural Areas

The natural area concept was used with considerable advantage in the many studies in urban sociology carried out at Chicago. The concentric zones of the city are by no means homogeneous either in terms of land use, or in terms of their population, but the ecologists offer no standard definition of the natural area save that it forms a segment of a zone, and about the nature of such segmentation there appear to be two distinct schools of thought. Zorbaugh considers the natural area as essentially the product of patterns of land utilisation modified by topographical and other special features peculiar to individual cities, within the framework of zonal development.

'The structure of the individual city . . . while always exhibiting the generalised zones described . . . is built about a framework of transportation, business organisation and industry, park and boulevard systems, and topographical features. All of these break up the city into numerous smaller areas, which we may call natural areas, in that they are the unplanned, natural product of the city's growth'[1]

McKenzie, on the other hand, in *"The Metropolitan Community"* defines the natural area in terms of the characteristics of its population, race, language, income and occupation; that is, as a *cultural* rather than a physical isolate. Both Zorbaugh and Mc-Kenzie are agreed that the natural area is an observable territorial phenomenon; the disagreement it would seem is about the relative importance of purely symbiotic and cultural factors in its creation. One may perhaps also note that in a territorial sense it is a relative concept, varying from the districts of a city to regional subdivisions of a continent.

Burgess comes nearest to a synthesis of the two opposing views for as he sees it, community life, as conditioned by the spatial distribution of population and institutions, has three distinct aspects, ecological, cultural and political. Physical location, and such end products of symbiotic competition as land use and the level of rents tend to have a selective effect upon population. The

[1] H. Zorbaugh, 'Natural Areas of the City', in *The Urban Community* ed. Burgess, Chicago, 1925.

development of social relationships may be promoted or impeded by locational factors such as transport facilities, and geographical distance may become a symbol of social distance. Such factors he regards as characteristic of an *"ecological" community*. A *cultural community* exists when there arises a social system or culture which is characteristic of locality. Finally, when it is possible to isolate political action on the basis of locality, one may speak of the *"political community.*"[1]

The inhabitants of the natural area form, in the ecological sense, a community. When they are human, their relationships are more than symbiotic, they are also social or cultural, yet if we accept the conceptual distinction between "community" and "society" already mentioned, the term "cultural community" is self contradictory. Obviously, if the term "local community" is to have any valid meaning in sociology it cannot be limited to a group whose inter-relationships are wholly symbiotic and non-social. It must be extended to cover groups whose existence and survival depends upon the transmission of a cultural heritage through social communication.

II

The irony of ecological theory — if one may use that term — is that in spite of its contradictions in definition and the ambiguity of certain of its concepts, some of the most important studies in urban sociology have been carried out within its framework. Our problem is to examine those of its propositions and concepts which relate to the physical distribution of crime and criminals and attempt to evaluate them in terms of (a) their validity and (b) their usefulness as tools of investigation.

The criterion of validity which must be used is simply the test of whether ecological investigations measure or describe what they *intend* to measure or describe. If a study of mental disorder in a city, for example, shows that occupation or social class is a more significant factor than residence, then it would seem that *prima facie*, an ecological investigation was an invalid procedure. For an exclusive ecological explanation of a situation to be valid, it must be conclusively demonstrated either that no other factors

[1] Burgess, *Basic Social Data in Chicago; An Experiment in Social Science Research,* ed. Smith and White, Chicago, 1929.

are at work, or that they are comparatively unimportant, and this is not always easy or reasonable to assume.

The standard by which working concepts ought to be judged is usefulness. To suggest that a concept is true or false as an accurate or innaccurate description of a process or constellation of facts is not particularly meaningful. No physicist would suggest that there are "things" called "gravity" or "force", they are merely convenient ways of describing and understanding certain phenomena, that a brick will fall if dropped from the hand, or that it is easier to close a door if it is pushed by the handle and not close to the hinges. Concepts are tools, which if properly designed, are the best equipment with which a problem may be solved. No-one would attempt to cut down a tree with a razor blade nor paint a house with an artist's brush, to quote extreme examples. But in other situations tools may be misused, but misused succesfully. It is quite possible, for instance, to split small logs with the aid of a hammer and a table knife. In sociological inquiries it is also possible to use concepts in analysing data which will produce some kind of result, but which will not necessarily be the best adapted to the problem in hand. If they are too crude, the results may even be misleading. The clarification of concepts or categories of analysis is therefore fundamental in any research and in this the Chicago ecologists cannot be said to have been conspicuously successful.

Alihan's criticisms of ecology are largely based upon the marked inconsistencies of expression in the literature of the Chicago School, but also upon the fact that the theory of human ecology rests in great part upon a series of completely false analogies beginning with the direct comparison of human and plant communities.

The plant community is characterised by the relationships of symbiosis, controlling influences over individual members which are both physical and external. Such relationships are co-operative and competitive; co-operative in that by their interaction the organisms help to establish a state of equilibrium in which conflict is minimal, and competitive in that each organism struggles against others for resources. Park quotes Darwin to illustrate such a situation by referring to his example of the humble bee and the red clover. Humble bees alone, on account of their size, pollinate the red clover and make their nests on the ground. These nests are a favourite food of the little field mice, who in turn are a delicacy for the local cats. In this way the quantity of red clover in a district might be expressed as a mathematical function of the number of local cats or even the spinsters who kept them. This interdependence of species within a common habitat through competitive co-operation seems to epitomise the struggle for existence which for Darwin was the quintessence of the theory of natural selection.

Superficially there appears to be an analogy between symbiosis in the plant community and the economic system of human society. Just as the insects or plants which share a common habitat affect both each other and the character of the total community without being fully aware of the significance of their individual activity so human beings may participate in a system of production distribution and exchange or may marry and have children, and yet be largely unaware of the objective consequences of their actions in shaping the nature of the economic system or in determining the rate of population growth. Park, in his mention of the classical economists, hinted at the similarity between symbiosis and the procedures whereby wealth and the factors of production are allocated in a perfectly free market. Indeed, as Western society has learned to its cost, there are remarkable parallels between *laisser faire* and the processes by which equilibrium is reached in the jungle and the depths of the ocean. "Competitive co-operation" is discernible in human society in spheres beyond economics, for not only do firms compete for markets, but political factions and social classes compete for power and religious associations for converts. Competition is co-operative in an objective sense; it might be argued, for example, that lively sectarianism implies an interst in religious ideas, and it is a familiar slogan in British politics that a vigorous opposition is essential for good Government and a healthy democracy.

The distinction between symbiotic community and cultural society, is however, of limited value in the study of human groups. The operations of the market are by no means as free as the classical economists would have them, for the restrictions and agreements which arise between competitors are legion. Such restrictions as develop arise essentially out of social relationships and are maintained by a consensus rather than by purely external pressures. One may take the case of land development as an example. Although certain tracts of land may be obtained by the exercise of effective demand, others cannot be acquired in such a way. Burial grounds and common lands which have existed for centuries are the subject of attitudes which regard them as sacred and inviolable. In the last resort no-one may seize land, for even compulsory purchase must result from due process of law as the railway moguls of the last century discovered. The respect and recognition of legal rights is a cultural phenomenon, and litigation in relation to them is not a symbiotic process but a form of social communication. It is doubtful whether there are any human relationships which can be described as "symbiotic" in the sense of symbiosis in the plant or animal community, although McKenzie writes as if there were.[1] If symbiotic relationships are "the factors involved in living together independently of communication"[2] as Burgess suggests, "communication" must be defined in terms of direct or face-to-face contacts, for even in a global society some comprehensive system of communication may usually be observed. In the economic sphere, in particular, the growth of a "world" economy has been accompanied by a growth in social contacts, and indirect communication through the mass media of advertising is of increasing importance in determining the character of the market.

The conceptual sequence of "invasion", "dominance" and "succession" must be critically examined in a similar way. One cannot say that industry "invades" and ultimately "succeeds" to a tract of land in the same way that insects or plants may "invade" and "succeed" to a physical habitat, for changes in land utilisation are not achieved by a kind of *force majeure*, but through the operation of socially approved techniques the use of which is regulated by the rule of law. Nor can one compare too closely population movements within a given territory with the migrations of insects and animals. If an immigrant group comes gradually to dominate a neighbourhood, it is because the indigenous population decide of their own free will to go when they do not like the newcomers. The change is a relatively gradual process by which as residential property becomes vacant by emigration it is acquired by the newcomers. The old inhabitants do not flee in a mass exodus like frightened creatures before a column of driver ants.

[1] McKenzie, *Encyclopaedia Soc. Sc.*, 1942.
[2] See Alihan, *Social Ecology*, p. 41.

Perhaps the most patently false analogy of the Chicago ecologists is that concerning the growth of cities. The problems of population movements and changes in land utilisation as we have seen, bear only superficial resemblance to ecological processes in the plant community, the city is an organic structure only in respect of such features as its political and economic organisation. If blocks of streets are grouped into wards which are the basis of political representation as the City Council, or a central shopping district is a market for durable consumer goods such as clothes and furniture, while neighbourhood shops sell bread and vegetables, one might be able to speak of the functional differentiation of parts within a total system. But to suggest that local communities or "natural areas" are functioning entities in their own right yet related to the city as the lungs or digestive system are to the body, or to compare transportation routes thronging with buses and tramcars with the pulsing arteries of a living organism, is to carry analogy too far. The point is not that an analogy does not exist, but that the ecologists lost sight of it as a conceptual tool and came to look upon it as a *fact*. The physicist may for some purposes conceptualise light as a series of waves and for others as a stream of particles; neither is true or false in terms of fact, but merely more or less adequate for the problem in hand. Similarly, the organic conception of the city is merely a way of looking at the facts of urban growth.

The zonal hypothesis in ecological theory is clearly regarded as if it were a *statement* of fact rather than a way of *considering* facts. Zorbaugh, for example, writes "Ideally this gross segregation may be represented by a series of concentric circles, and such tends to be the *actual fact* (italics mine) where there are no complicating geographical factors."[1]

Park and his followers held that this pattern held good, not only for Chicago, but for most American cities and some non-American cities as well. This view has been seriously challenged by Edith Abbott, a member of another faculty in the ecologists' own University. Quoting such contemporary sources as Chamberlain (*Chicago and its Suburbs* 1874), Colbert and Chamberlain (*Chicago and the Great Conflagration* 1871) and an important secondary authority, Homer Hoyt (*One Hundred Years of Land Values in Chicago* 1933) she writes that

[1] Zorbaugh, *Natural Areas of the City*, 1925.

' . . . early accounts of the growth of Chicago do not confirm the rather popular theory of city growth which portrays different population groups lying in a series of concentric circles around the business district. The theory that population density is greatest in a semi-circle around the central business district in Chicago, and that it regularly decreases through a graded series of semi-circles to certain outlying points; or the theory that poor districts of a city are to be found in one circle . . . are theories that seem to be purely theoretical and not realistic.'[1]

She continued by pointing out that Chicago was originally surrounded by satellite towns and villages, all of which grew and were finally incorporated within the city boundaries. The prosperous middle class tended to be housed in long lines parallel with the lake shore and not in a semi-circular arc.

Looking at a map of Chicago we find that the concentric zone system is a generalisation considerably removed from reality. Lake Michigan occupies virtually half the total circle, and the lake shore by reason of its littoral position is an area of very desirable residence notwithstanding its location in Zone II which is supposed to be the zone of transition containing the rooming houses, the brothels and the underworld dens. Like so many American cities, Chicago is planned on the block system of main streets running east to west and north to south, with the result that development tended to be along these lines of transportation rather than along radii from the central business district. To be fair, one must admit that Zorbaugh at least was conscious of the extent to which topography may make the pattern of urban growth unique to any given city.

'Of course, no city quite conforms to this ideal scheme. Physical barriers such as rivers, lakes and rises of land may modify the structure and growth of the individual city as is strikingly illustrated in the cases of New York, Pittsburgh and Seattle. Railroads and their belts of industry, cut through this generalised scheme, breaking the city up into sections and lines of transportation along the more travelled of which grow up retail business streets.'[2]

[1] Edith Abbott, *The Tenements of Chicago*, 1908-1935, Chicago, 1936.
[2] Zorbaugh, *Natural Areas of the City*, 1925.

The question which appears here to have been asked is whether it is particularly fruitful to continue to use the zonal hypothesis in describing the development of cities where topographical features have played such a predominant role in shaping the pattern of settlement. As a tool of analysis it can have only limited usefulness and on occasions may in fact impede rather than assist in research. Clifford Shaw in his work on delinquency areas in Chicago found the square mile area a convenient geographical unit for the computation of delinquency rates, but to fit the square mile areas into the scheme of concentric zones can only be described as the problem of fitting square pegs into round holes in its most literal sense!

The radial growth of the city then, is perhaps more apparent than real. It is true that the fine squares of London have come to be dominated by business organisations or private hotels and that the merchants and bankers have abandoned the metropolis for quieter surroundings in Surrey or the Chiltern Hills, from which they may travel each day by fast trains into Cannon Street, Waterloo, Moorgate and King's Cross. It is true that while the City clerk of the 1850's walked to his office from semi-rural surroundings in Peckham or Camberwell Green, his modern counterpart travels from Croydon or Sanderstead by electric train. But the pattern of development has been by no means one of the city spreading uniformly from a single centre. Traditionally, settlement in London has had two centres, Westminster and the City. In its growth the metropolis has absorbed villages like Charing, Kensington and Chelsea, but at the same time it has met with other towns which were themselves growing. The case of Croydon, an ancient market town is a good example. Croydon began rapidly to expand in the 1880's, and to the north began to reach out towards the expanding outer districts of London, Streatham and Sydenham. Finally in the 1920's the last vestiges of open space were built upon so that on the Brighton Road from Purley Fountain to London Bridge there is now an unbroken mass of bricks and mortar for nearly fourteen miles.

In ecological accounts of the city, it is the natural area which stands out as a concept of obvious value by comparison with other tools of ecological analysis. The most elementary social relationships in human society depended upon physical proximity, and although one may now enjoy social contacts with friends in the Antipodes, such contacts are only possible through man's technological conquests over distance. But notwithstanding the range of contacts made possible by modern systems of communication, it remains that there are many social relationships which are locally based, and as Burgess observed, the physical environment may play an important role in shaping their characteristics. At the biotic level the habitat has an undoubted influence upon the relationships between the species it contains through the process of their selective adaptation; man has gone far to limit the effects of his environment but selectivity remains, not at the biotic, but at the cultural level.

The railway tracks, canals, main road, and natural features which determine the physical pattern of the city's growth divide it into "natural areas" which tend to exhibit distinctive socio-economic characteristics. Their economic differences relate not only to land utilisation but variations in land values expressed either directly in terms of the cost of land on the market or indirectly in rateable values or rentals. Such economic factors play an important part in selecting the populations of different areas and it follows naturally that the weakest groups in the market, the poorest families or the near destitute, will seek housing at lowest possible cost in the deteriorating areas of the city where rentals are relatively low. Because our society is one in which social differentiation is based upon wealth and the outward signs of it, and the cost of living proportional to an individual's income and status varies from area to area in a city, it may be inferred that residence is a factor closely connected within the phenomenon of social class. The contention is that "cultural differentiation" i.e. differences in institutional behaviour and the values underlying it, is determined very largely by the facts of social class. The natural area as a cultural isolate is to a considerable degree the coincidental product of the economic differentiation between different physical areas. No-one aspiring to the higher levels of social status in the city chooses to live in an area dominated by industry and commerce (a) because the smoke, grime and noise are physically unpleasant and (b) because rentals are proportionately lower and to live there would give the impression of inability to validate, in money terms, the status to which a claim has been made.

The immigrant or "ethnic" group presents a somewhat different problem. In some instances choice of residence may be determined by the level of rentals, but in others the formation of a cultural enclave seems to be more related to the provision of what might be termed "specialised cultural equipment" such as churches and synagogues, or schools and cafes where the native language is spoken, or shops where traditional foods may be bought. Once a "bridgehead" has been established fresh waves of immigrants come to the area where their special needs can be best satisfied. Where a distinctive cultural or "ethnic" group is itself clearly stratified on a socio-economic basis, then both the cost of housing and the provision of cultural facilities help to determine the pattern of residence. There are, for example, Jewish enclaves in Whitechapel and Mile End, and also in Hampstead and Golders Green.

Park contended, not unreasonably, that the physical neighbourhood is usually transformed into something approaching a community, in the sense in which the latter term is generally understood. Partly on account of the processes of social selection, and partly in view of the "contagious nature of cultural patterns" he argued that " . . . people living in natural areas of the same general type, and subject to the same social conditions, will display on the whole, the same characteristics."[1] Such a general proposition seems to be borne out by the facts. The dwellers in semi-detached houses in the tree lined avenues of West Wickham are not markedly dissimilar from their counterparts in Woodford Green; life in the bay-windowed terraced streets of Clapham is much the same as it is in Leytonstone. It is important to note, however, that the extent to which social relationships are locally based, varies between different types of area. Social behaviour in Bermondsey and Bethnal Green is qualitatively distinct from that in Clapham. West Wickham is distinct from St. John's Wood and both are lacking in features common to Kensington and Westminster. The organisation of behaviour in the local community is, however, a subject for later discussion.

---

[1] Park. 'Sociology'. in *Research in the Social Sciences*. ed. Gee. New York 1929.

II

DELINQUENCY AREAS

I

ALTHOUGH Henry Mayhew in the 1850's had been aware that certain districts of London housed an unduly high proportion of the criminal population of the metropolis, it was Clifford Shaw in Chicago who first used the term "delinquency area" to describe those parts of the great city which seem to throw up criminals and delinquents with the same ease with which they produce instances of poverty, overcrowding and disease. In Shaw's view, the "delinquency area" is a natural area of the city as is the ghetto or Chinatown; it arises in the process of urban and growth and it is conspicuous for its characteristic patterns of anti-social behaviour. Within its confines, delinquent or criminal behaviour is a norm of expectation among its inhabitants; a hostile attitude is developed towards social agencies and the police and it comes to be a cultural enclave at odds with the rest of the city. Its formal characteristics are physical deterioration, overcrowding, a mobile population and a proximity to the areas of industry and commerce. Its social characteristics are primarily a lack of informal agencies of social control whereby the norms accepted by the wider society may be maintained. The cultural milieu is such that

'Children who grow up in these deteriorated and disorganised neighbourhoods of the city are not subject to the same constructive and restraining influences that surround those in the more homogeneous residential communities farther removed from the industrial and commercial centres. These disorganised neighbourhoods fail to provide a consistent set of cultural standards and a wholesome social life for the

19

development of a stable and socially acceptable form of behaviour in the child. Very often the child's access to the traditions and standards of our conventional culture are restricted to his formal contacts with the police, the courts and the school and the various social agencies. On the other hand his most vital and intimate social contacts are often limited to the spontaneous and undirected neighbourhood play groups and gangs whose activities and standards may vary widely from those of his parents and the larger social order. These intimate and personal relationships rather than the more formal and external contacts with the school, social agencies and the authorities become the chief sources from which he acquires his social values and conceptions of right and wrong.'[1]

Shaw's concept of the delinquency area then, derives directly from the natural area concept of ecological theory, the epithet "delinquent" relating to the dominant pattern of behaviour exhibited by a high proportion of its inhabitants. If the delinquency area concept is to be a useful tool of criminological analysis, ·however, we must attempt to define it clearly and unambiguously.

At a strictly semantic level, the delinquency area ought to be the area where *delinquent acts are committed*. Shaw, on the other hand, considers it primarily to be the area where delinquents *live*. In this he is not alone. Sir Cyril Burt, for example, in *"The Young Delinquent"* makes a point of illustrating variations in "the local distribution of juvenile delinquency" in order to consider the problem of environmental conditions, though this too is a distribution of delinquents' homes. This would seem to be an unfortunate use of the term, for the location of the offence is just as important, sometimes more important, than the location of the offenders' home. It is, in fact, necessary to distinguish between two types of delinquency area, areas of *crime commission* and areas of *delinquent residence*. Dr. Hasan El Saaty, in his study of Cairo, Egypt, has illustrated this point very well. The real slums of Cairo, Bab-El-Shariya and Bulaq have very low average proportions of arrests, but this is due to the fact that most of the juvenile delinquents flock to the wealthier districts nearby where they are often caught. The slums he designates as "breeding

---

[1] Shaw and McKay. *Social Factors in Juvenile Delinquency*. Washington. U.S. Govt. Printing Office. 1931. (The Wickersham Report.)

areas" while the shopping centres of Abdin and Muska he describes as "attracting areas."[1] Now it may be argued that very often, and especially in the case of juveniles, the two types of area may be geographically indistinguishable. In great cities like Chicago, Liverpool, or London, this is very broadly true, but to ignore the logical distinction which must exist in any effective analysis of delinquency, simply because there is no empirical distinction, is to ignore a point which, incidentally, Shaw himself makes though somewhat obliquely.

In his view, one of the formal characteristics of the delinquency area is the proximity or presence of an unduly high proportion of commercial and industrial property—factories, warehouses and railway yards—which, in the absence of facilities for vigorous and exciting recreation, provide a constant source of temptation to youngsters to break and enter or pilfer, by way of compensation or substitution. The existence of these temptations arising out of the physical development of the area are as important as the absence of effective informal agencies of social control in understanding the phenomenon of delinquency. There appear to be two distinct sets of factors which require separation for the purpose of analysing delinquency in any complete sense. Firstly, one must consider the factors which *pre-dispose* the individual towards committing a delinquent act. Absence of social control, "social contagion", a local criminal tradition combined with bad housing and a lack of adequate facilities for constructive recreation and lawful amusement are social facts which must be regarded as defining the limits, and in no small degree the character, of social action within the area. Nor can psychological factors be ignored here; systems of child rearing, the development of personality and the role and incidence of psycho-pathological individuals in the local population are no less important. But such pre-disposing factors result in a state of affairs which is characterised by *potentiality* rather than *actuality*. Delinquents do not become such until they have committed a delinquent act, and therefore the practical opportunities for crime afforded by an area require a distinctly separate consideration.

Many areas in which pre-disposing factors may be observed do indeed contain opportunities for crime, and the areas of deterioration offer the low rentals which tend to attract the "marginal" or

---

[1] El-Saaty. Doctoral Thesis on *Juvenile Delinquency in Egypt*. Faculty of Arts, Univ. of London, 1946. (Unpub).

social problem groups in the city. But as Shaw has noted in such works as *"The Jack Roller"*[1] and *"The Natural History of a Delinquent Career"*,[2] besides breaking into local warehouses and stealing from the freight wagons in the railway sidings near their homes, the young delinquents travel down to the central business district and steal from market stalls or the big department stores. The majority of crimes committed are larcenies, and in view of the predatory character of thieving it seems clear that the most fruitful areas of activity will not always be near the offender's home if it is in a district characterised by poverty and dilapidation. It is necessary to go further in considering areas of crime commission and distinguish between them on the basis of the types of crime and the types of criminal they attract.

The most profitable housebreaking for example is done, not in the depressed city slum but in the well-to-do residential districts; not, for example, in the poverty stricken streets of Stepney or North Paddington but in the tree lined avenues of Hampstead or the quiet mews's of Chelsea. Warehouse and factory breaking in contrast must be confined by definition to the less desirable districts adjoining docks, railway yards and other industrial plant. Frequently one may notice differences in the location of the crimes of adult as distinct from juvenile lawbreakers, the latter being less skilled and choosing areas in which crimes may be most easily committed. In the course of the author's empirical study, a tendency was noticed for housebreaking in the poorer areas to be rather more often the work of juveniles, while the more prosperous residential districts attracted the attentions of more skilled adult criminals. One possible explanation of this may be that in the poorer districts, terrace houses, the multiplicity of backyards, sheds and alleyways, and the general physical congestion of the area make breaking and entering relatively easier in that it is much easier to get away if the alarm is given, especially at night. In the daytime, it may be easier still, for not only will all the menfolk be at work and the children at school, but many of the women will be out shopping or at work themselves. In the well-to-do districts, on the other hand, the spaciousness of the streets and gardens and the detachment or semi-detachment of every house make concealment more difficult, even at night, while in the daytime any suspicious character loitering is doubly conspicuous. Shoplifting is another

[1] Chicago, 1931. [2] Chicago, 1931.

example of "localised" crime. It is much easier to steal from the open counter of a multiple store or in a market thronged with people than from the quiet "shop on the corner". The West End stores in London suffer from the depradations of shoplifters rather as a field of growing crops does from a swarm of locusts who descend upon it. The anonymity of the central business district reduces the risks of detection sometimes to vanishing point, particularly when the offenders concerned are nimble children who can quickly lose themselves in a crowd.

With the development of considered town planning which separates housing areas from industry and commerce, the degree of geographical coincidence between areas of crime commission and areas of delinquent residence seems likely to diminish still further. In the case of urban areas with large council housing estates there may be scarcely any overlap for it would seem that planners have sometimes gone out of their way to remove families as far away as possible from the factories, shops and offices which are the scene of their daily toil. In the old un-planned areas of the city the large degree of overlap tends to obscure the distinction we have made, and the definition of delinquency areas in terms of the pattern of residence is less likely to lead to difficulties in the interpretation of the factors involved in the problem. If, however, we were to assume delin-quent residence to be the primary criterion of identification of a delinquency area absurdities might result. If successful racketeers decide to live in wealthy and respectable neighbourhoods in which they can conceal their true activities these can scarcely be classed as "delinquency areas". This brings us to the point where, in addition to the qualitative, we must also concider the quan-titative aspects of definition.

II

In order to compare areas of the city we must first define them; this therefore brings us back to the question raised in our first chapter, namely whether the natural area is primarily a cultural or a physical isolate. If we adopt the former view, then in demarcating the area on the map physical features such as rivers, canals or open spaces may have to be ingored; alternatively no geographical area may display sufficient cultural homogeneity for it to be called a natural area. In defining an area in physical terms on the other hand, precisely the reverse may be true, that is the area so conveniently defined by railways, main roads, or canals may be completely heterogeneous in a cultural sense. It is, of course true, as Park suggested, that physical areas often tend to assume cultural characteristics, but it must be borne in mind that this is but a tendency and not a fact which can be assumed in every case. There are a variety of criteria by which cultural homogeneity—or heterogeneity—may be assessed. One may use such socio-economic variables as house type, room density, median rentals, occupation, or home ownership, or, and this might prove more difficult to obtain, social-psychological data such as child rearing practices or patterns of leisure.

Socio-economic variables are more easily obtainable because the research worker normally needs only to have recourse to census data, but unfortunately, census tracts do not always coincide with the specific areas in which the researcher is interested. In Britain census tracts normally relate to local government areas the boundaries of which are designed primarily to achieve an equitable distribution of electors and which frequently cross lines of physical demarcation such as railways or main roads in an arbitary way. Because of changes in the size of the electorate, local government boundaries may shift considerably over the years and the material of one census may be only comparable in very broad terms with that of another. If the census tract is fairly small, it may be possible to re-arrange the tract data to conform more precisely with the "natural" area. In Britain this is sometimes possible by re-grouping the smallest geographical units of the census, the enumeration districts, or even the streets which compose them, but it is a laborious and highly expensive business. In the United States, rather more attention seems to have been given to the problem of establishing census tracts which are small enough to be fairly homogeneous socially and economically, and which can be used to make comparisons over the years. This problem is dealt with in some detail by Lander in his study of delinquency in Baltimore.[1] When adjacent census tracts or enumeration districts display common social or cultural or economic features and are so located that they share, for example, a common system of transportation, we may consider them

[1] Bernard Lander. *Towards an Understanding of Juvenile Delinquency*. New York. 1954.

broadly to constitute a natural area with homogeneous characteristics. There is, however, no reason why homogeneity should be a necessary characteristic of the natural area, in fact, as we shall discuss later, social and economic heterogeneity may have important effects upon the patterns of behaviour of people who share the same physical neighbourhood.

For the purpose of comparing the incidence of crime and criminals in different parts of the city, it would seem most useful to distinguish between areas on the basis of both physical features and general social and economic characteristics. This must clearly be an ad hoc procedure and take into consideration the special features of the town or city under consideration. The chances are that in practice it may be possible to delimit a few areas which are distinct, either in terms of physical location, or their dependence upon a particular system of transportation, or their housing characteristics, while at the same time the remaining tracts of the city seem scarcely to exhibit any distinctive characteristics which distinguish them one from another. The Chicago ecologists tended to assume that every city could be broken down for analytic purposes into distinctive areas; indeed this is a corollary of the organismic zonal theory of urban structure. It may of course be argued that nondescript areas are natural areas nevertheless, and that such a characteristic is in itself significant in the study of human behaviour within the urban environment. Any division of the city into natural areas must be based to some extent on boundaries which are arbitrarily drawn, and it is fortunate that local government boundaries do often coincide with "natural" boundaries. For better or worse, the research worker is largely compelled to use ward divisions in the absence of data for other more convenient territorial units. In making comparisons between wards therefore, some attempt must be made to achieve a common denominator by which variations in the distribution of crime and criminals may be observed.

In considering variations in the pattern of delinquent residence the most obvious step is to calculate rates of offenders on the basis of the ratio of known offenders to the total population. Such rates were called *delinquency rates* by Shaw, and although in terms of our argument this title is something of a misnomer, it is perhaps now too well established in the literature for another term to be substituted without confusion. In the calculation of delinquency rates there is one point which needs especial care, that is, the definition of the population *at risk*.

It is not enough simply to calculate the rate as the percentage of offenders in the total population, for within that population will be numbers of very small children, sick, infirm and aged persons, and individuals incarcerated in institutions whose chances of committing offences may be negligible or non-existent. In considering a given area, it is necessary to ascertain whether there are, for example, any old people's homes whose inmates might reasonably be excluded from the population at risk. Similarly, an attempt must be made to exclude very young children from the calculation. Although estimates of hospital and institutional populations are perhaps more difficult to obtain, it may be, in a criminological sence, rather less important to exclude them than the very young and the very old. Individuals in institutions do, on occasion, commit offences, and although they are not "at risk" in the sense that they may be unable to shoplift or break and enter, they may still be able to commit larcenies and a variety of crimes against the person.

Delinquency rates are most meaningful when the population is divided into age groups, for two reasons. The first is that it makes the exclusion of the young and the old more easy, and the second, that a rate for the total population may mask important variations in the criminality of different age groups.

Table I relates to the year 1954, and demonstrates the point numerically.

TABLE I

Made Persons in England and Wales found Guilty of Indictable Offences.*

Age Group	Estimated no. in E & W. in thousands	No. found guilty of indictable offences	Rate per 100,000
8 and under 14	1,904	18,383	965
14 ,, ,, 17	865	13,387	1,548
17 ,, ,, 21	1,041	10,152	975
21 ,, ,, 30	2,611	20,149	772
30 and over	11,964	29,932	250
All ages, 8 and over	18,385	92,003	500

* Source: Criminal Statistics for 1954.

On the basis of numbers found guilty the 17-21's appear to be the most law abiding age group, whereas in fact their rate is second highest and almost double the rate for the whole population.

By the calculation of rates of this kind, not only may the relative criminality of different age groups in the population of a city be observed, but a more realistic picture of the criminality of the population of different districts be obtained. For local rates a percentage calculation is probably more useful than a proportion per thousand or hundred thousand. Ideally, comparisons between rates would be most accurate if the size of the local populations were standardised, but although the total populations of Wards tend to be similar, the proportions of their populations in different age groups may vary considerably. Where, for example, the number of adolescents in the population is very small, the rates for those age groups is somewhat less meaningful in criminological terms. Antisocial behaviour in this age group must have a different sociological significance in an area in which there are a large number of adolescents, than in an area where there are but few, for their role in terms of the total social structure of an area seems likely to vary with their numerical strength in the population.

In considering the pattern of crime commission we are faced with a rather more difficult task. Our initial distinction between areas of crime commission and areas of delinquent residence implied that crime in a given area is to a considerable degree a function of its physical and economic characteristics. In looking for a common denominator for the purpose of comparison some variable must be sought which reflects these characteristics. For delinquency rates, population is an obvious choice, simply because offenders are people. Crime rates in contrast are not related to population in the same way. A central business district may, in fact, be as thinly populated as a rural area, but its total volume of crime will be considerably more. Two variables immediately suggest themselves, acreage, and the proportion of commercial and industrial property. Density of crimes per acre is in fact the basis of one rate used by the Metropolitan Police, but its use is open to certain objections. If the areas compared are of similar size and are equally densely developed, then the rate undoubtedly reflects the concentration of crimes in a physical sense. If, however, an area contains large expanses of parkland or water, the rate may give a false notion of dispersion, whereas crimes may be highly concentrated in a particular part of the area.

Alternatively, rates might be constructed upon the basis of the number of crimes per monetary unit of commercial, industrial, or residential rateable value but such rates might also give a misleading impression. An area might have a high rate per unit of industrial rateable value because of the relative absence of industry, and the same criticisms hold true of rates based upon units of commercial and residential rateable value. Even a rate based upon units of total rateable value produces difficulties. An area with say 100,000 units of rateable value and 5,000 offences will have only half the rate of an area with 50,000 units of rateable value and 5,000 offences. Superficially it would appear that one area experiences more crime than another whereas the difference may simply be due to the fact that the property in the first area is rated twice as high as in the second. A similar objection might be made of rates expressed in terms of crimes per acre, but in so far as the rate is a measure of the physical distribution of crimes it is at least a realistic one, for it reflects the differences in the frequency of crimes between one area than another in a way in which other rates do not. The use of rateable values as a basis for crime rates is of course only meaningful in relation to crimes against property, in that implicit in their use is the assumption that the number of crimes will tend to vary with the wealth and prosperity of different districts in both relative and absolute terms.

Because it is so difficult to measure the incidence of crimes in terms of socio-economic variables such as rateable value in a manner which is criminologically meaningful, the density of crimes per acre rate would appear the most appropriate to use. It is nevertheless possible to analyse the relationship between the incidence of crime and such variables as the proportion of commercial, residential or industrial property by means of the correlation coefficient, but such procedures are not relevant to the task of comparing one area with another.

Assuming that the two major difficulties are defining first the areas to be compared and then the basis of their comparison, there still remains a number of questions unanswered. Unless, for example, criteria can be established whereby "delinquency areas" can be distinguished from other areas the terms "areas of crime commission" and "areas of delinquent residence" cease to have any real value. In a sense the terms could apply to all areas where crimes are committed or where criminals live. The situation would then be similar to that in Hans Andersen's *"Tinder Box"* in which the attempts of the Princess's nurse to identify her whereabouts by means of a cross of the door of the soldier's lodging were frustrated by the Dog with Eyes as Big as Saucers who chalked crosses on every door in the town. Shaw did not attempt to establish criteria on the basis of his delinquency rates whereby some areas could be designated "delinquency areas" and others "non-delinquency areas", but rather tended to regard their identification as something virtually self evident from a glance at his spot maps of Chicago. Lander, on the other hand, establishes a mean census tract rate for the city of Baltimore and makes comparisons between census tracts upon this basis. The questions which need to be asked then are how many crimes and how many criminals must there be before an area can be regarded as a delinquency area of one kind or the other?

Broadly speaking, a mean rate is of considerable value in this respect. Where, for example, the delinquency rates for all age groups in given areas are above or below the mean rate for the city, one may classify them with some confidence. Here again though, classification is to some extent arbitrary and it may be questioned, for instance, whether an area with a rate 1 % above the mean may be validly classified with one which has a rate 15 % above the mean. The use of statistical measures of dispersion does not solve this problem entirely, which is primarily one of criminological definition. It would be unwise to attempt to establish criteria applicable to all cities because the highest rates recorded in some cities may be but a fraction of the highest rates in others. Delinquency rates are relative and not absolute, in the sense that although there may be areas with no registered or known offenders and therefore with delinquency rates equal to zero, there are no areas where the proportion of offenders equals unity. Even in the worst blighted areas of Chicago Shaw did not establish rates higher than 20 %.

III

So far we have taken the definition of crime and delinquency as given, but in important ways, variations in their definition affect the validity and meaning of crime statistics. The source of the enumerator in an area's crime rate is no less important than that of the denominator if the rate is to be at all useful in inter-

preting the criminological facts. This problem then falls into
two parts (a) the question of how to define crime and delinquency, and (b) the selection of an appropriate statistical source
of crime or delinquency registration.

(a) *Definition of Crime and Delinquency*

Wyld's Universal English Dictionary offers the following
definitions.

Delinquency: fr. Lat. delinquentia, "a fault, crime" fr. delin-
quere, "to fail, be wanting; commit a fault".
Fault, offence, omission of duty.

Delinquent: One who neglects a duty; one who commits a
fault; a criminal.

Crime: fr. Lat. crimen, "judicial decision, charge, crime",
An act which is an offence against human law, of
a grave character, and punishable by death,
imprisonment, or fine.

Criminal: Of the nature of crime, wicked; criminal neglect;
a criminal offence; criminal conversation.

The early usage of these words may be noted showing that as
terms descriptive of social realities they are well established in
both language and our system of ideas about social behaviour.
The current usage of the terms "delinquent" and "criminal"
nevertheless sometimes seems to make nonsense of such established definitions. The mark of delinquency is generally an
appearance in court or a "brush with the Law"; furthermore, it
is a term used almost exclusively to describe the juveline law-
breaker. A boy of sixteen who breaks into a house or who commits robbery with violence is invariably described as a "Juvenile
Delinquent", yet his actions are clearly something more than
mere "faults", "misdeeds', or "violations of duty". On the
contrary, the citizen who parks his car in a yellow band area or
who infringes the provisions of the Town and Country Planning
Act by building a shed in his garden without a licence, is guilty
of a *criminal* offence. In common parlance we hesitate to describe
him as a criminal, yet it is a fact that of all persons prosecuted in
the criminal courts of England and Wales, over half are charged
with traffic offences, only a few of whom are "criminals" in the
accepted sense of the word.

The term delinquency can apply to behaviour which is

contrary to the established moral code, whether it happens to be an offence in law or not. For example, a petty theft is both a delinquent and a criminal act, contrary both to the provisions of the Larceny Act (1916) and to a normative system of social values about property. It is perhaps significant, nevertheless, that as Westermarck observed "the laws themselves command obedience more as customs than as laws."[1] Adultery, on the other hand, is not an offence in law, yet it is still a delinquent act in so far as it is a transgression of a system of moral rules regulating the social aspects of sexual behaviour. That it is not a criminal offence is to a very great extent an historical accident, for in some states with a high degree of theocratic government, like Calvin's Geneva, it was a capital offence. Not all delinquent acts are criminal, nor in a sense, are all criminal acts delinquent, for much depends upon the circumstances of the act and the current climate of moral opinion. If a man indulges in a violent altercation with his mother-in-law indoors he does not break the law; nevertheless he infringes a social norm. If he does the same thing in the street he may possibly be charged with "using insulting words and behaviour likely to cause a breach of the peace" contrary to the Metropolitan Police Act 1839 Section 54 (13) or an appropriate local bye-law. Either action in so far as it were negatively sanctioned by the consensus of moral opinion in the community would seem to be a "delinquent act", whether the sanction carries the force of law or not.

With the progressive extension of the activities of the State into the social and economic life of the community there has been a vast and unprecedented growth of administrative regulations which, though sanctioned by law, have no place in the long established body of rules which may be termed the moral order. Although obedience to the State is in general terms incumbent upon every citizen, few of its administrative rules have any intrinsic moral content. In former days the majority of crimes were also delinquencies in a social and moral sense. Thieving was against the law and against a set of primal rules about property supposedly handed down from Moses. The injunction that cyclists shall carry a red rear light, or that cars shall have two independent systems of braking has no such moral quality. Besides being arbitrary in nature, such rules may be instituted or

---

[1] E. Westermarck. *The Origins and Development of Moral Ideas*. London, 1906, Vol. 1. p. 9.

abolished according to political circumstances. Many of the
controls instituted by one government may be swept away over-
night by its successor in office.

How then may we usefully distinguish between crime and
delinquency? The most reasonable distinction would seem to be
on the basis of the seriousness of the action judged by the normative standards of conduct in the community. The parking
motorist would then be delinquent and the armed robber a
criminal. The term "juvenile delinquent" has grown up, not
because the activities of juvenile offenders are relatively trivial,
but because they are adjudged to be less responsible in a social
and moral sense. Much of the difficulty arises through the
equation of "crime" with "illegal actions". Diagramatically, the
situation might be illustrated by two intersecting circles, that on
the left representing anti-social behaviour negatively sanctioned
by moral opinion, and that on the right behaviour negatively
sanctioned by law.

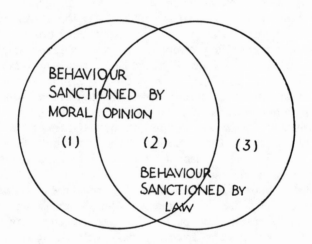

Such an analysis provides us with three categories of behaviour.

1   Anti-social action which is not illegal, and sanctioned only
     by public opinion.
2   Anti-social action which is illegal, and sanctioned by both
     law and public opinion.
3   Illegal behaviour sanctioned by law, but which is not
     commonly considered anti-social.

Category (1) may be said to correspond to delinquency, and behaviour in category (2) criminal or delinquent depending upon its gravity, while behaviour in category (3) may be termed quasi-criminal or quasi-delinquent. This is of course only valid where adult members of the community are concerned, for it is one of the paradoxes of our society that although young persons are accorded the benefit of diminished responsibility, their actions are often more circumscribed. Sexual promiscuity, for example, which for an adult would fall into category (1) could easily bring an adolescent girl into court as being "beyond control", "in need of care" or in "moral danger". It is of little purpose to argue that the Juvenile Court in such cases acts not as a criminal court but a court of chancery and that proceedings taken under the Children's Acts are not criminal. As far as the girl is concerned, she is being constrained by the community through the agency of the law, and if she is committed to an approved school the distinction between her and the girl who steals becomes academic. The extent to which the refractory behaviour of young persons comes within the scope of the law varies between different countries, and in the United States especially, comparisons between different cities are difficult because of the way in which the legal definition of delinquency and the scope of the law varies from one state to another.[1]

To consider the concept of behaviour negatively sanctioned by the consensus of moral opinion in the community we must examine the terms "consensus" and "community". Consensus may be reasonably defined as the measure of agreement expressed by a social group in its evaluation of behaviour; "community" however may mean a variety of things. Clearly its use cannot be limited in the way some of the Chicago ecologists have suggested to groups whose inter-relationships are wholly symbiotic and non-social. On the other hand, if we accept McIver's definition[2] as the group within which it is possible though not imperative for an individual to live his whole life, the division of labour has made communities out of whole continents embracing groups with differing social values and standards of conduct. In ecological terms it is the local group, or neighbourhood which comes nearest to being a community in having a characteristic culture

---

[1] For a fuller discussion of this problem see Milton Barron, *The Juvenile in Delinquent Society,* New York, 1954.
[2] McIver, *Society,* London, 1937, p. 9.

or social system. Social control, however, is not exclusively vested in local groups. It is possible, for instance, to talk of the "business community" which exercises control over its members who need not live in physical proximity.

Neighbourhood and locality have nevertheless an important significance in understanding the mechanisms of informal (as distinct from formal or legal) agencies of social control, which, because they depend so much upon face to face contacts must almost invariably operate at a local level. In some neighbourhoods, the consensus of local opinion may seem to justify certain forms of behaviour such as petty thieving or the indiscriminate use of physical violence, but no locality is ever a complete social universe, and the behaviour of its inhabitants must be judged with reference to other more widely accepted norms.

(b) *The Selection of Sources of Crime and Delinquency Registration*

Because there may be disagreement about what constitutes anti-social behaviour it is probably unrealistic to attempt to define norms on a statistical basis for a whole society; not only are wife-beating and promiscuity apparently acceptable in a minority of local communities or neighbourhoods, but there are often grave discrepancies between ideal norms and actual behaviour. In the category of behaviour not sanctioned by law but by public opinion alone, individuals are free to choose their own moral rules. They are not free, however, to choose their own laws, and for this reason it would seem most practicable to use records of transgressions against the law which buttresses such a wide variety of moral rules as an index of serious anti-social behaviour. From this area of behaviour it is reasonable to extract only those offences which are the subject of moral judgment, and disregard what we have termed quasi-crimes and quasi delinquencies.

To calculate rates of *crime commission*, the obvious source of the enumerator is the statistic of "crimes known to the police". Although this source is considerably more reliable nowadays as a result of greater care in the recording of crimes,[1] it is not completely so. Much depends upon the efficiency of the police in discovering offences and upon the attitude of the public in reporting them. Broadly speaking, the "dark number" of offences

[1] See H. Mannheim, *Social Aspects of Crime in England between the Wars*, London, 1940, Ch. 2.

which do not come to light varies according to the nature of the offence. Few homicides escape the notice of the police for most citizens are likely to bring such things to official notice, but there are many other offences which are less likely to be immediately reported. Petty larcenies may be so trivial that it seems hardly worthwhile to report them, or the victim may be eager to give the offender another chance. Occasionally the victim of assault or blackmail may be reluctant to report the offence simply because of the damage to his reputation caused by publicity. Although the margin of unreported crimes is probably smallest in the case of offences against the person and the more serious offences against property, it is likely to be greatest in respect of those offences which make up the largest single category in the records, namely simple and minor larcenies.

The sources of the enumerator of a rate of *delinquent residence*[1] are more varied, but equally subject to error. Shaw uses two sets of data, the numbers of persons in an area charged in court and the number of charges or "delinquency cases" involved, the former providing an estimate of the size of the lawbreaking population and the latter some indication of its relative criminality. Court appearances, like "crimes known to the police", are based upon what is known, and the reliability of a rate based upon them is impaired by a similar margin or "dark number" of unknown offenders. Furthermore, they relate only to *alleged* and not *proven* offences and do not include persons known to be concerned in crimes yet against whom no proceedings are taken, either because of lack of evidence which would secure a conviction, or because the person offended against declines to prosecute.

Where refractory children are concerned, who may be dealt with under the Children's Acts in this country, or under some of the wider legal definitions of delinquency in the United States and elsewhere, the social class factor is an particularly important variable to be considered. Different groups in the community tend to select different means of dealing with this problem, and relatively few resort to preferring court cases against their own children. The system of warnings to first offenders given by certain Chief Constables, and such systems as the Liverpool Juvenile Liason Scheme tend to reduce the validity of the charge statistics in a similar way. The record of persons prosecuted and

---

[1] In this context the word 'delinquent' must be taken as synonymous with 'criminal'.

convicted must also be viewed with caution for not only are a few innocent persons found guilty, but a proportion of guilty persons manage to be acquitted. Again, if the problem is that of constructing local rates of delinquent residence, the situation is further complicated by the fact that charges are brought in the area in which the offence is alleged to have been committed, and this may be many miles from the offender's home. Short of searching court records on a country-wide basis, there is no way of ensuring that the figure of alleged offenders in a specific area is completely accurate. Notwithstanding its drawbacks, in the absence of a more reliable set of data the record of court appearances is probably the most practical source of a rate enumerator. Whether persons charged, or the number of charges or cases preferred is used depends largely upon the nature of the problem of analysis in hand, though each would seem to be a useful complement of the other.

III

SOME ECOLOGICAL STUDIES
OF THE 19TH CENTURY

CRIMINOLOGICAL studies in the 19th century were very largely based upon published social statistics or upon the results of investigation by zealous social reformers and administrators, anxious about the moral welfare of the community. By and large they could be described as sociological in that they attempted to identify regularities in the pattern of criminal behaviour or that they tackled some of the vexed problems of social causation. In the last fifty years, however, the field has been as much the preserve of psychiatrists, psychologists and geneticists as sociologists and social statisticians. Indeed, studies confined strictly to the sociological aspects of crime have been relatively few, while the results of what might be termed the "psycho-social" approach have been both widely disseminated and fruitful. Burt's *Young Delinquent* for example, is a classic with much that is interesting and relevant to the present day, while the Gluecks have helped to open up new vistas in penology by their development of techniques of social prediction. It seems that Criminology is approaching that stage at which it may at last achieve recognition as a discipline with scientific status by arriving at some synthesis of the theories of other disciplines concerned with the phenomenon of crime. If it cannot have distinctive and unique research techniques, it can at least have methods of study which are both valid and acceptable for sociologist, physiologist, psychiatrist, psychologist and statistician alike.

Certain ideas about crime, which are essentially sociological, often appear to be overlooked in an enthusiasm for psychology. The consideration of crime trends, for example, such as gave rise to Quetelet's notion of an "annual budget" of crime, is of secondary importance today to the problems of criminal motivation. A similar fate has overtaken certain other forms of sociological conceptualisation; suicide, for instance, is almost invariably considered from the psychiatric standpoint, not as Durkheim saw it as a problem of social integration, but as one of mental health.[1]

It is reasonable to inquire how this state of affairs has come about, that criminology has become a discipline increasingly concerned with the problems of individual motivation rather than the collective phenomenon of "crime". There seem to be two general answers, complementary rather than alternative to each other. Firstly, social scientists have often felt under some moral obligation to provide the answers to social problems, and often too the basis of social policy. In order to do this, there has been an intensification of the search for "causes". Where the earlier sociologists or social scientists were interested in the classification of social data by painstaking applications of the comparative method in order to investigate such hypotheses as "evolution" or "progress"[2] nowadays psychologists and social statisticians are employed to inquire into such things as the dynamics of racial prejudice, the nature of social class, or to predict actuarially the chances of success or failure on release of a group of Borstal trainees.

The question "why" is posed so frequently, and human beings are so notoriously eccentric in doing similar things for a variety of reasons that it is not surprising that the individual has become the primary unit of analysis, and his distinctive behaviour, therefore, the primary field of investigation. Sociality implies, by definition, a plurality of individuals; therefore, any scheme which isolates the individual for analytic purposes is essentially psychological rather than sociological in character. For example, the analysis of a criminal act need not *necessarily* involve consideration of the social implications of that act as such, except in an ancillary sense; it might conceivably be considered in psychoanalytic terms as the end product or expression of an inner and unconscious conflict.

The second answer to the question is there has been a reaction

---

[1] One welcome exception to this is P. Sainsbury's *Suicide in London,* London, 1955.

[2] One might cite here the works of Comte, Spencer, Tylor, Morgan, Rivers and Hobhouse to name but a few.

to Lombroso, (whose greatest contribution to criminology was probably the shifting of the emphasis from crime to the criminal). The biologists' approach to the study of criminal behaviour was one which, though attractive in its apparent comprehensiveness and relative simplicity, touched at the very roots of human belief in the ability of man to control his own destiny. The logical inference from the theory of atavism was that the criminal was not a free agent but a mere automaton, destined by his genetic inheritance to tread an anti-social path. Not only did this run counter to the notion of free will, but it made nonsense of morality, for the ideas of praise and blame, innocence and guilt, are meaningless without the ideas of freedom and responsibility. The untenability of his original formulations became so apparent, that Lombroso himself so qualified them as to reduce them to what one might describe as "theoretical impotence." But attention having once been focussed on the criminal and his behaviour, rather than on the more abstract notion of "crime", and the biological avenue of inquiry having proved to be fraught with many difficulties, it is hardly surprising that attention turned from the examination of the criminal's genetic constitution to that of his psychological constitution.

Psychological inquiry into the nature of criminal or anti-social behaviour is nevertheless, perfectly valid; indeed, if one wants to understand why a little boy steals from Woolworths the psychologist, or more strictly, the psychiatrist, may supply a variety of interesting answers. The boy may, for example, be performing a symbolic act, a result of his emotional deprivation, alternatively he may be attempting to bolster up his own sense of adequacy by performing an action which has an element of danger in it. On the other hand, he may be attempting to validate his social status in the eyes of his companions, or pilfering may be a normal activity in his peer group. The latter two explanations bring us definitely into the field of sociological inquiry; while it is not suggested that any of the worthwhile work on the psychology of delinquency has failed to consider such facts, the complaint is that they have been considered primarily from a psychological point of view, and due recognition has not been given to them as sociological phenomena in their own right.

In order to develop this theme one ought to distinguish clearly between two levels of abstraction or analysis. At one level we may consider individual behaviour and its motivation. Here choice and action are the subject matter of psychology, for except in so far as the perception of situations and individual value systems are socially determined, decisions can be made without reference to any other individual. At a second level, however, we must consider not only the determinants of individual perception, and values or norms of conduct, but the objective consequences of individual action. These are essentially social facts which can be considered apart from the motivations of individuals; some of the norms can be seen crystallised in the Criminal Law, and the objective consequences of action may be observed in the oscillations of the Criminal Statistics.

To say that social facts constrain the individual is to say nothing new, but it seems important to say that systems of social values which vary between different sections of the community in important details bear vitally upon the alternative forms of behaviour which are open to the individual. For instance, is it merely a coincidence that amongst working class children delinquency is often the concomitant of emotional deprivation or maladjustment, while amongst middle class children—among whom there is no reason to suppose that these things occur any less frequently—delinquency, at least as measured by criminal proceedings, is minimal?

The objective consequences of individual action, the pattern of which is socially determined even if its motivation is unique and psychological, may be observed as a system of regularities. The incidence of one type of crime may be compared with that of another. Similarly, the relative criminality of different age groups, occupational groups or the two sexes is a valid field of, inquiry. Indeed, for the purposes of determining social policy it is vital to discover "how much crime?" "what kind of crime?" and "what kind of criminals?" there are, questions which stand quite apart from considerations as to why individual criminals commit particular crimes.[1]

The purpose of these introductory paragraphs is to justify the validity of criminological research into the nature and interrelationship of factors which are essentially sociological in character, such as crime patterns and trends, the age and occupa-

---

[1] The opposite view is held by William Healey who wrote, "The dynamic centre of the whole problem of delinquency and crime will ever be the individual offender". *The Individual Delinquent,* Boston, 1915, p. 22.

tional structure of the criminal population, the variations in crime rates between different geographical areas, and the possible existence of a consensus of anti-social values in "criminal districts". Such matters were the subject of a considerable amount of painstaking research in the nineteenth century, the most important of which we shall be considering in a moment. The appearance of Lombroso, and the founding of a school of "criminal anthropology" seems to have resulted in the total or near total eclipse of the work of sociologists in the criminological field. The genetic theories of crime which have been subsequently replaced by psychological theories of crime seem to have excited so much interest that sociological theories, particularly in Europe, have been of secondary importance. Indeed, one might say that Lombroso lives on in the work and writings of Sheldon and Hooton, the latter still defending him against Goring a quarter of a century later.[1]

What reasons might one offer for this eclipse? Firstly, the importance of Darwinism in the late nineteenth century can hardly be overestimated. Evolution and natural selection were concepts adopted and adapted wholesale in almost every field of intellectual inquiry from biology to sociology, or what Mill called more properly the "moral sciences". "Positive" was an attractive term and almost limitless in its application. Furthermore, studies of motivation were more attractive partly because they came nearer to the vitality of human behaviour, and partly because by existing at a lower level of abstraction they required less intellectual effort, a fact which led to the vulgarisations of popular pseudo-science, the notion of the "born criminal" being a case in point. Secondly, Lombroso and his followers embarked on a wide programme of propoganda, and to quote Lindesmith and Levin

'After Lombroso's attempt to appropriate criminology to biology and medicine had attracted wide publicity in Europe, physicians and psychiatrists were attracted to the problem in greater numbers and gradually displaced in public attention and prestige the magistrates, prison authorities, lawyers, philanthropists, journalists and social scientists who had previously dominated the field . . . The Lombrosian myth arose,

[1] Hooton, E. A. *The American Criminal, an Anthropological Study*. Cambridge, Mass. 1939.

therefore, as a result of the "seizure of power" so to speak by the medical profession.'[1]

The same authors go further and relate the popularity of Lombrosianism to the state of public opinion;

'It may be that the theory of the born criminal offered a convenient rationalisation of the failure of preventive effort and an escape from the implications of the dangerous doctrine that crime is an essential product of our social organisation. It may well be that a public which had been nagged for centuries by reformers, welcomed the opportunity to slough off its responsibilities for this vexing problem.'[2]

Much of the research of the nineteenth curenty which must be regarded as sociological, and which was largely totally obscured by Lombrosianism, may also be regarded as ecological. The term "ecological" is not intended to suggest that Guerry, Rawson, Fletcher and Mayhew can be strictly classed with say, Park, Burgess, Shaw and McKay, for while the latter worked within the confines of a specific body of theory, the former worked not only in isolation but upon a series of *ad hoc* hypotheses, or as it appears in Mayhew's case, upon none at all. But there are a number of points of similarity between their work which might be summarised as follows.

1 A primary interest in crime as a social or collective phenomenon of which individual behaviour is a component, rather than in the motivation of crime in the individual.
2 The quantification of data relating to crime and criminals to illustrate qualitative variations in both time and place.
3 The role of objective socio-economic factors such as poverty, education, density of population and external value systems, in determining and perpetuating criminal behaviour.

In their work the nineteenth century ecologists were concerned with the geopgraphical location of crime and criminals within the total physical environment, and the differences in

[1] Lindesmith, A. and Levin, Y. 'The Lombrosian Myth in Criminology', *Am. Journ. Sociology,* 42, 1937, p. 669.
[2] *Ibid.* p. 670.

criminal behaviour which could be associated with differences in the pattern of social institutions or the character of social values. Although modern statistics can demonstrate with ease the fallacy of assuming an association between two variables as necessarily indicative of some specifically *causal* relationship, one can at the same time measure the extent to which the association is purely fortuitous. The value of their work, even after subtracting for a certain degree of naievety, seems to be that they not only used quantitative techniques with some skill to reinforce their arguments, but that they stated so categorically that whatever the nature of individual motivation might be, the objective consequences of individual action, and the modes of its expressions are social phenomena par excellence, characteristic not of the individual, but of the collectivity of which he is but a part.

That criminology, no less than any of the other social sciences, was originally speculative rather than empirical was perhaps understandable in the absence of adequate and reliable sources of statistics. Mayhew, in particular, had strong views on this subject though personally he had some contempt for the "arm chair" theorists and preferred to augment his information by field research. He wrote,

'In a subject like the crime and vice of the Metropolis and of the country in general, of which so little is known—of which there are so many facts but so little comprehension—it is evident that we must seek by induction, that is to say, by careful classification of the known phenomena, to render the matter more intelligible; in fine, we must, in order to arrive at a *comprehensive* knowledge of its antecedents, consequences and concomitants, contemplate as large a number of facts as possible in as many different relations as the statistical records of the country will admit of our doing.'[1]

Relatively accurate social statistics began with the publication of Census Reports, but statistics relating to crime and criminals were rather less systematic than the census data, and tended to be *judicial* rather than *criminal* statistics as we nowadays understand the term. In this country they appeared in increasing numbers as House of Commons Papers from the 1790's onwards. These reports may similarly be regarded as the response to a demand

---

[1] Mayhew, H. *The Criminal Prisons of London,* London, 1862.

for some accurate assessment of the state of social unrest particularly in the years following Waterloo. It was France, however, that set the standard for official statistics on crime and criminals with the first publication of the Compte Générale in 1825. The civil servant responsible for the comparatively efficient collection and analysis of the data was one M. Guerry de Champneuf who unfortunately lost his position when Charles X was deposed by the Revolution of 1830. In 1829 a Monsieur *A. M. Guerry* was appointed to collect and collate the judicial statistics for the City of Paris, and it is he who is remembered rather than his predecessor; to whom he was apparently quite unrelated. A. M. Guerry was helped in his work by the geographer *Adriano Balbi*, and together they published in 1829 a statistical map comparing the extent of education with the extent of crime in France. In 1833 Guerry published his "*Essai sur la Statistique Morale de la France*". The most novel feature of the book was the use of the cartographic method of presenting the statistical material, a technique which was to be widely used not only by ecologists and social statisticians of those times but later by the Chicago School. He felt that the different kinds of shading on the maps would not only enable the reader to see the facts more quickly but to appreciate more readily the essence of the comparison. J. S. Mill, in the sixth book of the *Logic* continually refers to the "moral sciences"; for Guerry the social facts he considered were essentially "moral facts"; crime, suicide, illegitimacy and levels of education.

The statistics of crime were based upon the Quarterly Returns of the local Public Prosecutors in all parts of France. These in turn were collated on a Departmental Basis, and the Departments grouped into five great regions, each comprising seventeen Departments, viz., North, South, East, West and Centre. The implicit notion in the comparisons between these regions is that variations are due to regional factors, but there arises the difficulty that the figures are essentially *judicial* statistics, "accusés" or "charges".[1] It is possible that not all persons charged in an area are natives of it, in which case the area must be considered as an area of crime in relation to such of its characteristics as provide opportunities for crime, rather than an area of criminal

---

[1] Guerry preferred 'charges' to 'commitals'; he regarded these as a better measure of crime as the courts were not always consistent in their application of the law. 'Essai sur la Statistique Morale de la France,' p. 6.

production or "delinquent residence". Guerry regarded the problem as one of enumerating areas of criminal production and his analyses seem to indicate that he was more concerned with factors which predispose the individual towards crime rather than those which precipitate its commission. In order to justify his procedure on the basis of local statistics he cites the Compte Générale for 1828 which established that on an average 72% of the persons charged in any Department were natives of that Department and that for all France 97% of all persons charged were of French origin. The author of a critical notice at the time regards this evidence as conclusive,[1] nevertheless an average, particularly for all the 86 Departments of France is likely to be misleading, and in so far as such a parameter represents an index of residential mobility for the criminal population, one might justly ask for more detailed figures. In the Departments of Seine, Seine et Oise and Eure, for example, one would expect a larger proportion of "non natives" in the population at any given time than say in the sparsely populated Massif Central.

The data collected in this work is listed under the following headings. Each section is amply illustrated with shaded maps and the tables on which are based.

1 Crimes committed in France for each year 1825-1830, subdivided by type.
2 The influence of sex differences on crime, i.e. analysis of male and female crime.
3 The influence of age, i.e. analysis by age groups.
4 Seasonal variations in crime rates.
5 Motives for capital crimes. } (as established by the Court)
6 Motives of crimes against the person. }
7 Comments on the maps showing the local distribution
8 of crimes (7) against property and (8) the person.
9 Comments on the map showing the variations in educational levels in France.
10 Comments on the map showing distribution of illegitimacy.
11 „ „ „ „ „ „ charitable donations.
12 Comments on the map showing distribution of suicides.
13 Consideration of crimes peculiar to age levels.

Perhaps the most interesting of Guerry's analyses is that of the variations in rates of crimes against the person and against property between the different regions of France.

TABLE 2

CRIME IN FRANCE 1825-1830

Crimes against the Person All France = 100

	1825	1826	1827	1828	1829	1830	Average	Population
North	25	24	23	26	25	24	25	8,757,700
South	28	26	22	23	25	23	24	4,826,493
East	17	21	19	20	19	19	19	5,840,996
West	18	16	21	17	17	16	18	7,008,788
Centre	12	13	15	14	14	18	14	5,238,905
	100	100	100	100	100	100	100	31,672,882

Crimes against Property All France = 100

	1825	1826	1827	1828	1829	1830	Average
North	41	42	42	43	44	44	42
South	12	11	11	12	12	11	12
East	18	16	17	16	14	15	16
West	17	19	19	17	17	17	18
Centre	12	12	11	12	13	13	12
	100	100	100	100	100	100	

From this table it can be seen that not only do there appear to be regional variations in the type of crime committed but also variations in the per capita rate of crimes. For example, crimes against property in the North were almost twice as numerous as crimes against the person (respective averages 42 and 25 %). The South, on the other hand, was responsible for an average of 24 % of crimes against the person but only 12 % of crimes against property. But whereas the average for crimes against the person in the North was 25 % and the average in the South almost as great (24 %), the *population* of the south was only just over half that of the North. In the case of crimes against property, the South is far below parity with the North, responsible for only slightly more than a quarter as much, 12 % compared to 42 %.

In other words, the North was characterised by crimes against property rather than crimes against the person. In the South, not only did crimes against the person exceed those against property (considered as percentages of the total for all France), but the *per capita rate* of crimes against property was lower than in the North while the per capita rate of crimes against the person was about double that of the North.

The inference to be drawn from this is that in the Southern region of France the pattern of criminal behaviour was uniquely different from that of the more populous regions. An excess of crimes against the person over those against property suggests that it was the South which was atypical in this respect, for in France as a whole crimes against the person were only a fraction of those against property.

Guerry's comments are not only directed towards the regional variations in crime patterns but towards the regularities in the yearly regional totals, for instance, to the fact that the average for the five year period is seldom ecxeeded. Besides this there was a consistency from year to year in the level of criminality in each age group, and in the proportions of the sexes. A further apparent regularity persisted in that most crimes against the person were committed in summer, whilst most crimes against property were committed in winter. He writes:

'Now, if the infinite variety of circumstances which lead crime to be reflected upon, together with the extraneous or personal influences which constitute its greater or less depravity, these invarying results are what nobody would have dreamed of; and it is a matter of astonishment that acts of free will should rigorously assume no uniform a character. On such a view there is no reasonable ground to deny that moral as well as physical events are subject to invariable laws, and that in many respects judicial statistics afford a sure guide to the judgment. In spite, therefore, of the frequent misuse of statistics by some reasoners, and of the objections of others whose speculations this science does not bear out, it has naturally attracted general attention and given a new direction to ,criminal legislation and to the inquiries of the moral philosophers.'[1]

Guerry was not content to postulate some explanation in terms of sociological determinism like his contemporary, Quételet, he tested empirically three of the commonest hypotheses as to the causes of crime which were held in the nineteenth century, and which, indeed, have some currency today, namely

[1] Guerry, A. M. op. cit. p. ii. Translated and quoted in *Westminster Review*, Vol. 18, p. 357.

1) Crime is due to poverty
2) Crime is due to ignorance i.e. lack of education
3) Crime is due to population density

The first hypothesis seemed difficult to substantiate when the wealthiest region,[1] i.e. the North had the largest proportion of crimes against property, while the poorest, the South and Centre, had the smallest proportion of such crimes. Guerry was quick to point out that the general level of wealth in a Department might easily mask the variations in levels of wealth between different social classes. The existence of a relatively small number of millionaires is often concomitant with a much larger number of people in extreme poverty. This would be particularly true in the North of France at this time when the industrial revolution was just beginning, and wealthy manufacturers lived in much closer proximity to their employees than is probably true today. It would also be true to say that urban poverty is often more pressing than rural poverty, for the starving peasant may live in some measure by poaching, or off the hedgerows, sources of supply not available to his town cousin. In order to refine the relationship between wealth and crimes against property, Guerry mapped the distribution of patents throughout France, establishing that the larger the number of patents held in a particular Department, i.e. the greater the concentration of manufacturing industries, the larger the number of crimes against property. The two exceptions to this were Brittany, a Region largely concerned with maritime activities, where there was much thieving but little manufacturing, and in Meuse and Cote-d'Or, wine growing areas with much trade but little thieving.

The original hypothesis was that men stole because they were poor and needy, but if the figures for larceny were examined for the regions most poverty stricken, the suggestion seemed disproved. But as has been pointed out, the most prosperous regions might also have a considerable amount of poverty. The real answer seems to be forthcoming only if we consider the *opportunities* for crime. In the poorest Departments there will be little to steal; in the wealthiest there will be a great deal. (Such a type of explanation might in fact also explain why larcenies occured most frequently in winter, during the long hours of

---

[1] Poverty and wealth were measured by the amount of direct taxation.

darkness.) His most pertinent observation seems to be that there
was a kind of "stage army" of professional thieves who operated
in the large urban centres like Paris, and in the seaports. This
explains, for instance, how St. Nazaire, Brest and other places in
Brittany had a high level of larceny, and at the same time, the
relationship between concentration of industry and larceny, viz.
professional criminals operate in densely populated urban centres
such as tended to grow up in manufacturing districts.

His rejection of the idea that increases in population density
resulted in increase in crime as too hasty is not altogether
convincing. He argues that the great urban centres of Toulouse,
Montpellier, Nîmes, Marseilles, Nantes, and Bordeaux are
situated in Departments noted for a relatively few crimes
against property, whilst Troyes, Chalon-sur-Marne, Arras,
Evreux and Chartres, less populous towns, are situated in
Departments with many more such crimes. This argument
disregards differences within each Department, both in the location of crimes and the distribution of population. The larceny
figures for Marseilles, for instance, might have been half the
total for all Provence, quite a likely thing in view of its being a
seaport. The example of his second set of towns is rather more
substantial, though one might add that each was, and still is, a
commercial centre being at an important route junction, and
that the population of say, Toulouse and Nîmes was not all that
much greater than that of say, Arras or Chartres.

His evidence as to the relation between education and crime is
considerable, and his general conclusion was that the popular
view that education would prevent crime, though well-meaning
was mistaken. His criterion of education was literacy and he was
fortunate in that in 1827 it became compulsory for all conscripts
into the French Army to be examined on entry as to their ability
to read and write.

TABLE 3

EDUCATION IN FRANCE 1827-29

% of literate conscripts			% of literate criminals			Proportion of boys in school to total pop.
1827	1828	1829	1828	1829	1830	1829
East	51	56	58	52	52	53	1 in 14
North	48	53	55	49	47	47	1 in 16
South	32	33	34	31	28	30	1 in 43
West	26	27	27	29	25	24	1 in 45
Centre	24	25	25	25	23	23	1 in 48

From the fact that the best educated Departments had the largest proportion of crime and, one might suspect, the largest proportion of criminals, education did not appear to be a bulwark against crime. Guerry also noted that crimes against property appeared to be the concomitant of "education", and those against the person the concomitant of "ignorance." The relationship between delinquency and educational attainment is still today somewhat enigmatic.

The peculiar relationship demonstrated in Guerry's tables is not difficult to explain. In the populous urban centres which provided opportunities for crime, the facilities for education were more adequate than in the thinly populated rural areas where criminal opportunities were somewhat more restricted. The test of simple literacy was a crude one, but the best available to him in 1830; if one applied a similar test today one would still find that the areas with the best educational facilities (the urban ones) also had the largest proportion of criminals.

Finally, Guerry notes the distribution of suicides, finding a higher incidence in the more urbanised areas. His critic in the *Westminster Review* remarks with some wit "The ignorant portion, in the centre of France, attack other people's throats, but take especial care of their own. On the subject of suicide they represent a great white patch."[1]

The importance of Guerry's work would seem to be two-fold. Firstly, he appears to have been the first to utilise relatively accurate criminal satistics to test certain "arm-chair" hypotheses concerning the nature of crime and to find them misleading and sometimes erroneous in the light of the facts. Secondly, he demonstrated that social facts have an objective aspect which justifies their consideration as the end products of human behaviour independently of any reference to analyses of individual motivation. Hitherto, crime had been considered in terms of the moral turpitude of the offender; Guerry, without personally dropping the mask of the scandalised bourgeois, had raised the level of inquiry from arguments about particulars, in ignorance of the facts, to a discussion of general and further reaching principles in an atmosphere approaching that of scientific enlightenment.

He considered the problem of crime in France in terms of geographical units and social institutions, an approach which

[1] *Westminster Review,* loc. cit.

cannot but earn for him the title of the first of the social ecologists. Quételet, whose work is rather better known than that of Guerry, carried the latter's concept of an "analytique morale" a stage further. Like Guerry, he was impressed by the regularity of social data, and noticed their degree of concomitance with such variables as age, sex, and climate. Quételet's notion of "social physics" is a milestone in the theory of sociological determinism. Montesquieu had hinted at a similar idea in his *"Spirit of Laws"* when he had suggested that criminality increases in proportion to proximity to the Equator, but the idea might not be so naive as it first sounds. There is evidence that geography and habitat affect both technology and social institutions; it is possible to say, therefore, that forms of behaviour might conceivably be related to such factors. Quételet's ideas were by no means disregarded; Jevons in 1897 postulated a relationship between the occurrence of sun spots and the Trade Cycle, and Mayo Smith[1] went to some trouble to re-examine Quételet's findings. Grant Dexter's study of crime and the weather[2] suggests that meteorological conditions do have a definite effect on the behaviour of some individuals, though one suspects that situations other than heat-waves might be equally effective in reducing the extent of their self-control.

'Social physics' and its developments are, however, marginal to our theme, and do not come fully within the scope of social ecology, the study of the spatial relations of people and institutions within a given habitat. While Quételet's concepts of the "average man" and the "annual budget of crime" gave an important impetus to the progress of social statistics, Guerry's work particularly in respect of his method of presenting data in cartographic form gave direction to studies in the local distribution of social phenomena, particularly crime, which grew in number from 1830 onwards. He himself, turned his attention to England and at the Great Exhibition of 1851, a series of maps drawn by him based on the criminal statistics of the years 1833-50 were shown. He read a paper before the British Association at about this time, and in 1860 he published a comparative work on the "moral statistics" of France and England.

It appears to have been Guerry's cartographic method of

---

[1] Mayo Smith, R. *Statistics and Sociology,* New York, pp. 271-272.

[2] Grant-Dexter, E. *Weather Influences; An Empirical Study of the Mental and Physiological Effects of Definite Meteorological Conditions,* 1904.

presenting data which appealed to so many writers in the field of social research at this time, rather than his observations upon the regularity of social data which appeared to be independent of individual motivation. *D'Angeville's* extremely comprehensive social demographic study of France published in 1836[1] contains 16 "cartes graphiques" of the type designed by Guerry, illustrating the tabulated data. Although little known, it is an excellent work, and in such details as format and typography many modern works of a similar kind would compare unfavourably. *Eduard Ducpétiaux*, the Belgian writer on eduction and social economics, and incidentally, the author of one of the early treatises on the futility of Capital Punishment, also used the cartographic method to present some of his data, as did *W. R. Greg* in his *Social Statistics of the Netherlands*."[2]

In 1837, *Parent-Duchatelet*, a friend of Guerry, and being what one might describe as the "Medical Officer of Health" for Paris, published two remarkable volumes on the subject of prostitution in the city. His treatment of the subject was comprehensive in that it dealt with the social, medical, moral and administrative aspects of the problem from the beginning of the fifteenth century up to 1830. Because of the official control of brothels in Paris, he was able to amass a considerable volume of data on the "filles publiques" from 1817 to 1827 including the districts of France from which they came. These data were presented in map form. Although it showed that certain Departments were the catchment areas for Parisian prostitutes, while others provided none, it did not, of course, allow any valid inferences to be drawn concerning the local conditions which resulted in girls turning to prostitution for a livelihood. One suspects that some southern districts which had few of their daughters on the streets of Paris were well represented on the quays of Marseilles, just as those from the Massif Central probably found their way more easily to Lyon.

On the Continent, the remaining works which followed closely on Guerry's model were Robriquet's study of Corsica[3] in which he made comparisons on a departmental basis of rates of

[1] D'Angeville, A. Comte, *Essai sur la Statistique de la population Française,* Bourg, 1836.
[2] Greg, W.R. *Social Statistics of the Netherlands,* 1835.
[3] Robriquet, F. *Crimes commis dans la Corse.* Paris, 1841.

various crimes in Corsica and France, and Niceforo's study of Sardinia.[1]

In England, members of the then Statistical Society of London had turned their attention to the study of crime at an early date. In its *'Journal'* for 1839 may be found a paper on the "Criminal Statistics of Preston" by the chaplain of its House of Correction, and a short abstract on the "Number and Nature of Robberies in London and Liverpool in 1838". The most interesting contribution for our present purposes is by *Rawson W. Rawson,* a prolific writer on a wide variety of topics ranging from the railways in Belgium to the then new French colonies in North Africa. Rawson's paper,[2] in two sections, was originally read before the Statistical Section of the British Association on August 27th and 28th, 1839.

In the first part he set out to defend the notion that "moral" (that is "social") phenomena are subject to established general laws as evidenced by the regularity and uniformity of recorded social data. Judging by his remarks, this must have been under severe criticism in some quarters, though it is difficult to understand how many of the sincere religious opponents of science in the last century rejected such an idea, when it was based upon empirical evidence, yet accepted the notions of "God's Will" or "Divine Providence" though they were the products of metaphysical speculation. Rawson attempts to reconcile the view that these are general laws to which human behaviour is subject and at the same time free will, by saying that unless there were a limit to the powers of mind " . . . man would be able to counteract the order of nature and to disturb the harmony which the Creator has established."

His reasoning, nevertheless, matches his casuistry. He notes that all human beings are endowed with basically the same characteristics except "such differences as may be accounted for by the varieties in the physical condition". It is the socialisation of the child which determines the character of the individual's responses to basic social situations.

'If we had the means of ascertaining correctly the amount and nature of crime in the several countries of the world, and all the circumstances of their social condition, we should be

[1] Niceforo, A. *La Delinquenza in Sardegna,* Palermo, 1897.
[2] Rawson, R. W. 'An Inquiry into the Statistics of Crime in England and Wales' *Journ. Statistical Soc. London,* Vol. 2, 1839, pp. 316-344.

able, by comparison to ascribe to each circumstance its relative power of inducement to crime and arrive at the laws which regulate criminality.'

Taking the judicial statistics for the years 1835-39 as a base he examines them in terms of the number of offences, their classification, the influences of age and sex upon the total volume of crime, and upon particular types of offence.

The second part of his paper is a comparative view of crime in various districts. He points out that whilst variations in the number and types of crime committed in say Northern and Southern Europe might be explained in terms of climatic differences, no such explanation would account for such variations in England and Wales. He rejects the idea of distinguishing between districts on an ethnic basis on the grounds that any differences that might have existed have long since disappeared. Rawson, therefore, argues that since, in his view, "the employments of the people exert the most important influence upon their physical condition", it is not unreasonable to suppose that they have some bearing upon their social and moral character, of which crime is one of the strongest evidences of such an influence. Accordingly, he divides the counties of England and Wales into four groups, agricultural, manufacturing, mining and metropolitan (those around London) on the basis of the material of the 1831 Census. On the basis of his analysis of crimes distributed among the four groups he sets out the following propositions.

1 Crime prevails to the greatest extent in large towns.
2 The difference between manufacturing and agricultural counties, in which the influence of large towns is not much felt, is not very great.
3 Crime is very much below the average in mining counties.
4 It is even less frequent in Wales and in the mountainous districts of the North of England.

Today these generalisations may seem trite and obvious, because we are accustomed to an enormous disparity between the size and density of rural and urban populations. In Rawson's day, however, there were still many people alive who could remember the time when rural and urban population was much more evenly balanced, but probably more important was the fact that riots, rick firing, and the larceny of crops, cattle and game, existed in quite serious proportions in the agricultural counties due to the political unrest and economic distress which affected rural England at this time. Rawson, himself, notes that riots and assaults on peace-officers were actually most frequent in the agricultural counties, exceeding the proportion for either the manufacturing or the metropolitan group of counties. The Industrial Revolution and the growth of the great conurbations was then still in progress so it was probably to some point that Rawson concluded to his audience " . . . the collection of large masses of the population in crowded cities conduces more than anything else to the creation of those causes, whatever they be, which stimulate the commission of crime."

It is worthy of notice that he did not attribute crime *directly* to the density of population; rather he suggested that the level of population determined only the causes, or perhaps more accurately, the precipitating factors. Rawson qualifies for the title of social ecologist by virtue of his views that the regularity and pattern of social behaviour is the result of the pattern of social institutions, which themselves vary between different districts. The analysis of the distribution of industries and the postulate that industry has some bearing upon social and moral facts appears to be an analysis of the spatial relations of individuals and institutions.

Joseph Fletcher, a barrister, and Rawson's successor as Honorary Secretary of the Statistical Society of London, using a modified version of Rawson's division of the English and Welsh counties on the basis of their industries, investigated at some considerable length the problem which had originally interested Guerry and Balbi, namely the relationship between education and crime.[1]

It will be remembered that the results of Guerry's analysis of the relationship between education and crime had been inconclusive; Fletcher, on the other hand, concluded that the extension of "Christian education" was not a powerful antidote to crime, though his evidence appears equally inconclusive. His data was later divided under two headings, "indices to moral influences" and "indices to moral results" apparently at the suggestion of the Prince Consort who heard one of the three original papers

[1] Fletcher, J. 'Moral and Educational Statistics of England and Wales', *Journ. Statistical Soc. London* Vol. 11, 1848, pp. 344-366 and Vol. 12, 1849, pp. 151-335.

read before the Statistical Society of London on March 19th, 1849.

<table>
<tr><td rowspan="4">Indices to Moral Influences</td><td>1</td><td>Dispersion of the Population</td></tr>
<tr><td>2</td><td>Real property in proportions to the Population</td></tr>
<tr><td>3</td><td>Persons of Independent Means in proportion to the Population</td></tr>
<tr><td>4</td><td>Ignorance, as measured by the percent of signatures by marks in the Marriage Registers</td></tr>
<tr><td rowspan="8">Indices to Moral Results</td><td>5</td><td>Crime, as indicated by the Criminal Commitments of Males</td></tr>
<tr><td>6</td><td>Commitments for the more serious offences against the Person and malicious offences against Property</td></tr>
<tr><td>7</td><td>Commitments for all offences against property, excluding the malicious</td></tr>
<tr><td>8</td><td>Commitments for assaults, and miscellaneous offences for males in proportion to the total male population</td></tr>
<tr><td>9</td><td>Improvident marriages, i.e. those entered into by males less than 21 years old</td></tr>
<tr><td>10</td><td>Bastardy, as indicated by the Registrar of Births</td></tr>
<tr><td>11</td><td>Pauperism</td></tr>
<tr><td>12</td><td>Deposits in Savings Banks in proportion to the population.</td></tr>
</table>

Each of these tables was accompanied by a shaded map showing the relative importance of these variables for the counties of England and Wales, and followed by no fewer than eighty pages of minutely detailed comparative tables.

Some of his observations are worthy of mention. It is interesting to note that he believed that crime was as much a product of idleness, itself a sin, as of anything else.

' . . . it will appear that (the excess of commitments in bad times) result rather from idle habits, acquired in an atmosphere of rude discontent, than from the pressure of actual want, which is so largely relieved by our institutions of public and private charity.'

The latter part of this proposition would appear to have been open to some question, on the basis of such varied evidence as Dicken's "Oliver Twist" or the testimony of Matthew Davenport Hill, Recorder of Birmingham, to the Select Committee on

Destitute and Criminal Juveniles in 1852. Nevertheless, Fletcher noted, albeit obliquely, the importance of changes in the pattern of social institutions, particularly those connected with economic organisation which affected public morality. The ability of women and children to earn, and so relieve the burden of financial responsibility upon the head of the family Fletcher saw as a moral evil because it led in his view to earlier marriages, to an increase in illegitimacy, and a general increase in improvidence. Not only social change, but its rapidity was important:

'. . . it would appear that a rapid progress in material civilisation, without a proportionate moral advancement, has thrown new and more frequent incentives to disorder among the people at large, which produce their worst effects on the recoil of each wave of industrial prosperity, amidst those classes whose moral ties to the existing framework of society are feeblest and least felt or understood, and to many of whom Socialism, or any other destructive theory would appear as consistent with their well-being, as the most cherished axioms of political science, or even the words of Christian truth itself'.

The "social problem group" as far as Fletcher was concerned were those who were least oriented to the value system which was a by-product of the social structure of early Victorian England, and as a result the thief and the advocate of radicalism belonged to the same general category insofar as they each rejected part of the existing value system. This concept of *'anomie'* in relation to the social structure remains a fundamental problem in the study of social action whether the deviant behaviour one considers is criminal or political in character.

The studies which we have so far considered might be described as "regional" studies in the spatial relationship between crime and social and economic organisation. But as is clear from the work of the Chicago School in the present century, the most fruitful studies in social ecology have been of a "local" rather than a "regional" character. A study of the criminal statistics of Preston in 1839 has already been mentioned, but it did not deal either with the question of variations in crime rates within a given area, or with the relationships, if any, between crime and the social environment.

This last matter had been touched upon by Fletcher, and in

September, 1855, *John Glyde*, another member of the Statistical Society of London, read a paper before the British Association in Glasgow entitled *"The Localities of Crime in Suffolk."*[1] His paper was based upon an analysis of the local judicial statistics for the years 1848-1853, that is, upon the records of persons committed for trial. Of the regional studies a major criticism is that the county was the smallest territorial unit considered, but Glyde, by breaking Suffolk down into its seventeen Poor Law Unions was able to demonstrate that the "County Aggregate" masked considerable differences between the smaller geographical units of which it was composed. In the Mutford Union, for example, there was but one alleged criminal per 1,344 of the population, while in Cosford the rate was 1 in 464. The Unions contained the towns of the county besides its villages, and in order to demonstrate the variations between the towns, as distinct from the Unions, he drew up a table showing the criminality of the nine towns of importance which ranged from one offender in 1,320 in Southwold to 1 in 309 in Halesworth. The population of none of these, excepting Ipswich exceeded 7,000.

He examined the hypothesis that crime increased with density of population, and found that in Suffolk, at any rate, the relationship was by no means as simple. Ipswich, for example, produced only slightly more criminals than the little town of Debenham, while the differences between the small towns are equally inexplicable in terms of population, Southwold and Halesworth, though of the same approximate size, being at the opposite ends of the scale.

TABLE 4

CRIME IN THE COUNTY OF SUFFOLK 1848-1853

Rates of Alleged Offenders 1848-1853

Town	Population in 1851	Ratio of criminals to population
Southwold	2,109	1 in 1,320
Framlingham	2,450	1 in 1,020
Debenham	1,653	1 in 555
Ipswich	32,914	1 in 557
Lowestoft	6,580	1 in 565
Sudbury	6,043	1 in 475
Hadleigh	3,338	1 in 405
Bungay	3,841	1 in 370
Halesworth	2,529	1 in 309

[1] Glyde, J. 'Localities of Crime in Suffolk', *Journ. Statistical Soc. London*, Vol. 19, 1856, pp. 102-106.

Inquiring into the relative criminality of the urban as distinct from the rural districts he found further evidence to suggest that crime was not simply the result of the corrupting influences of the herding together of people in towns. A group of fifteen towns, each with an average population of 5,000 furnished an annual average of 1 criminal per 593 persons, while a group of fifteen villages, average population 820, furnished an annual average of 1 criminal per 317 persons. In view of the fact that about 30% of the population of the county were town dwellers, the figure of 17% which represents the proportion of town residents in the total seems surprisingly small.

TABLE 5

COMPARATIVE CRIMINALITY OF RURAL
AND URBAN DWELLERS IN SUFFOLK 1848-1853

Offences	Town residents	Country residents	Total
Murder	5	19	24
Malicious wounding etc.	3	9	12
Stabbing, shooting with intent	3	11	14
Highway robbery	2	2	4
Burglary and Housebreaking	16	41	57
Arson	4	72	76
Rape	4	9	13
Assault with intent	1	15	16
Unnatural offences	—	7	7
Sodomy	—	1	1
Bestiality	—	5	5
TOTAL	38	190	228

In considering this table one must bear in mind the fact the countryside at this time was in a state of unrest, and in East Anglia, political consciousness amongst the agricultural proleteriat was developed and probably often demonstrated by rickfiring which would account for the large number of crimes of arson.

Glyde was aware of the limited validity of his study, and appealed at the end of his paper

'We respectfully solicit the attention of statistical inquirers to the facts we have brought forward and earnestly hope that some five or six gentlemen will make an experiment in mining, manufacturing and agricultural counties, so as to ascertain whether the same differences in the ratio of criminals exist therein, and whether the town populations are, in all cases, so free from committing those grave offences that form the most serious blots on the moral character of the present age.'

A review of ecological studies of crime in the nineteenth century cannot be complete without some mention of the work of *Henry Mayhew*. Mayhew, as a person was quite unlike any of the other authors we have considered in that his whole life and work were dominated by an encyclopaedic interest in social data which he presented in a distinctly journalistic manner which would have seemed out of place in the staid pages of the Journal of the Statistical Society of London. He is notable for three considerable literary enterprises, *London Labour and the London Poor* originally issued in part form from 1854 onwards, and published in book form in 1862, *The Criminal Prisons of London and Scenes from Prison Life* written with John Binny and published in 1862, and his part in the founding of *Punch* in 1841.

London Labour and the London Poor is not specifically a criminological treatise, but rather a comprehensive social survey of early Victorian London. To the social historian, its accounts of the various London street trades are invaluable, and to the criminologist some of his remarks about the character and causes of crime in the metropolis are worthy of consideration. Mayhew was indeed unique in that he not only rejected the notions popular among his contemporaries that crime was due variously to poverty the growth of towns or illiteracy, but that he anticipated Lombroso and rejected the theory of biological determinism in favour of a distinctly sociological explanation.

'But crime, we repeat is an effect with which the shape of the head and the form of the features appear to have no connection whatever. Again, we say that the great mass of crime in this country is committed by those who have been bred and born to the business . . . living as systematically by robbery or cheating as others do by commerce or the exercise of intellectual or manual labour.'[1]

In his view it was professional crime which was the root of the problem and there is indeed much modern evidence to suggest that it is the hard core of persistent offenders who present the most serious problem to the community in that it is they who

[1] Mayhew, H. *The Criminal Prisons of London*, p. 383.

show the least response to all the various techniques which modern penology has devised.

The preceeding quotation comes from *The Criminal Prisons of London* but there is in fact a very considerable amount of duplication between this work and *London Labour and the London Poor*. Besides certain arguments which are repeated there is a set of maps and tables of the kind now very familiar from the works of Guerry, Rawson, Fletcher and others, showing the distribution by counties of fifteen variables which are very similar to those of Fletcher. This is certainly the least original of Mayhew's work, and it seems somewhat irrelevant when considered in conjunction with the rest of his material. Mayhew's work is, however, broadly based, not upon arm-chair speculation, nor upon ingenious analyses of published statistics, but upon data he obtained by going into the streets and taverns of London and interviewing those who were the subjects of his research. In this way he amassed an enormous amount of biographical material which went far to demonstrate his main hypothesis, that crime was essentially a social phenomenon which was perpetuated by anti-social attitudes and ways of behaving being transferred from one generation to the next in a social setting characterised by poverty, drunkenness, bad housing, and economic insecurity. A quotation serves better than a synopsis to illustrate the intensity with which he expressed himself.

'Thousands of our felons are trained from their infancy in the bosom of crime; a large proportion of them are born in the homes of habitual thieves and other persons of bad character, and are familiarised with vice from their earliest years. Frequently, the first words they lisp are oaths and curses. Many of them are often carried to the beershop or gin palace on the breasts of worthless drunken mothers, while others, clothed in rags, run by their heels . . . In their wretched abodes they soon learn to be deceitful and artful, and in many cases are very precocious. The greater numbers are never sent to school; some run idle about the streets in low neighbourhoods; others are sent out to beg throughout the City; others go out with their mothers and sit beside their stalls, while others sell a handful of matches or small wares in our public thoroughfares.'[1]

---

[1] Ibid. p. 273.

Besides providing the reader with a most illuminating series of authentic case histories, in *"The Criminal Prisons of London"* is given an account of the building and contruction of the then new London prisons which were coming from the fertile drawing board of Colonel Jebb, R.E., of the condition of their inmates, and a minute description of their penal regimes. Mayhew and Binny's account of conditions in the Metropolitan prisons is in fact the only authoritive but non-official account of the early days of the new prison system which followed upon penal reform and the abolition of transportation. A foreword to the book by the Rev. William Tuckniss, chaplain to the Society for the Rescue of Young Women and Children, gives a good account of the number of social agencies engaged in preventive and rehabilitative work in the field at that time.

Mayhew's case histories are the material substance upon which his arguments are based, rather than illustrations of a set of *a priori* notions. Probably only Shaw has brought home the poignant truths about the delinquent as a person with comparable skill. But it is his study of the distribution of delinquents in London which, though not exhaustive, marks him out clearly as an ancestor of the ecologists of the twentieth century. London was then divided into seven Metropolitan Police Divisions, and Mayhew discovered that in the years 1841-1850, two of these divisions, which included the districts of Hoxton and Westminster, produced no less than 65 per cent of all the alleged criminals of the Metropolis. His comparable analysis of the distribution of crimes bears out the view that the incidence of crime is in some degree a function of the opportunities afforded by the area. Essentially a journalist, Mayhew provides a vivid description of the areas concerned which he gathered in his usual way by first hand observation. Particularly interesting in his account of the area east of what is now Kingsway around Clare Market—then a street market of the "Petticoat Lane" variety, surrounded by low taverns and lodging houses, the haunt of thieves and prostitutes.

Mayhew's contribution to the science of criminology is perhaps not fully appreciated, partly due to the relative obscurity of his work, although there were some extracts from *"London Labour and the London Poor"* republished in the late 1930's. One might summarise it as follows:

1 His work provides a unique source of information about

crime and its social setting in early Victorian London, and the "new" prison system, which seems to suggest that the basic problems facing the social worker and the penologist have changed relatively little in the passage of time.

2 He was one of the first advocates and successful exponents of the technique of collecting first hand material by direct inter-views and observations which would have delighted both Park and Malinowski alike.

3 His view that the root of the crime problem is a cadre of professional criminals who are trained in an intsitutional manner by their parents and/or other criminals suggests that notwithstanding the validity of psychological investigations of criminal motivation, the sociological aspects of crime, in respect of the transmission of a code of anti-social values and criminal techniques are equally worthy of our attention.

While Rawson, Fletcher and Glyde were moralists and schol-ars, Mayhew was essentially a reformer and an investigator with dynamic energy. His primary view was that crime was not the result of moral laxity alone, any more than of some supranatural forces of determinism,[1] but very largely of contemporary social conditions, a view re-echoed in the writings of other reformers of that time, like Mary Carpenter[2] and Walter Buchanan.[3]

Since Mayhew there have been no exclusively sociological studies of the local distribution of crime until perhaps the Cam-bridge Study during World War II.[4] So many other studies, like Burt's *"Young Delinquent"*, and Mannheim, Carr-Saunders and Rhodes' *"Young Offenders"* take into serious account factors which might be described as genetic and psychological.[5] This is not, of course, an implied criticism for it is becoming increasingly clear that any valid aetiology of crime must result from a syn-

---

[1] As exemplified by Quetelet, e.g. ". . . society bears in its womb the embryo of every crime that will be committed, because it creates the conditions which stimulate crime; it prepares for crime, so to speak, while the criminal is merely the tool." *Essai de Physique Sociale.* Brussels, 1869, pp. 176-177.

[2] Carpenter, M. *Juvenile Delinquents, Their Condition and Treatment,* London. 1853.

[3] Buchanan, W. *Remarks on the Causes and State of Juvenile Crime in the Metropolis, with Hints for Preventing its Increase;* London, 1846. See also Quetelet's remark abore.

[4] Mannheim, H. *Juvenile Delinquency in an English Middletown,* London, 1948. A number of local studies of a quasi-sociological character are listed on pages 6 and 7

[5] Mannheim, H., Carr-Saunders, A. M., and Rhodes, E. G., *Young Offenders* Cambridge, 1942.

thesis of research in a number of sciences, medical and biological as well as social. It remains true, nevertheless, that the sociological approach developed by the ecologists of the nineteenth century was almost totally eclipsed by Lombroso's theories, and because the arguments against the theory of atavism lay primarily in the psychological field it has never, in spite of its revival, enjoyed any measure of its former exclusiveness.

IV

EARLY AMERICAN STUDIES:
CLIFFORD SHAW
AND THE CHICAGO SCHOOL

I

ALTHOUGH the theories of Lombroso achieved a truly remarkable degree of acceptance among those actively concerned in the study of crime, they were not immune from criticism. The most effective answer to this particular variety of scientific determinism came partly in the painstaking work of Goring, and partly in the results of psychological inquiry into criminal motivation. Perhaps it is significant, nevertheless, that the earliest effective criticisms of Lombroso were of a sociological nature, of which he clearly took note in his later work,[1] notwithstanding the fact that his revised theories virtually destroyed the validity of the original.

In 1886 *Tarde* and *Lacassagne* founded in Lyon the *"Archives d'Anthropologie Criminelle"*, a journal in which much of this criticism was voiced. In his books,[2] Tarde formulates a theory which though perhaps not without a psychological flavour, is nevertheless, sociological in character. The statistical regularity of social data, he argued implied the non-existence and lack of exercise of free will, man living in society imitates far more than he innovates.[3] Criminal methods, for example, are disseminated by means of press publicity, but social imitation in general is in proportion to the degree to which men are in close contact

---

[1] See, for example, *Crime, Its Causes and Remedies,* Turin, 1906. trans. Boston, 1911.
[2] Tarde, G., *La Criminalité Comparée,* 1886. *Les Lois d'Imitation,* 1890. *Penal Philosophy,* 1890, trans., London, 1912.
[3] *Ibid.,* 1912, p. 297.

with one another. There is a considerable body of evidence to support this view, indeed the maintenance of the fabric of social institutions may be said to depend in no small measure upon imitation. Although institutions are supported by sanction, the precise forms which they take can vary according to the prevailing fashion. Methods of child rearing in this century may be cited as a particularly striking example. How far criminal behaviour can be said to be the result of imitation alone is doubtful, for although it may be true that a boy may steal because it is the "done thing" in the group from which he takes his system of values, one cannot disregard the factors which predispose him to accept those values in the first instance. Tarde did not distinguish effectively between the imitation of criminal behaviour, i.e., the decision to emulate a criminal and commit an offence, and the imitation of criminal methods, i.e., whether to carry a gun or a cosh.

The problem of the relationship between free-will, and the apparent regularity of social patterns can be explained in terms other than those of the laws of imitation. The premise underlying much of Durkheim's theory for example, would seem to indicate that such regularities are the result of coercion rather than imitation. Whether or not there exists coercion within a criminal group to adopt anti-social patterns of behaviour is another question but one which does not directly concern us here.

In America at this time there developed a movement which though not principally academic, was to have a considerable effect upon the future of sociological research in the criminological field. In an earlier chapter, mention has been made of the fact that Chicago, the "capital city" of the Middle-West was the focal point at which so many of the social changes in American society in the years 1870-1925 could be observed. The rapidity of social change brought the same basic problems as were associated with the Industrial Revolution and the growth of cities in Britain, France and Germany. Chicago became, as a result, the centre for social work pioneers in the field of housing, education, social medicine and delinquency. Chicago led the world in 1899 by the establishment of the first Juvenile Court in Hull House, a settlement designed to fulfil in addition the functions of a remand home. Jane Addams, the founder of Hull House may be compared with such people as Charles Booth and Canon Barnett who were attempting in similar ways to awaken the social conscience of the community to the needs of the poor and delinquent of London.

Jane Addams, and Merrit Pinckney,[1] for some years the principal Justice of the Chicago Juvenile Court, together with their disciples continually emphasised, both in their treatment of young offenders, and in their propaganda work, the importance of social and economic factors in precipitating social breakdowns, not only of a delinquent kind, but in mental and physical health. Side by side with a campaign against delinquency and the influences of drink, gambling and sexual vice, went a campaign against bad housing, poor sanitation and inadequate medical and educational facilities, for all of which Chicago had earned an unenviable reputation. Their work was made incalculably harder by the fact that so many of the new immigrants, particularly such groups as the Negroes from the South, the Irish, and the southern Italians and Sicilians came from poverty stricken rural districts with equally low standards of housing and hygiene. This fact, added to the strangeness of city life and difficulties of language made it difficult to arouse them to protest vigorously against such social evils.[2]

These social workers were, of course, not discovering new phenomena. Humanitarians and reformers in nineteenth century England had been faced with similar appalling facts, and had experienced many similar difficulties in their attempts at reform. The enforcement of social reform which does not depend wholly upon idealism, requires compulsive legislation, but such is anathema to the advocates of *laissez faire*, who abounded in the warm climate of unrestrained capitalist expansion in America, just as they had done in Britain some three-quarters of a century earlier.[3]

Two women who were later to become internationally famous in the teaching of social work and administration in the University of Chicago were associated closely with the movement for

[1] See Addams, J., *The Spirit of Youth and the City Streets,* New York, 1909. *A New Conscience and an Ancient Evil,* New York, 1912. Also the statement of Judge Pinckney in Breckinridge and Abbott, *The Delinquent Child and the Home,* Appendix 2, pp. 202-246, and in *The Child in the City,* ed. Breckinridge, New York, 1912, pp. 315-354.
[2] For an excellent account of immigration conditions in this period see Abbott, E., *Immigration, Select Documents and Case Records,* Chicago, 1924 and *Historical Aspects of the Immigration Problem,* Chicago, 1926.
[3] See Breckinridge, S.P., 'Tenement House Legislation in Chicago' in *The Tenements of Chicago 1908-1935,* ed. Abbott E., Chicago, 1936.

social reform. In 1912 the results of their field research, which was directly connected with the practice of social work in the city, was published as *"The Delinquent Child and the Home"*.[1] Their study was undertaken with the approval of the United States Federal Children's Bureau, whose Chief, Julia Lathrop, herself connected with Hull House in Chicago, contributed a pertinent foreword. Its aims were twofold: (a) to achieve a better understanding of the needs of all children, based upon a more exact knowledge of the conditions surrounding the special group studied, and (b) to arrive at a more intelligent judgment with reference to the possible usefulness of the Juvenile Court in serving children and the lines along which that institution might be developed. Children brought before the Cook County Juvenile Court in the period 1903-4 were selected for study, and the field work carried out in the years 1907-8. In this way they obtained data, not only applicable to the time of the court proceedings, but to the subsequent four years in which the results of casework might reasonably have been expected to show themselves.

The data seemed to suggest that immigrant groups were especially prone to produce delinquent children, whose delinquencies were clearly related to problems of social adjustment in a new culture, particularly those which developed from the differential rate of assimilation between immigrants and their children.[2] It is interesting to note how one of Lombroso's earlier notions is borne out by the fact that while the boys were mainly thieves, the vast proportion of girls were amateur prostitues or in what would now be termed "moral danger". Perhaps the most significant relationship brought out by the study is the relationship between delinquency and low economic status. The authors classified the families of their delinquent group as below.

There was evidence of considerable exploitation of children by their parents to commit petty offences, particularly to provide food and fuel for the home. The majority of mentally and physically handicapped delinquents came from the poorest families, and the illiteracy and educational retardation which results from

---

[1] Abbott, E. and Breckinridge, S.P., *The Delinquent Child and the Home,* New York, 1912.

[2] For the classic account of this problem see Thomas, W.I. and Znaniecki, F., *The Polish Peasant in Europe and America,* New York, 1927. The case history of Nick quoted by Shaw is perhaps an even better account. Shaw, C. R., and McKay, H. D., *Social Factors in Juvenile Delinquency,* Washington, 1931, pp. 3-20.

		% of Total in Study	
		Boys	Girls
1	Very poor families	38·2	68·8
2	Poor families	37·9	21·0
3	Families in fairly comfortable circumstances	21·2	7·6
4	Families described as "quite comfortable"	1·7	1·3
5	Homeless children	1·0	1·3
	Total in numbers	584	157

roaming the streets in search of food or firewood was naturally conspicuous.

Breckinridge and Abbott appeared to place more emphasis on the facts of economic deprivation, than on the problem of social adjustment in the home and the neighbourhood. They write for example,

'When we see all the background of deprivation in their lives, the longing for a little money to spend, for the delights of the nickel theatre, for the joy of owning a pigeon, of for the glowing adventure of a ride of the train, it is not hard to understand how the simple fact of being poor is many times a sufficient explanation of delinquency.'[1]

There are two area maps showing (a) the location of the delinquents' homes and (b) the relative density of population between the wards of the city. There is a clear coincidence between the location of delinquents homes, and physical congestion, the absence of play spaces, and the proximity of railway yards. These facts appeared to provide the immediate stimulation of delinquency, while the problems of social adjustment and social control, shaped largely by socio-economic considerations created its predisposition. Because of poverty, many of the immigrant mothers had to work in order to supplement the family income, and in so doing used up the time and energy which ought to have been expended in looking after homes and families. What is perhaps more important was the fact that *over half* the working mothers were employed *away* from the home.

[1] *Op. cit.,* p. 89.

Chicago in 1912 was not an inspiring city from the viewpoint of the social reformer, but one feature was noted by Breckinridge and Abbott as a hopeful sign. In the midst of a situation which was later to be described by the term "social disorganisation" the gang, though frequently an association noted for its anti-social tendencies was seen as a "social phenomenon of hopeful significance and promise when once understood and utilised".[1] Thrasher's study of the gang published some fifteen years later was to show that it was probably unique as an effective agency of social control in certain districts. Later, the Chicago Area Project was to attempt to make direct use of such indigenous forms of social organisation to develop local solidarity and advance schemes of communal self help.

II

The criticisms which must be made of the work of Breck-inridge and Abbott are that they worked almost completely without reference to a coherent body of social theory, and as a result tended to overstress the *theoretical* importance of poverty in the aetiology of delinquency, as distinct from its practical importance at that specific point of time. Shaw's work might be described as the successful amalgam of the social work tradition and the theory of human ecology, both of which had developed at the University of Chicago in the period 1915-1925. (In the United States in the 1920's, however, the crime problem began to assume quite new dimensions.) Before the First World War, lawlessness was a feature of America's "Wild West", and the problems of urban crime, those which stemmed largely from economic deprivation in appalling social conditions.

The Volstead Act or "Prohibition" as it is more familiarly known, created a state of affairs which was to assume the proportions of a national emergency, in that hosts of America's hitherto law abiding citizens became criminally involved in the illegal traffic in liquor. The economic functions of distributive and retail concerns in the drink trade were taken over by highly organised gangs, and the laws of supply and demand enforced by the revolver and the Thompson sub-machine gun. City districts became terrorised by gang leaders who "controlled" an area by a system of petty chiefs and lieutenants which was distinctly

[1] *Ibid.*, p. 156.

feudal. The established agency of law enforcement was fought openly if necessary and policemen died in alarming numbers. It was as if the robber barons of medieval Europe had become re-incarnate in the twentieth century. It is perhaps a tragedy that the type of legislation which was so conspicuously unsuccessful in relation to alcohol has been introduced to deal with the narcotic problem. The criminal organisation of the drug rackets, with its emphasis on the spread of addiction, would appear to be having even more disastrous social consequences than Prohibition.

Shaw was not primarily concerned with the problem of gang lawlessness, but with the conditions which surrounded delinquency and crime. Largely these were the same as had been studied by Breckinridge and Abbott in 1907-8, but there was now an important difference, in that the chances of a delinquent child graduating to the ranks of an adult criminal gang were immeasurably greater. Because liquor was forbidden, it was dear, and under conditions of relatively inelastic demand there was big money to be made in its illegal traffic, an attractive prospect, especially to those whose lives had hitherto been blighted by poverty. Crime and delinquency became the subject of social research par excellence, and by 1931 the National Commission on Law Observance and Enforcement had produced no fewer than fourteen substantial volumes, one of which was the work of Shaw and Henry McKay.

The fact that certain areas of a city produce not only the majority of lawbreakers but a more than average number in proportion to their population was not a new discovery; it had, for instance, been noted by Mayhew in the 1850's, and it was implicit in Guerry's material even earlier. For Shaw this was the point of departure in his analysis, and although he appeared to be merely retracing the steps of earlier ecologists, he had at his disposal not only more accurate basic social data, but more refined statistical techniques with which to handle them. In addition he had the advantage of being able to work within the confines of a body of social theory, the theory of human ecology developed by Park, which by virtue of its sophistication was superior to the somewhat primitive notions of such writers as Mayhew. If the basic postulates of human ecology were valid, that human behaviour and institutions can be purposefully studied in terms of their spatial relations within a given physical area, which in itself determines to a considerable degree the genesis and character of those relations, then specific kinds of behaviour can also be studied within such a frame of reference.

The social system[1] within a given area, may be seen as the resultant of a number of variables, such as land use, population density, and age structure, besides such factors as ethnic and religious groupings, nationality and social class. In this way behaviour, in the sense of standardised responses to regular stimuli (the overall pattern of social institutions), can be seen as a function of these variables. Shaw believed that factor analysis could reveal much of the character of social institutions if considered in this way, but more important was his belief that to make the understanding of behaviour complete, it was necessary to employ what he called "situational analysis", that is of the response of the individual basically conditioned by what he describes as "culture" to a specific social situation. In his introduction to "*Delinquency Areas*"[2] he stressed the importance of *individual* attitudes, as distinct from *generalised* attitudes, as subjective factors in the process of interaction between the person and the social world in which he lives. Shaw's work is an attempt to combine a kind of factorial analysis of objective social data, with situational analyses of individual behaviour. Besides investigating the relationships between land utilisation, poverty and delinquency, it is also necessary to investigate the "inner world" of the person through detailed life histories. There is a close parallel here with the methodology of psycho-analysis, and indeed much of the most illuminating data is to be found in these life histories.[3] This was, undoubtedly, an advance upon the original formulations of ecological theory, in that it attempted to accommodate the fact of individual motivation within an objective scheme of social action. The regularity and consistency of social facts at a societal level may have been responsible for the ecologists assumption that within a given area, behaviour, even at an individual level was completely standardised. Without Shaw's refinement of "situational analysis" it would be quite impossible

---

[1] 'System' is used here rather than 'structure' for the latter tends to suggest rigidity, whereas fluidity, as will be seen, is often a more apposite description of social relations in certain urban areas.

[2] Shaw, C. R., *Delinquency Areas; A Study of the Geographic Distribution of School Truants, Juvenile Delinquents and Audlt Offenders in Chicago*, Chicago, 1929.

[3] Similar methods are advocated by W. I. and Dorothy Thomas, *The Child in America*, New York, 1928, p. 571.

to explain why not every child in a delinquency area is delinquent, and why even children from upper middle class districts occasionally come into direct conflict with the law.

The ecological study of such a problem as juvenile delinquency necessarily begins with the study of its geographical location, but in Shaw's view this step is equally fundamental by reason of the fact that it reveals "*the areas in which delinquency occurs most frequently*", and therefore marks off the communities which should be studied intensively for factors related to delinquent behaviour.[1] Here one must note that his somewhat slipshod phraseology produces an unwanted element of ambiguity. "Areas in which delinquency occurs most frequently" are literally those in which crimes are committed, while it is clear that he is primarily concerned with the problem of delinquent attitudes, or predisposition, as evidenced by his plotting cartographically the home addresses of offenders. The importance of this theoretical distinction has already been discussed in our first chapter.

Given the modifications of the "cultural approach" and "situational analysis" as discussed in his first chapter, Shaw outlines the by then familiar story of the growth and configuration of the city of Chicago in ecological terms.[2] This constitutes *Part I*. *Part II* of the work is a study of the geographical location of individual delinquents, consisting of eight series as follows, illustrated by spot maps.

Series 1 Distribution of male school truants brought before Juvenile Court 1917-23 aged 10 - 17.
Series 2 Distribution of delinquent boys dealt with by Juvenile Police Probation Officers during 1926.
Series 3 ,, ,, ,, ,, ,, 1927.
Series 4 Distribution of delinquent boys brought before Juvenile Court 1917-23
Series 5 Distribution of delinquent boys brought before Juvenile Court 1900-1906.
Series 6 Distribution of male offenders brought to Boys Court on Felony Charges 1926.
Series 7 Distribution of adult male offenders in Cook County Jail in 1920, aged 17 - 75.

[1] Shaw, *op. cit.*
[2] Viz., the 'zonal analysis' formulated by McKenzie and utilised by Park and Burgess.

Series 8 Distribution of delinquent girls brought before Juvenile Court 1917-1923.

Part III consists of the distribution of delinquency cases, i.e., of offences, but not in the sense one would expect in that the maps do not show where the offences were committed, but the home addresses of the offenders. These maps are really no more than illustrations of the geographical location of delinquents, assuming a ratio of 1 offence to 1 delinquent consisting of,

Series 9 Distribution of cases of male delinquency brought before Juvenile Court 1917-1923, and
Series 10 Distribution of cases of male delinquency brought before Juvenile Court 1900-1906.

Finally *Part IV* considers the problem of recidivism among male delinquents coming before the Juvenile Court in the periods 1900-1906 and 1917-1923, in terms of the excess of delinquency cases over the numbers of individual delinquents.

Because of the differences in population size and density, in age structure, and the ratio of the sexes which exist in the various areas of the city, comparisons between them need to employ a device which will take these differences into account yet not obscure the essential facts which need to be compared, in this case, the relative incidence of crime and delinquency. The device employed by Shaw was the *delinquency rate*. Essentially this is a simple ratio between a number of offenders and a total population of the same sex and age group. In Shaw's work the population bases are related to each census tract in the city. These census tracts he combined into square mile areas with a corresponding area rate. The object of calculating a delinquency rate was to demonstrate the qualitative differences between different districts in the matter of law observance among their inhabitants, which could not be perceived from a simple distribution of alleged offenders between districts which varied in population, density, age and sex structure.

No ecological study would be complete without a series of maps, and in this matter, it is undoubtedly true that Shaw made great advances upon the cartographic technique used by nineteenth century ecologists which was basically the same as that used by the geographer Humboldt in the eighteenth century. The maps are divided into three kinds.

74

1 Spot maps showing the actual geographic distribution of offenders.

2 Rate maps, showing the variation in rates between the square mile areas.

3 Radial maps showing variations in delinquency rates or "gradients" drawn from the city centre.

4 Zone maps showing the averages of the rates in the square mile areas.

The spot maps Shaw considered important because they not only showed the areas in which delinquents were concentrated, and the relation of those areas to the city as a whole, but the extent of the actual problem of delinquency with which each district was faced.[1] The radial maps, on the other hand, were intended to illustrate the variations in the delinquency rate between the "natural areas" which had resulted from the radial expansion of the city.

That juvenile delinquency, adult crime, recidivism, and truancy are all associated is suggested by the fact that the ten series of data appear to be positively correlated, in some instances to the extent of $+0.8$ and $+0.9$. Similar variations between areas can be seen from the rates of different series. Unless one can at the same time, however, estimate the degree to which such a relationship may have come about by chance, these positive correlations might be no more useful in understanding our major problem, than is the positive correlation between the number of storks and the Swedish birth rate to the demographer.

Shaw's choice of truancy, as one of the variables to be compared with delinquency and adult crime was founded in the belief in the relationship between the two, which has been demonstrated by quite a formidable number of studies. The New York State Crime Commission had conducted an inquiry[2] into the subsequent careers of 248 boys and 3 girls committed to the truant school in the period 1921-23, the findings of which were worthy of some attention. 51 % of this number had by 1928 re-appeared in court as follows

[1] Shaw, *op. cit.*, p. 31.
[2] Summarised in 'From Truancy to Crime' *Survey*, (New York) Vol. 61, No. 8, 1929.

	% *of total*
Re-appeared as Juvenile Delinquents	21
Arraigned for misdemeanours	16
Charged with Felony, e.g., burglary, armed robbery, etc.	14
	51

Of those among the remaining 49 % who were again charged with truancy, some 43 % had families with a criminal record, i.e., criminal parent(s) and/or sibling(s). The geographical distribution of the truants in Shaw's Series (1) showed the greatest concentrations to be in the areas adjacent to the Loop, (the central business district) and near large industrial districts like the Union Stock Yards and the steel mills by Lake Calumet.

The distribution of delinquent boys (Series 2, 3, 4, 5, 9 and 10) shows a markedly similar concentration in these same districts. It is interesting to note that in areas where the concentration is not so great, small constellations of "spots" can be seen, and these often occur in juxtaposition to railways, and commercial and industrial properties.[1] The adult offenders (Series 7) tended to come from the "rooming house" districts which were also close to the central area of commerce and industry.

The characteristic common to "high rate" areas, whether considered in terms of truancy, delinquency or adult crime is physical deterioration. For Shaw "deterioration is the frame of reference for his interpretation; other writers have linked the fact with the concept of "social disorganisation", though even if we admit the validity of this latter concept, it is by no means established that physical deterioration and "social disorganisation" invariably go together. It has been suggested that human ecology is no more than another name for geographical determinism, and Shaw attempts to dispel this notion by insisting that

'It should be clearly understood that this study is not an attempt to show that delinquency is caused by the simple external fact of location. We are pointing out here that delinquency tends to occur in a characteristic type of area. More intensive analysis of these areas is necessary before the factors that characterise delinquency-producing situations can be indicated.'[2]

[1] See Shaw, *op. cit.*, p. 55. [2] *Ibid.*, p. 21.

Clifford Shaw

Shaw's findings in this original Chicago study may be summarised as follows:

1) There are marked variations in the rates of truancy, delinquency and recidivism between different areas which cannot be explained in the terms of population size and density. It is likely that the distribution of socially maladjusted children throughout the city is relatively uniform, but because of variations in methods of controlling children and in the characteristic modes in behaviour only maladjustment which shows itself in a criminal manner is likely to become known as delinquency.

The theory that variations in area rates—which are based ultimately on police prosecutions—reflect differences in the extent of police activity is rejected by Shaw on the grounds that the variations in police strength are very slight; there was one policeman per 482 persons in a typical high rate area and one per 506 in a low rate area. The differences between rates were quite out of proportion to these differences in police strength. Whether there exist variations in police *attitudes* to offenders from different areas (essentially different social classes) is, however, quite another matter.

2) Rates of truancy delinquency and adult crime vary inversely with distance from the city centre. Shaw does observe that this radial pattern may not be characteristic of all cities and that even in Chicago there are certain deviations from the pattern.
3) There is a similarity in the distribution of truants, delinquents and adult offenders and similar variations in their rates for different areas.
4) Differences in rates reflect differences in community backgrounds. High rates Shaw noticed occurred in areas characterised by declining population and physical deterioration.
5) High rate areas have been characterised by high rates over a long period of time (1900-1927) irrespective of changes in the national, racial, or cultural composition of their populations.

On the basis of (2) and (4) above, Shaw concludes that delinquent behaviour is very closely related to certain community situations which arise in the concentric process of city growth.[1]

[1] *Ibid.,* p. 204.

Under the pressure of disintegrative forces which are endemic in this process, the community ceases to function effectively as an agency of social control, and as resistance to criminal behaviour diminishes, it becomes not only tolerated but even sometimes accepted. He rejects the notion that such factors as bad housing, overcrowding and low living and educational standards have any causal significance *in themselves*; it is likely that they merely reflect a type of community life; " . . . by treating them one treats only symptoms of more basic processes. Even the disorganised family and the delinquent gang which are often thought of as the main factors in delinquency, probably reflect community situations."[1]

Perhaps more important for our consideration is the suggestion that once delinquent and criminal patterns of behaviour have arisen in a neighbourhood, they are transmitted socially just as any other social and cultural pattern is transmitted. In time these anti-social patterns may become dominant and shape the attitudes and behaviour of the majority of persons living in the area, which thus becomes a "delinquency area".[2]

Shaw's second major publication, in 1931,[3] in collaboration with Henry McKay goes a good deal further to investigate the relationships between the social system of a neighbourhood and the social values underlying it, delinquency and crime. It would appear that the demographic, cultural and economic changes wrought by the process of city growth in neighbourhoods with an appreciable delinquent population had made a basic form of social solidarity impossible. The desire of some to move out of the area as soon as they were sufficiently prosperous, and the pressure of various immigrant groups with diverse cultural backgrounds at various stages of assimilation to their new life, have already been suggested as contributory factors to this situation. The case of Nick, an American born child of Italian immigrant parents, in violent conflict with the older members of his family is a poignant example of the problems resulting from differential rates of assimilation,[4] but this is only a problem in

[1] *Ibid.*, p. 205.
[2] *Ibid.*, p. 206.
[3] Shaw, C. R. and McKay, H. D., *Social Factors in Juvenile Delinquency; a study of the community, the family and the gang in relation to delinquent behaviour*. National Commission on Law Observance and Enforcement. Report on the Causes of Crime. Vol. 11, U.S. Govt. Printing Office, Washington, 1931.
[4] *Ibid.*, pp. 3-20.

cities with large immigrant populations. The absence of a
consistent set of cultural standards or the existence of a set of
anti-social norms in any district, will mean that the child's
access to conventional traditions and norms will be restricted to
formal contacts with the school, with various social agencies and
probably the police. On the other hand, his most intimate social
relationships are likely to be in the local play group, whose
activities and norms may differ as widely from those of his family
as from society at large. In Shaw's opinion these relationships
rather than formal external contacts, are likely to be the chief
source from which the child acquires his social values and the
conception of right and wrong.[1] How far Shaw disregards the
family entirely as a factor in this situation is not clear, but the
evidence of Piaget would seem to suggest that the play group is
at least as important, in that it is within it the child learns that
values or moral judgments are not apocalyptic but based upon a
form of social consensus.[2] From the data on the activities and
traditions of delinquent groups, and on family relationships,
consisting mainly of case histories and interview records, and
autobiographical material, it seems fairly clear that the existence
of disharmony within the home was an added incentive for the
child to look to the play group as a relief from his anxiety. Its
activities were often of a character which provided an outlet for
pent-up feelings, and in its goals and discipline he could perceive
and enjoy a consistency of action and purpose which was so
singularly lacking at home.

Besides the data on the distribution of delinquents in Chicago
which is reproduced from Shaw's original work *"Delinquency
Areas"*, the accounts of the geographical distribution in six
other American cities, Philadelphia, Richmond, Cleveland,
Birmingham, Denver and Seattle, suggest that the pattern is
fundamentally the same as that found in Chicago. The areas of
high and low rates of delinquents are also differentiated in much
the same manner while the general tendency for rates to decrease
along the "gradients" from the central business district to the
periphery is equally marked. In his view this similarity reflects
the process of differentiation and segregation of neighbours
resulting from the natural growth and expansion of the city.
Unfortunately, these six additional studies merely amplify the

[1] *Ibid.*, p. 111.
[2] Piaget J., *The Moral Judgment of the Child,* London, 1932.

original statement of the problem, and do not tell us anything more about the relationship between the characteristics of the local environment and behaviour, but simply that American cities of widely differing size, age, location and ethnic composition have tended to develop in the same way under the "natural conditions" of free enterprise.

The continuation of this comparative survey of American cities throughout the 1930's finally resulted in the publication of data on other cities[1] in 1942 under the title Juvenile Delinquency and Urban Areas.[2] The importance of this work lies perhaps not so much in its comparative aspect, but in the refinements and reformulations of certain theoretical issues which Shaw and McKay had made in the period of a decade. With the exception of three cities, Birmingham, Omaha and Boston, the gradient of delinquency rates from the centre to the periphery was observed; in these exceptional cases rates were still high in areas adjacent to industry and commerce, which had for topographical reasons developed in areas other than the centre of the city.

The introduction to this book by Burgess may be regarded as the authoritative criticisms of the work by a senior ecological theorist. In his view the fact that such variables as population change, bad housing, poverty, foreign birth and negroes, tuberculosis, adult crime and mental disorders all correlate highly with juvenile delinquency and are highly inter-correlated would seem to suggest that they are all manifestations of some general basic factor. The basic factor he considers to be "*social disorganisation*" or the lack of community effort to deal with these problems, and that the solution of them lies in the development of community organisation.[3] Thus far Burgess appears to give his *imprimatur* to Shaw and McKay's conclusion. But in the matter of the definition of delinquency there appears to be some measure of inconsistency between them. Burgess argues that it is a mistake to extend the term delinquency to include cases of behaviour problems which are brought to Child Guidance Clinics, or to children whose mischeivous behaviour is controlled

---

[1] Philadelphia, Boston, Cincinnati, Cleveland, Richmond, Columbus, Birmingham, Little Rock, Denver, Seattle, Portland, Vancouver, Spokane, Evansville, Peoria, Omaha, Baltimore and Minneapolis and St. Paul.
[2] Shaw, C. R. and McKay, H. D., *Juvenile Delinquency and Urban Areas,* Chicago, 1942, with chapters by Norman S. Hayner, Paul Cressey, Clarence Shroeder, T. Earl Sullenger, Earl R. Moses, and Calvin Schmid.
[3] Shaw and McKay, *op. cit.,* p. xi.

by parents or neighbourhood action.[1] Shaw on the other hand writes, "It is, by definition, a departure from the behaviour code or norm approved by the larger society, even when representing, for the child concerned, conformity to the standards of his immediate social group or groups."[2]

The terms "behaviour code" and "norm" do not have a specific legal connotation. It is difficult to see how a child addicted to pathological lying, temper tantrums or persistent bed wetting would not be departing from the behaviour code or norm of, say, a middle class family. If the definition "delinquency" were uniformly applied or it were unmistakably different from "maladjustment", one could accept Burgess' argument. But even within the United States, different states have different definitions, and in this country one cannot really deny the unreasonableness of describing a thief of eight years as a delinquent, and one of seven years eleven months as a "child in need of care and protection". Shaw had suggested earlier[3] that though it was probable that maladjustment among children could be found all over the city, those living in low rate areas did not appear to get involved in such behaviour difficulties as the larceny of motor vehicles and armed robbery. His case documentation, however, would appear to suggest that delinquency in a high rate area was no less often precipitated by emotional stress.[4] To suggest that delinquency and maladjustment are different phenomena, on the basis of differences in specific forms of behaviour, some illegal and others merely anti-social, when there is evidence that both may be precipitated by a common factor, namely emotional stress or disturbance, seems altogether too arbitratry. It seems all the more unsound in the light of the facts that the "white collar criminal", the tax evader and the fraud, come mainly from those groups in the community which are regarded as relatively respectable; in other words, anti-social individuals from low rate areas can actually become criminals, though their offences may be of a less spectacular kind.

In this later work the authors have treated the subject of recidivism with rather more care. In *"Delinquency Areas"* Shaw considers that the difference between the rate of delinquents and

[1] *Loc. cit.*
[2] *Ibid.,* p. 86.
[3] *Delinquency Areas,* p. 199.
[4] See the cases quoted in *Social Factors in Juvenile Delinquency* and in *Delinquency Areas.*

the rate of delinquency cases (charges) could only be due to recidivism. 'The surplus of delinquency cases over individuals in the city as a whole, or in a given area, will be referred to as cases of recidivism.'[1]

Now whether Shaw's use of the term recidivism in this way is legitimate, on the grounds that at least he defines his concept is a matter for individual judgment, but it must be admitted that this is not the usual definition of recidivism. Recidivism is generally understood to be the repetition of offences by an individual offender, the recidivist is in fact the "habitual" criminal.[2] It is quite likely that in any of Shaw's series, some of the excess of charges over individuals must be due to some individuals appearing during the period on several occasions, there is the possibility of individuals being charged with several offences at the same time. An examination of the 1917-23 Juvenile Court Series (9)[3] shows that this is possible, though not very likely.

Admitting that the excess is due to recidivism, in this instance, though he defines it in a somewhat roundabout way, the theoretical criticism stands that the excess *could* be in part accounted for by multiple charges on single occasions. In this country, such a practice would be highly suspect as a valid procedure, particularly in the instance of adult offenders in which the number of offences which are "taken into consideration" (T.I.C.) is sometimes considerable.

What is perhaps more important is that in his original work the largest time span used is six years, 1900-1906 and 1917-1923. These periods would cover children who were between eight and eleven years old at the beginning and fourteen and seventeen at the end. Such recidivism as can be deduced from the Juvenile

---

[1] *Delinquency Areas,* p. 175 *et seq.*

[2] See the various Statutory definitions of the habitual offender, e.g., Prevention of Crimes Act, 1908 and Criminal Justice Act, 1948.

[3] Shaw, *loc. cit.,* pp. 181-186. Tables XXI and XXIII.

a) No. of Individual delinquents   8,141
b) ,, ,, delinquency cases   12,029
Excess of (b) over (a)   3,888

c) No. of recidivists   2,392
d) ,, ,, court appearances   6,280
e) ,, ,, individuals not recidivist $= (a) - (c) = 5,749$
f) ,, ,, appearances by non-recidivists $= (b) - (d) = 5,849$

therefore no. of cases per non-recidivist $= \dfrac{f}{e} = 1 \cdot 0001$ (approx)

This is assuming that one appearance on the part of a recidivist is one case, that is, relates to one charge. Unfortunately the authors do not define these terms.

Court Series only relates to the period of childhood and adolescence, but there is no direct evidence that delinquent behaviour ceased with the onset of adulthood. The usual concept of recidivism, however, relates to the fact that anti-social behaviour may persist over a longer period than six years, and from childhood and adolescence into adulthood. Most adult recidivists were in fact, once juvenile delinquents.

This deficiency in the original Chicago material is to a great extent rectified in the latest publication. A one third sample of boys brought to court on truancy charges during 1920 was followed up with interesting results. In the ensuing eighteen years 60% of them had re-appeared in court as adult offenders. The variations in rates of recidivism between different areas shown in the original material were again demonstrated by the follow-up study. The proportion of delinquents subsequently charged as adults in the part of the sample drawn from high rate areas was 70.7%, whereas that for the low rate areas was 53.9%.

In the latest presentation of the Chicago material a number of objective indices to describe the community situation have been developed. It had earlier been suggested that the social problems constituted by bad housing and low living standards were like delinquency, symptomatic of some communal disorder. The objective indices[1] devised by Shaw and McKay not only appear to demonstrate this, but also provide an adequate means of describing the different areas of the city. Decrease of population, the incidence of dependency (families on relief) of demolished buildings, of the foreign born, of infant mortality, tuberculosis and mental disorder all correlate highly with delinquency and crime rates. Population increase is characteristic of low rate areas, while the proportions of home ownership and median rentals correspond accordingly with variations in the delinquency rate.

Finally, the work points a scheme of action which in the authors' view will at least arrest the process of deterioration and disorganisation in the blighted areas of the city. The Chicago Area Project was inaugurated in 1932 to develop positive interest by the inhabitants in their own welfare, to establish democratic bodies of local citizens who would enable the whole community to become aware of its problems and attempt their solution by

[1] Relating to square mile areas.

common action. The rationale of this Project makes the assumption that delinquency is a direct result of conditions in the community, though it pointed out that there was no conclusive evidence to suggest that local conditions in themselves *caused* delinquency.[1] Rather, the suggestion was that they, like delinquency were symptomatic of a common problem. It might well be that the most communal action can do is to cure symptoms, leaving the malady untouched.

[1] *Juvenile Delinquency in Urban Areas,* p. 198.

V

GENERAL CRITICISMS OF
SHAW'S WORK

SOME comments upon the validity of Shaw's[1] concepts
have already been made, notably his failure to distinguish
between areas of criminal production and areas of crime
commission. The most serious criticisms have, however, been
made of the validity of his *delinquency rates* and some of his
conclusions about the significance of the cultures of local
communities and the nature of the physical environment itself.

Among his earliest critics was Sophie Robison,[2] who not only
felt that the gradient of delinquency rates from the city centre
outwards was merely coincidental with a particular type of
urban development, but that the rates themselves, because they
were based upon court appearances could hardly provide a
reliable index of the extent of delinquent behaviour. In her view
the factors in delinquent conduct are too complex to crowd into
a single symbol, court appearance. The customs of diverse
cultural groups, she argues, are such that irrespective of the
location of the groups in the city the proportions of their
populations who come before the courts will inevitably vary.[3]

It would appear that Robison's concept of delinquency is
somewhat broader than that of Shaw, and extends to cover
behaviour which is generically described as anti-social. Her
argument would seem to run that the higher the parental income
the fewer the child's chances of coming into court, partly because
of the greater importance of familial or pedagogic agencies of

[1] When reference is made to Shaw, his collaborators are implicitly included unless
otherwise stated.
[2] Robison, S. M., *Can Delinquency be Measured?*
[3] *Ibid.*, p. 4.

social control higher up the social scale.[1] In other words, the delinquency rate measures only

(a) the specifically illegal and known delinquencies

of (b) those children who have no opportunities to express their wayward desires in technically legal ways.

This point could also be presented in slightly different form, by asking what is the relationship between the amount of apprehended and unapprehended delinquency, and are there certain constant factors which affect the registration of delinquency? Allowing the narrowest definition of delinquency,[2] differences in income level might conceivably affect the official registration of delinquency, for example, middle class parents might be less eager to prosecute their own children for stealing in the home, and be prepared to "square" offended persons or policemen with hard cash. Shaw's answer is that the behaviour of the "problem child" from Lakeshore Drive is qualitatively distinct from the robbery and car thieving of a boy from "Little Sicily", and in the matter of "squaring" membership of a gang is as useful as being the son of a company director.[3]

Robison's doubt as to whether objective factors such as population density and change, and the proportion of industrial and commercial property can be regarded in the same way as such subjective factors as local cultures, would appear reasonable in view of the fact that the efficiency of various cultures in controlling the behaviour of individuals can scarcely be measured in the same way. Notwithstanding the correlations which are visible between various features of the physical environment and delinquency, the importance of cultural factors cannot be overlooked. Although Chicago's immigrant groups were concentrated in the deteriorating "interstitial" areas of the city, and

---

[1] "There is no doubt that the official registration of a child's delinquency is affected by the extent to which families possess a considerable income margin. This margin may afford socially accepted outlets for children's energy and access to resources for the care of transgressors through other than official or voluntary agencies. Sometimes a psychiatrist solves the behaviour difficulties of the well-to-do. Boarding schools often deal effectively and constructively with problems very similar to those referred to in the Juvenile Court." *Ibid.*, p. 28.

[2] See Burges's introduction to *Juvenile Delinquency and Urban Areas,* p. xi and Robison, *op. cit.*, p. 204, *et. seq.*

[3] This would seem to be truest at the higher juvenile age levels. Breckinridge and Abbott noted that when adolescent prostitutes were in court there were invariably men in the public enclosure ready to pay their fines if necessary.

delinquency and deterioration correlate positively and highly, it remains that the negroes and Italians produced delinquents out of proportion to their numbers when compared with other "ethnic" or "cultural" groups. She contests the ecological view that social disorganisation is characteristic of all slum areas. Some communities through the agency of a priest or rabbi may possess a large measure of solidarity enhanced through the performance of a collective ritual and the possession of a common heritage.[1]

Robinson's criticisms of Shaw apply also to the New York State Crime Commission's study of the City of New York which was carried out along the "classical" ecological lines.[2] The addresses of male offenders in the 16 - 20 age group for the year 1929 were plotted over the health areas of the city. It was found that the "delinquency areas" were (a) characterised by decreasing population, (b) central rather than peripheral, and (c) those which combined industry, commerce and housing rather than being residential suburbs. A subsequent study appears to corroborate these findings.[3]

Her own study of New York was also based upon the health area as a local unit and began in 1931. The delinquents were drawn, like Shaw's subjects, very largely from the Juvenile Court records, but as many "delinquents" who were on the files of social agencies were also included. (This was justified in terms of the breadth of Robison's definition of delinquency.) The data was somewhat limited in that it referred solely to the year 1930.

According to Robison, the health area rates, which took account of differences in sex, age, colour, religious affiliation, and parental origins were compared, but Chis-quare tests (of the likelihood of differences having occurred by chance) revealed very *few significant* differences between the areas. One suspects this may be in part due to the artificiality of the health area boundaries which fail to correspond to neighbourhoods, or "natural" areas in the ecological sense. In addition, but without any evidence, she argues that the zonal pattern of delinquency

---

[1] See Zorbaugh, *The Gold Coast and the Slum,* also the detailed consideration of Catholicism in a Liverpool slum by Mays, J. B., *Growing Up in the City,* Liverpool, 1954.

[2] *The Youthful Offender,* New York State Crime Commission, New York, 1931.

[3] Maller, J. B., 'Maladjusted Youth', Report of Children's Court Jurisdiction and Juvenile Delinquency Committee, quoted by Burgess, *loc. cit.*

distribution could not apply to New York. This seems to ignore the significance of the zonal theory, in that the distribution of delinquency is concomitant with certain ecological characteristics of the various stages of city growth, (for example, the invasion of a housing area by industry and commerce which themselves tend to follow a zonal scheme. Radial development in itself is a factor of secondary importance.[1]

A delinquency index in her view is not feasible partly on account of the inadequacy of the definition of the basic unit of measurement, delinquency, and partly on the grounds that variations in group practices or cultural traditions affect the uniform registration of delinquency, even with voluntary agencies. Although, for instance, the population of New York in 1930 was fairly evenly divided between Catholics, Protestants and Jews, in the Court records there were seven Catholic children for every white Protestant child, and three for every Jewish child.

Robison's somewhat negative approach[2] to the ecological aspects of delinquency distribution is not helped by the all inclusive nature of her concept of delinquency. If one accepts a delinquent act to be specifically illegal, then the Court figures would seem to be a fair guide, for it is doubtful, as Shaw points out, whether group differences are likely to affect the registration of such delinquencies as robbery and car theft. (Failure to prosecute and "squaring" seem likely to be cancelled out between different groups.) The most valuable of her criticisms seem to relate to the fact that Shaw did not consider adequately the differences between groups of approximately the *same* socioeconomic status, living in *similar* areas.

The criticisms of Jonassen[3] are somewhat more substantial in that they do not suffer from any disagreement as to the acceptability of Shaw's definition of delinquency. They are largely directed at the diachronic aspects of the Chicago study, and the

---

[1] See, for example, the configuration of Birmingham, Alabama. *Juvenile Delinquency and Urban Areas,* p. 320.
[2] "Although the delinquency area technique of study, developed in Chicago and later extended to an examination of the locus of delinquency in other cities, has received official recognition, the suspicion persists that this method is not only essentially invalid to indicate the extent of juvenile delinquent behaviour but that it does not furnish any very useful approach to the problem of understanding or preventing delinquent behaviour." Robison, *op. cit.,* p. 4.
[3] Jonassen, C. T., "A Revaluation and Critique of some of the Methods of Shaw and McKay", *American Sociological Review,* Vol. 14, 1949, pp. 608-615.

validity of comparisons over a period of 30 years. There is no doubt that while the "ethnic" or "national" composition of the delinquency areas has changed, in overall terms the delinquency rates have remained consistently high. But the data upon which comparisons are made is not altogether uniform,[1] for example, some of the Census Tracts in existence in 1923-27 were not in existence in 1900 to 1906. Other factors such as variations in police policy, in the existence of various extra-legal procedures for handling of delinquents, and in such demographic factors as age and sex structure and marital status will also affect the comparison. The square mile area is in his view, too large, for if it embraces several culturally distinct communities their different-ial delinquency rates will be masked by the aggregate. At one period of time an area might show a certain rate, the aggregate of A and B (low rate groups) and C and D (high rate groups). Ten years later the same rate might exist, only this time as the aggregate of X and Y (low rate groups) and Z a high rate group. The area rate system, unless the area is culturally or ethnically homogeneous, fails to show not only the relative delinquency of specific groups, but that not all groups produce delinquents under the same conditions. This would appear to be substan-tially the same as Robison's point except in that it is made more explicitly.

The stability of a high delinquency rate in an area, the pop-ulation of which has changed in the course of time is an impor-tant piece of evidence to the ecologist, in that given certain specific ecological conditions particular social phenomena may reasonably be expected to follow. In this instance specific economic and cultural conditions combine with an environment which in its physical sense is the epitome of all that is sordid and unhealthy to produce such "pathological" social forms as delin-quency, crime, dependence and the like. At least this is how Jonassen interprets Shaw's conclusions about the significance of the localised persistence of delinquency. In *Social Factors in*

---

[1] Jonassen alleges an inconsistency in the age spans of the 1900-06 series and the 1917-23 series. It is true that in *Juvenile Delinquency and Urban Areas* the coverages are quoted as *10-17* and *10-16* respectively, (p. 60), but by reference to the orig-inal work it will be seen that the same 8,056 boys in the 1900-06 series are described as *10-16* (*Delinquency Areas*, p. 22). The matter is further complicated by the statement that in 1906 the upper age limit in the Juvenile Court was *15*! (*Juvenile Delinquency and Urban Areas*, p. 60) Shaw was also aware of the impor-tance of such factors as variations in court and police policy. *Ibid.*, p. 135.

Juvenile Delinquency Shaw stressed the importance of culture conflict between the child and his parents among the first generation of immigrants, the opposition of the Old World to the ethos of the New, as a precipitating factor in the breakdown of informal systems of social control and ultimately, in delinquency. In Jonassen's opinion this is inconsistent with Shaw's later claim that the local persistence of high rates demonstrates that "ethnic" factors are intrinsically unimportant and it is the area which counts.[1]

A number of his minor criticisms were answered by Shaw and McKay themselves in a rejoinder to his original article,[2] but it remains that Jonassen's interpretation of the text in this latter instance is hardly reasonable. To say that the delinquency factors are inherent in the community seems in no way inconsistent with the view that culture conflict may precipitate delinquency. That there is population mobility in the area over a period of time is an irrelevant fact; what is crucial is that "interstitial" or "deteriorating" areas by reason of (a) low rentals and (b) their opportunities for social anonymity attract a variety of social problem groups, whose difficulties will tend to be intensified by the nature of their environment. Those groups which achieve some measure of adjustment[3] are invariably those who become physically and socially mobile, leaving behind those who fail to adjust to be joined by a new generation with similar problems.

Finally, Jonassen argues that the "thread of ecological determinism is discernible all through the warp and woof of the theoretical formulations",[4] most evident in the statistical analyses and least evident in the case material. A superficial glance at the results of such an ecological study would indeed make human ecology appear a deterministic social theory. Shaw was perhaps

[1] "... the fact that in Chicago the rates of delinquents for many years have remained relatively constant in the areas adjacent to centres of commerce and heavy industry, despite successive changes in the nativity and nationality composition of the population, supports emphatically the conclusion that the delinquency producing factors are inherent in the community." *Juvenile Delinquency and Urban Areas*, p. 435.
[2] *American Sociological Review*, Vol. 14, 1949, p. 615, *et seq.*
[3] This is, of course, 'adjustment' measured by the criteria of society at large. Shaw makes the point, which is incidentally fundamental to Mays' interpretation of the Liverpool data (q.v.) that: "Within the limits of his social world, and in terms of its norms and expectations, he may be a highly organised and well adjusted person." Shaw, *op. cit.*, p. 436. The problem remains as to how far the criteria of adjustment are absolute or merely relative. See also, *Ibid.*, p. 86.
[4] Jonassen, *op. cit.*, p. 614.

anticipating this criticism when he emphasised that the discovery of correlations between ecological data and delinquency does not provide an adequate basis for causal explanations.[1] Determinism would surely imply that given a set of ecological circumstances, delinquency must inevitably result, yet it is clear from the evidence that if nowhere in Chicago are there rates of 100, circumstances are by no means so compelling. Shaw suggests that the concomitant variation of delinquency with another variable may be seen not as "cause and effect" but as the result of the influence of some third factor.[2] It would appear that this procedure is as valid as that employed by actuaries for many years to determine insurance risks. As a method of calculating the contingency of delinquency, clearly ecological analyses of this kind have an important contribution to make in the field of preventive action. It is unfortunately only too easy to slip into thinking of them as being of a quasi-causal character, and experimentation, particularly in the field of slum clearance and re-housing which has sprung from such thinking, has been met often with severe disappointments.

[1] See *Delinquency Areas*, p. 21, p. 198, and *Juvenile Delinquency in Urban Areas*, p. 134.
[2] Shaw, *ibid., loc. cit.*

VI

SOME AREA STUDIES SINCE 1930

BETWEEN 1929 and 1942, Clifford Shaw and Henry McKay with the help of others extended the scope of "delinquency area" research to cover a wide variety of cities in the United States. In addition to these studies which have been the subject of discussion in an earlier chapter, a considerable number of other research workers turned their attention to the subject of crime and delinquency in the context of both rural and urban sociology. Much of their material in its published form is unobtainable outside the United States, though some of it adds very little to the body of ecological theory except in so far as more comparative material provides further verification of certain basic hypotheses.[1] Our purpose here is to examine a few pieces of research which can be said to have made important contributions to the body of theory developed by Shaw from the teachings of Park and McKenzie at Chicago.

(a)   Perhaps the first question to come to mind is whether Shaw's basic postulates, which by 1931 had been verified for several other cities besides Chicago, would be applicable to cities and urban areas outside the North American continent. An early attempt to answer the question was made by *Andrew Lind* of the University of Hawaii.[2]

Lind established that in Honolulu, the spatial distribution of delinquents' homes, dependency cases, arrests related to organised vice, and suicides, tended to follow the same spatial pattern as in the cities of North America. Honolulu, like many American

[1] E.g., the association of such factors as delinquency, truancy, adult crime, dependence, etc., in specific localities.

[2] Lind, A. W., "Some Ecological Patterns of Community Disorganisation in Honolulu", *Am. Journ. Soc.*, Vol. 36, 1930, pp. 206-220.

cities, contained large numbers of immigrants, but whereas in America, the social pressures of the city and the wider society tended all the time to coerce the immigrant into the acceptance of a common set of cultural norms, the situation in Hawaii was quite different. The legally enforced norms of conduct were those of White America, but the indigenous population was Polynesian, with differing norms, especially in matters of sexual morality. In addition to the white Americans who were really immigrants themselves, there were substantial communities of Chinese, Japanese, Filipinos and Portuguese. The presence of such large groups with diverse cultural norms, in the relatively limited space of the islands tended to make the competition of the social and moral standards of each group more severe. In America, cultural assimilation had been accelerated by the fact that the majority of individuals accepted a common cultural standard; in Hawaii, the standards imposed by law, were in fact, only one set among several. Lind found therefore, that many so-called delinquents brought before the Courts were not regarded by their own communities as delinquents. Gambling and cock-fighting were culturally acceptable to Filipinos as was adolescent promiscuity among the Polynesians. The existence of institutionalised suicide among the Japanese, also altered the significance of suicide as an index of "social disorganisation".

The conservative pressures of the immigrant community, therefore, although tending to prevent the individual from suffering from the confusion of moral standards, tended often to bring him into conflict with the law.

(b) The second matter to which Shaw failed to give adequate consideration, was the location of crimes as opposed to the location of offenders homes, and relationship between the two. In Lind's view, the frequency of crime within the neighbourhood of the delinquent's residence is an index of the efficiency of the local community in maintaining social standards. He employs two concepts to discuss the relationship between residence and place of offence, namely, the "neighbourhood triangle of delinquency" and the "mobility triangle of delinquency".

The neighbourhood triangle represents the situation in which the homes of two or more delinquents and the place of their offence are found within the same neighbourhood. This he maintained was commonest in the slum where community standards are at their lowest ebb. Though this may be true of Hono-lulu, this does not necessarily follow however, unless the slum area provided opportunities for crime. The mobility triangle, on the other hand, is that in which the homes of two or more delin-quents lie within the same neighbourhood, while the place of the offence is located elsewhere. It is likely, he argues, to have its base in an area of "somewhat greater stability and more effective social restraints".[1] The neighbourhood pattern rep-resents a prior stage to the mobility pattern.

That the mobility pattern should be less characteristic of the slum than the neighbourhood pattern does not seem to be in keeping with the kind of information Shaw provides from his Chicago material, for while certain interstitial districts with their concentrations of business premises and railway yards provide opportunities for crime among the local residents, the interstitial slum areas are ecologically distinct from the central business district which is the scene of the crimes of many slum delinquents. The evidence would seem to suggest that crimes are committed where the practical opportunities are greatest rather than with specific reference to the attitudes of other members of the local community.

R. *Clyde White's* study of Indianapolis[2] confirms this view.

'The railroad as such does not appear to be associated with high felony rates, but at certain points on it where factories are located felony rate tends to be higher than the contiguous tracts at similar distances from the central business district. In general, then, the residences of felons and the location of their offences are associated with business and industry.'[3]

White's study used the same basic techniques as Shaw had done, and resulted in the same general conclusions. But by plotting residence and place of offence rates on the same logarithmic scale he was able to show that there is a distinction between them which has some bearing upon ecological theory in that the city has certain secondary business districts on its periphery. While

---

[1] *Loc. cit.*

[2] "The Relation of Felonies to Environmental Factors in Indianapolis", *Soc. Forces* 10, 1932, pp. 498-513.

[3] cf. Sutherland, "Petty crimes against property are ... concentrated near the places of residence of criminals but the more serious crimes against property are committed some distance from the place of residence of criminals." *Principles of Criminology*, Chicago, 1934, p. 39.

both residence and place of offence rates declined from the central business district outwards, offence rates declined more sharply in Zones II and III, but much less sharply in Zones IV and V.[1]

Whether the priority of the neighbourhood pattern over the mobility pattern has any real significance is doubtful, except perhaps in the case of the professional house or shopbreaker who tends to operate further away from home than the amateur or juvenile.

Stuart Lottier's analysis of the distribution of criminal homicide, rape, robbery, assault, breaking and entering, larceny and car stealing in the Metropolitan region of Detroit,[2] shows the same tendency for offence rates to rise slightly near the city boundary where the metropolitan district ends and the region begins. Lottier's contention is that just as the region surrounding a great city is socially and economically integrated with it, so the incidence of crime in both the city and its hinterland will form part of a common pattern. The reason for the "hump" in the curve, at least for crimes against property, would seem to be the presence of satellite business districts in the city suburbs.

(c) Without admitting any *causal* relationship between delinquency and crime on the one hand, and the existence of other factors usually described as "indices of social disorganisation" on the other, it is still necessary to establish their relationship in terms of the ecological process of social interaction within a spatial frame of reference. The question is whether the ecological environment tends to precipitate[3] delinquency among those who live and grow up in the neighbourhood, or whether it constitutes a complex of selective forces attracting those individuals who are prone to delinquency for a variety of reasons.

The findings of *Donald Taft*,[4] based upon research in Danville, Illinois, into this particular issue appear to be inconclusive. A

---

[1] The distance between place of residence and place of offence exhibited variations between different offences. The mean distance for offences against the person was 0.84 miles, that for offences against property 1.72 miles.

[2] "The Distribution of Criminal Offences in Metropolitan Regions", *Journal of Crim. Law and Criminology*, Vol. 29, 1938, pp. 37-50. Sutherland's analysis of burglary and robbery data for the banks and stores of the Chicago Metropolitan Region in 1931 and 1932 presents a similar picture. Sutherland, *op. cit.*, p. 122.

[3] Because one cannot neglect the importance of subjective personality traits, the term 'precipitate' is used here rather than 'cause'.

[4] "Testing the Selective Influence of Areas of Delinquency", *Am. Journ. Soc.*, Vol. 48, 1942, pp. 202-213.

sample of 109 felons (that is, serious offenders) from Danville who were committed either to the Pontiac Reformatory or the Southern Penitentiary were selected for study. Of this number 29 were found to be non-residents, and so excluded, and in 7 cases the information was incomplete. In the remainder, the numbers of "native" and "non-native" were respectively 13 and 60. About 40% of those not born in the city had previous criminal records elsewhere, while a further 8% had families with a delinquent background.

Although the size of the sample was small, the conclusions have a reasonably high degree of validity for the group of felons in the period 1928-1930. Unfortunately, they represent a relatively small proportion of all offenders, and Taft has no information on the subject of adult misdemeanants or juvenile offenders who are, both numerically and theoretically, more important to our problem. Perhaps the most significant point brought out by this study, however, was the transient residence of delinquents in the city, and their concentration in the rooming house districts. This would suggest that selective factors are at work in so far as these areas offer amongst other things, accommodation at lowest possible cost. Whether the fluidity of the population in militating against the development of local solidarity and the enforcement of conduct norms can itself be regarded as an environmental factor, is of course another matter. Elmer, in his study of Minneapolis and St. Paul had argued along these lines some years before, maintaining that it was the areas of rapid demographic change, rather than simply those of dense population which produced community problems, in that there were no effective social groupings to establish social norms or to act as informal agencies of social control.[1]

Further research into this problem was made by *Marshall Clinard* in Iowa,[2] on the basis of a sample of some 200 men sentenced between 1938 and 1940 for offences against property. Adopting Wirth's concept of urbanisation[3] as a mode of life characterised by size, density, heterogeneity and impersonality rather then merely an aggregation of population, he was able to consider villages and small towns as well as cities in which such

[1] Elmer, M. C., "Maladjustment of Youth in Relation to Density of Population", *Proceedings of Am. Sociological Society,* Chicago, 1925.
[2] Clinard, M. B., "The Process of Urbanisation and Criminal Behaviour", *Am. Journ. Soc.,* Vol. 48, 1942, pp. 202-213.
[3] Wirth, L., "Urbanism as a Way of Life", *Am. Journ. Soc.,* Vol. 44, 1938, pp. 1-24.

factors as physical mobility, local solidarity and differential association could be observed in varying degrees.

Two groups of rural offenders, those from outlying farms and those from villages, were matched against two control groups. The offenders were residentially more mobile than the controls, and were less well integrated with their local communities as measured by their participation in community organisations. Networks of criminal behaviour, or "differential association", were found to vary directly with the degree of urbanisation in the areas from which the offenders came. Leadership characteristics were rare among rural offenders, whose gangs, when they existed, were of a loosely organised kind. Definitely organised criminal behaviour and closely knit gangs, however, were an outstanding characteristic of city offenders. Clinard's conclusion is that such organisation can only exist in the degree to which social contacts tend to be impersonal.

' . . . as long as there exists a predominant measure of personal relations and informal social control in the farm and village areas, it will be impossible for a separate criminal culture to exist as is characteristic of large urban areas. For this reason it appears almost impossible to develop criminal social types in rural areas.'[1]

(d)   None of the researches considered above was implicitly critical of Shaw's principal techniques, or indeed of his general conclusions, except in so far as they sought to amplify certain theoretical issues which had arisen with the development of ecological theory as a whole, for example, the extension of ecological analysis to the metropolitan region around the city itself. A quarter of a century after the publication of *Delinquency Areas*, however, there has appeared a work which is not only a painstaking study of juvenile delinquency in Baltimore, but which raises a number of important issues which have never been properly resolved by Shaw or his colleagues. Among the most important of these is the precise definition of "social disorganisation" or *anomie*, and its relationship to socially deviant behaviour.

Bernard Lander's study[2] is based upon the 8,464 cases of ju-

---

[1] Clinard, *op. cit.*, p. 213. One might point out that highly organised criminal activity *is* possible in rural areas, providing it is to some extent socially acceptable in the community, e.g., the Ku Klux Klan in America's rural 'Deep South'.
[2] Lander, B., *Towards an Understanding of Juvenile Delinquency*, New York, 1954.

venile delinquency which occurred in Baltimore during the
period 1939-1942. The starting point was the analysis of delinquency rates by geographical areas and their relation to the
distribution of a series of socio-economic variables derived from
the U.S. Census of 1940, viz:

1 Education: median years of school completed by all persons
   aged 25 and over.
2 Median rental.
3 Overcrowding: percentage of persons living in homes with
   1.51 or more persons per room.
4 Substandard housing: percentage of homes needing major
   repairs and/or having no private bath.
5 Population composition: percentage of non-whites and foreign born.

Although delinquency rates decrease with distance from the
centre,[1] industrial land use in Baltimore does not conform to the
radial pattern, though this fact by itself would not necessarily
disprove the association between the numbers of delinquency
cases and the proportion of industrial property.[2] The rates
decrease irregularly from the centre, and near the periphery tend
to remain constant. The highest rates, well above the mean for
the city, occur in areas adjacent to commercial and industrial
property or dominated by it, but so also do some of the very
lowest. The zones of transition do not conform to the concentric
pattern noted in Chicago, and they too, have widely varying
delinquency rates. From the Baltimore evidence Lander concludes that the "invasion" of an area by commerce and industry
is not so crucial to the problem as Shaw has suggested.

It is in the analysis of the distribution of delinquency and the
socio-economic variables that the limitations of Shaw's theory
which leans so heavily upon the evidence of zero-order correlations become most apparent. The zero-order correlation assumes
a linear relationship between two variables, but this may be an
assumption which masks the truth. For example, in the analysis
of housing and delinquency in Baltimore the following correlations were obtained:

[1] "The delinquency rate declines precipitously from 10.2 per cent in Zone 1, to
   6.1 in Zone 2, and 2.7 in Zone 3. Beyond Zone 3 the rate remains substantially
   the same for the remaining four zones." Lander, *op. cit.*, p. 24.
[2] *Vide,* the instance of Birmingham, Alabama, p. 80 above.

delinquency and overcrowding $+$ ·73
delinquency and substandard housing $+$ ·69

By regression analysis, however, Lander is able to show that these relationships are not necessarily significant, and indeed some of the areas of worst housing have some of the lowest delinquency rates. Home ownership, on the other hand, is significantly (and negatively) related even on the 0·01 level of significance. If home ownership is a measure of social stability, then factor analysis seems to confirm the relationship between delinquency and social instability.

In Chicago Shaw found a positive correlation between delinquency and the proportion of negroes and foreign born; in Baltimore there appears to be an inverse relationship, a correlation of—0.16 at the 0.05 level of significance. Lander's detailed analysis of the population factor produces some surprising but important results. In areas of great negro concentration, where they are 90% or more of the total, the rates tend to be low.[1] Where negroes form between 50 and 100% of the population, the correlation with delinquency is negative, where they form less than 50% the correlation is positive.

Factorial analysis of the Baltimore material suggests that there are two independent variables underlying the situation. The first of these Lander calls *anomie*, following Durkheim in regarding differential crime rates as reflection of varying degrees of social cohesion or solidarity, and social control. This is of course, very similar to both Shaw and Burgess' concept of "social disorganisation". The *anomic* factors are, however, insufficient to explain all the inter-relationships in the matrix, and it appears that a second basic factor, socio-economic in character is also operative. In accounting for delinquency, Lander draws upon the evidence of the relationship between social and economic instability and delinquency. The physical characteristics of an area tend to be of secondary importance to the presence of absence of *anomic* factors.

Lander does not say precisely, what he understands by the term "socio-economic factor". It would seem, however, that it describes a factor or factors which tend to be objective, in contrast to "anomic" factors which appear to be much more sub-

---

[1] If all the ethnic groups lived in dense concentrations, and were like the negroes in this respect, the negative correlation between delinquency and percentage of "ethnics" would be readily explained.

jective. For example, the street play group is "socio-economic" in character in so far as it is (a) part of the general style of life of the working class child and (b) a group whose socialising function is to some extent the result of long absences by both parents during working hours. It derives from an objective class situation—a "sub-culture"—and the objective fact that many working class mothers go to work. Anomic factors on the other hand, because they are related to psychological perception and mental health tend to be more subjective and by no means uniformly distributed throughout a neighbourhood.

Throughout the work, Lander is constantly emphasising that correlations may be fortuitous, but as a scientist he is scrupulously honest with himself in admitting that even when we can be sure a relationship is not fortuitous, we still cannot say *why* it exists, or precisely what it represents. But by closely examining each factor in the matrix in terms of how much it contributes to the variance of the dependent variable, delinquency, he is in fact utilising a form of ecological analysis which may be used for for predictive purposes. The study of regression, of course, brings us fundamentally, no nearer to the goal of explanation than before. But whereas the ecological approach to the study of delinquency and other community problems has sometimes been regarded in recent times as having outlived its usefulness, particularly since the development of new theories in psychology concerning personality and social structure, Lander's work has shown that if it cannot answer completely the question "why delinquency?" it can at least answer with some accuracy the question "how much is there likely to be at a given time?" The predictive techniques developed by the Gluecks are now used in modified form as the basis of sentencing policy in at least two of the United States; whether a method of ecological prediction is likely to be employed in relation to delinquency or other forms of social pathology by social workers and administrators remains to be seen. It would seem largely to depend upon how soon techniques are devised which are neither cumbersome nor unreliable.

In Britain ecological research in the field of crime and delinquency has not followed the tradition of the Chicago School, perhaps because the impact of that School upon British sociology has not been particularly great, and because the study of criminology itself has never enjoyed more than a precarious foothold in the Universities from which the impetus of research must ultimately come. The situation is further complicated by the fact that most of the studies which have been carried out in the last 25 years have, strictly speaking, been *area studies*, rather than *ecological* studies, in that they have been concerned with discovering the dimensions of the problem in particular towns or regions rather than investigating the dynamics of delinquency within an ecological frame of reference. This is not of course a suggestion of their inadequacy, indeed the best of them stimulated a healthy and much needed interest among the local lay public.

In the mid-1930's *J. H. Bagot*[1] undertook a comparative survey of delinquency in England and Wales and the city of Liverpool. This was very largely a factual survey along lines not dissimilar from parts of Burt's *Young Delinquent*. The publication of Bagot's work was followed by that of a large scale survey of the London area by *Carr-Saunders, Mannheim and Rhodes*.[2] *Young Offenders* is perhaps the most comprehensive local statistical survey of delinquency conducted to date, although it appears somewhat unbalanced owing to the curtailment of the psychological side of the inquiry by World War II. The evacuation of the London School of Economics, however, provided *Mannheim* with the opportunity of continuing similar research on a smaller scale in the city of Cambridge.[3] This survey is interesting in that it provides interesting data about the wartime period which was subsequently blamed for much of the post-war delinquency which reached its peak in 1951. At the same time it supplies details of numbers of small contemporary local surveys.

The post-war crime wave which aroused considerable public concern and uneasiness about the growing problem of juvenile crime was frequently coupled with apprehension about the effects of full employment and the Welfare State upon attitudes to work and property and social responsibility in general. Previously it had been assumed that poverty and social insecurity were at the roots of a great proportion of crime; it was all the more bewildering then, that crime should continue to rise with the tide of post-war prosperity and social security. Many magistrates and

[1] Bagot, J. H., *Juvenile Delinquency: A Comparative Study of the Position in Liverpool and England and Wales,* London, 1941.
[2] Carr-Saunders, A. M., Mannheim, H. and Rhodes, E. C., *Young Offenders,* London, 1942.
[3] Mannheim, H., *Juvenile Delinquency in an English Middletown,* London, 1948.

not a few social workers, blamed the Welfare State as having sapped the foundations of personal responsibility. It was often forgotten that many of the old evils, especially overcrowding and bad housing remained, and that the problems arising out of mental defect or abnormality and emotional disturbance were as great as ever.

Against this background *John Mays'* recent study of Liverpool[1] is of especial interest. It is in no sense a statistical survey, nor is it an "ecological" study in that it is written within a theoretical frame of reference. Rather, it is in the style of W. F. Whyte's *Street Corner Society*,[2] concerned with investigating the phenomenon of the delinquent sub-culture of the city slum. It was precisely this kind of "situational analysis" that Shaw had advocated as a necessary adjunct to statistical inquiry, and which demonstrates the ecological aspects of the problem of the delinquency area. Based on his interviews with boys at the Liverpool University Settlement, of which he is Warden, Mays presents a striking picture of the cultural milieu in which delinquent activity in the form of shoplifting, malicious damage and petty larceny is for boys in certain age groups, "normal" behaviour which is passively accepted in the neighbourhood. He puts forward two suggestions about delinquency in a great city which are in many respects highly controversial.

In the first place he suggests a novel definition of the delinquent and the criminal. Those who submit to the temporary social pressures of the gangs and commit offences he calls "delinquent" as distinct from those "criminals" whose offences are the outcome of psychological disturbance and who tend to persist in this form of behaviour well into adolescence and early adulthood. Essentially these are ideal types and in practice they tend to merge imperceptibly in consequence of the fact that many "delinquents" have experienced some degree of emotional maladjustment and many serious and persistent offenders are "the victims of a criminogenic social background."[3] Accordingly, he expresses the concept in the form of two equations:

Personal + environmental factors = Crime
Environmental + personal factors = Delinquency

[1] Mays, J. B., *Growing Up in the City*, Liverpool, 1954.
[2] Whyte, W. F., *Street Corner Society*, Chicago, 1943.
[3] Mays, *op. cit.*, p. 20.

In adopting this viewpoint, Mays has adopted the offender rather than the offence as his point of reference. This is in complete contrast with the present author's own views, discussed earlier, and seems to run counter to the sense of the strict linguistic sense of the terms "delinquent" and "criminal". Much of his argument for the validity of such a distinction appears to rest upon the persistence of certain boys in their offences, but persistence by itself is scarcely a valid criterion: if it were, then the man who persists in minor traffic infringements from riding a bicycle on the pavement as a boy to parking his car in a restricted street as a man is "criminal" rather then "delinquent".

More important, however, is Mays' contention that delinquency as a form of sub-culturally prescribed behaviour during boyhood results in almost every boy committing offences likely to bring him to court at some time or other. From his informal interviews with boys he was impressed by the number who had in fact never been caught, and seems to suggest therefore that the problem of why not every boy from a delinquency area becomes a "legally defined" juvenile delinquent is less real than one would suppose. Almost all his boys told him that they had grown out of the delinquent phase although they had almost all been through it. If this is indeed so, and although the sample was not a random one there is little reason to suppose that it was wildly unrepresentative, it suggests that the sociological or "cultural" factors in the genesis of crime and delinquency have been gravely underestimated. Such a situation may have come about as a by-product of the psychological researches which have emphasised the need for legal recognition of the idea of diminished responsibility. It may well be that the social pressures to conformity are as important in a quantitative sense as the effects of emotional maladjustment, particularly as the gang, as Mays so ably points out, has frequently to act as a substitute for the emotional and intellectual poverty of both home and school life.

In Mays' view minor infringements of the law are part of a system of behaviour which is "normative" in the city slum among boys of a specific age group, those that fail to "grow out" of this anti-social phase consisting very largely of individuals from backgrounds which have endowed them with deeper and more permanent problems of social and psychological adjustment. The inference which is most readily drawn from his material is that the delinquent "sub-culture" is essentially a juvenile culture, and that social deviance in later life is psychological rather than sociological in character.

A contemporary study of a Midland mining town, however, does not appear to confirm this suggestion. The setting up of a committee for the prevention of juvenile delinquency in Nottinghamshire resulted in a research project the findings of which have been circulated under the title of *The Social Background of Delinquency*.[1] In "Radby" the same problem of the delinquent sub-culture was investigated, and it would seem that there is no small degree of continuity between the anti-social attitudes and behaviour of children and those of their elder brothers and sisters and parents. Professor Sprott, in his introduction argues that there has been too great an emphasis laid on the "pathological" aspects of delinquency, and too little on its sociological aspects, particularly within the family. The research began by recognising that differential amounts of legal delinquency exist, even within areas which are relatively homogeneous in socioeconomic status. The hypothesis it attempted to test was that "within working class areas different standards are upheld, and the differences between norms of behaviour contribute to differential rates of delinquency distribution".

The methods used by Miss Jephcott and Mr. Carter combined the techniques of the social survey with that of participant observation. The latter worked for some time as an unskilled worker in a local factory, while the former organised a play-room in one of the streets which provided unique opportunities for study and inter-action with the local children and their parents. Juvenile delinquency was found from the analysis of court records to be concentrated in five fairly small areas. In each area a pair of streets was selected for study, one with a heavy concentration of delinquency cases, the other with fewer cases. These "black" and "white" streets appeared to be superficially very similar and it was in individual families that the main differences were to be found. 225 families were interviewed and graded on a five-point scale according to four criteria, marital relationships, relationships with children, housekeeping standards, and education. The use of these criteria is open to some criticism, but it was reasonably established that within a single street there

---

[1] Carter, M. P., & Jephcott, P., *The Social Background of Delinquency*. Rockfeller Research, 1952-4. Director, Prof. W. J. H. Sprott. Typescript available on loan from the University Librarian, Nottingham.

may be wide variations in social norms and aspirations, although by and large the "black" streets contained a majority of families with low social standards without discernible social aspirations.

The picture of the "black" streets which the research workers draw is indeed a vivid one telling a story of domestic violence, street brawling, drunkenness and sexual promiscuity. The children are exposed to the influences of adults who very largely reject the norms of the wider society in favour of a way of life which is characterised by self-interest and a flagrant disregard of the rights of others. Indeed, Mr. Carter's description of the factory workers shows their lives to be in the words of Hobbes "nasty and brutish". The majority of the families in the "white" streets in contrast are houseproud and jealous of their good name; they keep a close rein on their children and place a premium upon education as a means to social and economic betterment.

It would appear that in Radby legal delinquency is merely one aspect of a way of life followed by families of low social status; furthermore, there does not seem to be a marked cleavage between the patterns of behaviour of the younger and older age groups as Mays' suggests is the case in Liverpool. It may well be, of course, that in Radby the boys stop stealing from Woolworth's and grow up to be workshy and sexually promiscuous young men. It may also be true that the adult criminals are also often psychologically disturbed, but from the factory study it would seem that petty larceny persists well into manhood, and is a socially accepted phenomenon.

Mays quotes a boy as having scruples about stealing from a corne shop but not from a big store; such an ethical distinction would be rare in Radby.

Implicit in the Radby material is the notion that delinquency and other forms of anti-social behaviour are a function of social class. But the establishment of such a relationship tells us little about the dynamics of the situation, in particular about the role of personality and psychological abnormality in the creation and transmission of a system of behaviour wich is unacceptable to the world at large Sociological explanations such as Merton's are not enough.[1] The great virtue of the Radby study is that it highlights the *family* in the process in both its sociological and psychological contexts.

[1] Merton R.K., "Social Structure and Anomie" in *Social Theory and Social Structure*. Glencoe Ill. 1949.

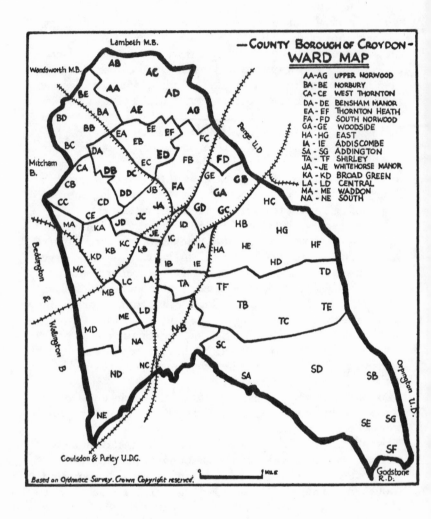

—COUNTY BOROUGH OF CROYDON—
WARD MAP

AA-AG	UPPER NORWOOD
BA-BE	NORBURY
CA-CE	WEST THORNTON
DA-DE	BENSHAM MANOR
EA-EF	THORNTON HEATH
FA-FD	SOUTH NORWOOD
GA-GE	WOODSIDE
HA-HG	EAST
IA-IE	ADDISCOMBE
SA-SG	ADDINGTON
TA-TF	SHIRLEY
JA-JE	WHITEHORSE MANOR
KA-KD	BROAD GREEN
LA-LD	CENTRAL
MA-ME	WADDON
NA-NE	SOUTH

Lambeth M.B.

Wandsworth M.B.

Penge U.D.

Mitcham B.

Beddington & Wallington B.

Coulsdon & Purley U.D.C.

Orpington U.D.

Godstone R.D.

Based on Ordnance Survey. Crown Copyright reserved.

MILE

VII

DELINQUENCY AREAS IN CROYDON

THE writer's reasons for selecting Croydon[1] as an area for study were several. In the first place the vast proportion of ecological studies dealing with the problem of crime and delinquency are confined to the United States; furthermore they relate very largely to the situation in large industrialised cities. Implicit in many of these studies, however, is the idea that certain propositions about the relationship between criminal or other forms of socially deviant behaviour and the ecological environment are likely to be valid for urban settlements in other parts of the world. A large British town with special *sub*urban as well as urban characteristics seemed a reasonable area for testing some of these propositions. In the second place it had been suggested in *Young Offenders*[2] that there was a need for some kind of ecological study in the London area:

> 'The limitations of the control method must be recognised.
> While . . . we may hope to find out whether there are significant differences . . . in respect, let us say, of the structure of the family, e.g., "broken" or "normal", we cannot expect to throw much light on such a question as the possible effect of the lack of paying fields and open spaces on delinquency, for all those attending a school generally . . . enjoy or endure the same topographical environment.[3]

[1] It is perhaps a departure from sociological tradition to refer to a town which has been studied by its own name, but anonymity in this instance would have been short-lived and might even have resulted in some distortion of the data. On the other hand, the material has been arranged in such a way that personal confidences have been respected and individual streets and families cannot be recognised.

[2] Carr-Saunders, Mannheim and Rhodes, see above, p. 101.

[3] *Ibid.,* p. 148.

Towards the end of 1952 the town achieved an unwelcome notoriety by what is now referred to by Croydonians as the "Craig and Bentley affair". One Sunday evening two local youths attempted to break and enter a wholesale sweet shop in the centre of the town; an alarm was given, and the police arrived on the scene, arresting Bentley almost immediately. Craig meanwhile had climbed on the roof in an effort to evade arrest and shot dead the police constable who was attempting to bring him down. At the Old Bailey, Craig, being but sixteen years of age, was ordered by the Lord Chief Justice to be detained until Her Majesty's Pleasure be known; Bentley aged nineteen was sentenced to death as an accessory on the grounds that he had incited Craig to murder by shouting "Let him have it Chris!" After a prolonged and unsuccessful appeal, Bentley was executed at Wandsworth Prison.[1] Among the effects of the affair was a front page article in a national daily—VICIOUS YOUNG FOOLS STILL PARADE IN A TOWN OF TRAGEDY. On balance, it seemed unlikely that the Teddy Boy population of Croydon was any larger or more troublesome than in any other large town, indeed the local Probation Service produced evidence to show that delinquency was rather less prevalent than in the County of Surrey. What seemed most provoking in this article, however, was the assertion that

> 'The "Craig" boys of Croydon are not ill-cared for little throw-outs from slum homes. They are a different problem altogether. They come from decent *middle class* (author's italics) homes where they parents would be mortally ashamed of any trouble with the police.'

This suggestion was indeed a novel one, for generations of research workers from the 19th century onwards have shown that crime and delinquency are almost exclusively the *metier* of the "submerged tenth", the socially deviant and "unrespectable". Craig, however, was not the son of an unskilled labourer but of a bank clerk; his home was not in a slum or a council housing estate but in a higly respectable district from which white collar workers went up to the City every day. Could it be then, that the

---

[1] For an account of the interesting legal aspects of the case, see Montgomery Hyde, H. (Ed.) *The Trial of Christopher Craig and Derek William Bentley*, London, 1954, and the review of this book by J. E. Hall-Williams, *British Journal of Delinquency*, Vol. VI, No. 2.

phenomenon of delinquency was spreading across the socio-economic barriers which had so far confined it, and if so, what were the forces operating to produce this change? To one who had been born and educated in the town and been later connected with Youth Work in it, the question posed was intriguing. It was hoped that an intimate knowledge of the area could be tempered by a degree of objectivity in a study which might provide an answer.

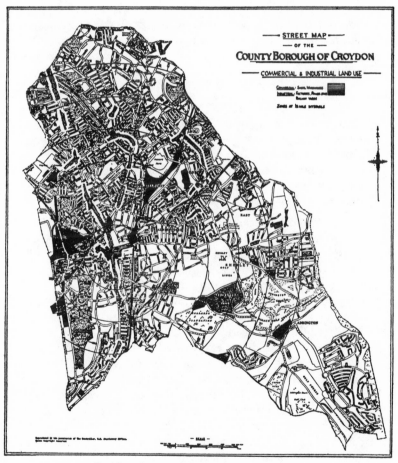

Croydon: Commercial and Industrial Land Use

SOCIAL AND ECONOMIC CHARACTERISTICS

Croydon's identity as an urban settlement is well established in history. Roman and Saxon remains have been excavated and there is a mention in Domesday Book. During the Middle Ages it grew to be a market town of some importance, largely due to the patronage of the Archbishops of Canterbury who came to reside there. It was the arrival of the railway in 1839, however, which heralded the period of most rapid growth. Between 1801 and 1851 the population had risen from some 5,000 to 20,000; by 1901 it had risen to over 130,000. Much of this increase in population was due to the popularity of Croydon as a suburban settlement for those who found their work in London and by 1887 no fewer than 14 railway stations had been built within the parish to accommodate the demand for commuting facilities. In a contemporary guide book we read:

'Purity of water supply, good roads, efficient sanitary arrangements with lovely surrounding scenery combine to render Croydon a desirable place of abode. Here the death rate is exceptionally low. Its proximity to the Metropolis to every part of which there is ready access from Croydon in all directions by means of train, adds to the attractions of the neighbourhood.'[1]

In 1883 the town became a Municipal Borough, and a County Borough five years later. In this period of "boom town" growth there were no fewer than ten local papers published both daily and weekly. Local life flourished at all cultural levels from the theatre where Bernard Shaw put on first nights to the Woodside race track (of such ill repute that public opposition secured its removal to Gatwick in 1890). Between the two World Wars a further period of expansion took place. By 1914 Croydon and Metropolitan London had already fused to the north by continuous urban growth; in the 20's and 30's Coulsdon, Purley, Caterham and Sanderstead were developed as dormitory areas and became to all intents and purposes suburbs of Croydon, though outside its administrative boundaries. Since 1945 most of the available building land in the Borough—almost all of it to the east in Addington Ward—has been used, the major proportion for new Council housing projects.

[1] Anderson, J. Corbett, *A Descriptive and Historical Guide to Croydon,* Croydon, 1887.

At the 1951 Census the population was recorded as 249,870 persons, one of the largest County Boroughs in England and Wales. Owing to its proximity to Metropolitan London, its identity as an urban entity in its own right tends to be masked, and in 1954 an unsuccessful attempt was made to secure a Royal Charter granting city status in order to reinforce this aspect of civic pride. The following table, derived from the material of the 1951 Census[1] illustrates some aspects of the town's relationship to the metropolis.

TABLE 6

Place of Work: Population Aged 17 and over

	Men	*Women*
Working in Metropolitan London	27,557	11,114
Working elsewhere, mainly Home Counties	9,007	2,641
Total	36,564	13,755
Estimated population aged 17 and over	89,300	103,100
Balance remaining in Croydon*	52,736	89,345

* It is clear, of course, that the bulk of women in this category are not gainfully employed, i.e., are housewives, and some of the men will not be in gainful employment for one reason or another.

It can be seen that rather under half the male population of working age is employed outside the town, for the most part in London. Not all these are necessarily white collar workers, though the fact that the Metropolitan Boroughs of Westminster, Lambeth and Holborn, and the City of London absorb between them some 15,000 men and 8,000 women suggests that most of them are employed in a clerical, administrative or professional capacity.

Croydon itself provides employment for a large proportion of its workpeople, and attracts others from immediately surrounding areas as a consequence of a highly developed network of road transport services. Employment in the town falls into three broad categories:

(1) Factory work, especially in light engineering of a skilled nature,

(2) Distributive trades, especially shop work,

(3) Clerical/administrative, e.g., in Local Government, and nationalised public utilities which have their regional headquarters in the town.

[1] Census 1951. *Report on Usual Residence and Workplace*, p. 251.

In terms of economic geography the town would seem to serve as a dormitory area for a large number of city workers, as an important shopping and business centre for its own well defined hinterland to the south, west and east, and also be a developing industrial centre, concentrating mainly on those forms of engineering and manufacture which depend largely on electric power.

The social class stucture, defined in terms of the Registrar General's *Classification of Occupations* appears to reflect these aspects of its economic structure.

TABLE 7

SOCIAL CLASS DISTRIBUTION OF OCCUPIED AND RETIRED MALES AGED 15 AND OVER*

	Class I	Class II	Class III	Class IV	Class V
Thousands	4,403	16,535	48,062	7,238	8,252
Proportions per thousand of Total	52	196	568	86	98

* Source 1951 Census. *Report for the County of Surrey.*

That there are more persons in Classes I and II than in IV and V suggests that the initial impression of Croydon as a "middle class" town is fairly correct, borne out by the fact that only once, in 1945, has a Labour member been returned to Parliament for any of the three Divisions and that on the Town Council the Labour Group has, apart from a brief period after the war, been for years outnumbered by about 3:1. Each of the 16 Wards in the town was analysed in terms of the Juror's Index,[1] a device originating from the Government Social Survey, which provides a reliable indication of the class structure of any given area. The

[1] Cray, Corlett, & Jones, *The Proportion of Jurors as an Index of the Economic Status of a District,* Social Survey, London, 1951. At the time of the research a person was qualified for Jury Service if he or she were:
(i)   Aged between 21 and 60
(ii) A registered Local Government Elector,
(iii) either (a) a resident beneficially possessed of £10 p.a. in real estate or rent charge, or £20 in leaseholds held for not less than 21 years or determinable on any life or lives, or (b) a householder residing in premises of rateable value of not less than £30 p.a. in the Counties of London and Middlesex or £20 p.a. elsewhere in England and Wales.
In their validation tests for the Index significant correlations were produced with other variables highly saturated with the social class factor, e.g.,
    with non-industrial rateable value per head   + 082
    with infant mortality (reciprocal)   + 0.71
    with proportion of Labour votes cast   — 0.85

"J. Index" showed that the wards to the east and south of the town had a predominantly middle class population, and as these wards are largely the areas of commuter residence it appears that the characteristics of the town's class structure are primarily derived from the fact that it is an important dormitory area of London.

TABLE 8

THE CROYDON JURORS' INDEX 1952

Source: Electoral Register, Nov. 20th, 1952.

	Upper Norwood	Norbury	West Thornton	Bensham Manor	Thornton Heath	South Norwood	Wood-side
Electors	13,359	12,528	12,064	13,082	12,268	12,491	11,304
Jurors	1,694	1,527	1,256	1,444	1,067	1,353	858
J. Index	12·7	12·2	10·4	11·0	8·7	10·8	7·6

	East	Addiscombe	Addington	Shirley	Whitehorse Manor	Broad Green
Electors	10,946	12,075	9,172	9,259	10,312	10,625
Jurors	2,102	853	1,498	1,549	460	458
J. Index	19·2	7·1	16·3	16·7	4·5	4·3

	Central	Waddon	South	CROYDON C. B.
Electors	8,853	11,739	10,818	180,895
Jurors	467	1,056	1,202	19,024
J. Index	5·3	9·0	11·1	10·52

It can be seen that there are certain wards with very high proportions of Jurors compared with the Borough Index-East, Addington and Shirley Wards, while others have J. Indices well below this mean , in particular Whitehorse Manor, Broad Green and Central. Those areas with high J. Indices are concentrated in the middle class areas east of the railway and in the outer residential zones on the western side of the town, while those with low J. Indices are old deteriorating areas in the central part of the Borough. The heterogeneity of certain wards is, however, masked by the index for the ward as a whole. For example, Thornton Heath falls only 1.2 below the Borough mean, but one polling district (EE) has an index of 5.25, some 5.27 below the mean. Similarly the CE district of West Thornton is ecologically an extension of a natural area which lies mostly in Broad Green and is quite dissimilar from the rest of the ward. Because the natural areas of the town do not exactly coincide with political boundaries which are drawn to secure parity of electoral representation, the J. Index had to incorporate certain refinements in the form of J. Indices for a typical District.

TABLE 9

J. INDEX FOR ATYPICAL POLLING DISTRICTS

Source: Electoral Register Nov. 20th, 1952

	West Thornton CE District	Thornton Heath EE District	Waddon MD District	South NC District
Electors	1,472	2,380	3,774	1,554
Jurors	22	125	197	52
J. Index	1·5	5·25	5·2	3·3
Ward Index	10.4	8.7	9·0	11·1

Further evidence of the town's class structure can be derived from an examination of the housing characteristics of the various wards. It is clear that the predominantly middle class wards have a room density which is below the Borough mean and are usually in a better position in regard to overcrowding, that is to say, the percentage of persons living at a room density of 2 or more.

TABLE 10

ROOM DENSITY AND OVERCROWDING

Source: Census 1951

	Upper Norwood	Norbury	West Thornton	Bensham Manor	Thornton Heath	South Norwood
Persons per room	0·67	0·64	0·67	0·66	0·71	0·69
% Persons at more than 2 per room	1·7	0·6	0·5	0·9	1·6	0·9
Persons per household	2·97	2·99	2·98	2·97	3·14	3·03
Rank order: J. Index	4	5	9	7	11	8
Rank order: overcrowding	4	10	11	9	5	9

	Woodside	East	Addis-combe	Addington	Shirley	Whitehorse Manor
Persons per room	0·70	0·65	0·69	0·81	0·64	0·75
% Persons at more than 2 per room	0·6	0·3	1·1	0·3	0·3	2·9
Persons per household	3·15	3·18	2·92	3·79	3·17	3·14
Rank order: J. Index	12	1	13	3	2	15
Rank order: overcrowding	10	12	8	12	12	1

	Broad Green	Central	Waddon	South	CROYDON C. B.
Persons per room	0·78	0·60	0·75	0·62	0·69
% Persons at more than 2 per room	2·4	1·5	1·9	1·4	1·4
Persons per household	3·30	2·77	3·37	2·92	3·10
Rank order: J. Index	16	14	10	6	
Rank order: overcrowding	2	6	3	7	

These data, of course, represent generalisations for each ward and in the case of certain wards give a somewhat misleading impression.[1] By and large those wards which have certain polling districts with a J. Index markedly different from the rest of the ward also have polling districts in which the housing situation is significantly different from the general picture. In addition to these localised variations, the true picture in such wards as Upper Norwood and South tended at the time of the Census to be somewhat distorted by the fact that there were distributed over a wide area numerous requisitioned properties, often inhabited by large families. The high room density in Addington would seem to be related to the two large council estates in that ward; the extent of overcrowding on the council estates is probably rather less than in the other working class areas because the Housing Department as the landlord, is able to keep a stricter control over the number of occupants in any one dwelling than is the private landlord or his agent who may have rather less interest in the enforcement of the housing regulations.

One of the problems of describing the social and economic characteristics of a town such as Croydon is that ward statistics tend to give the impression of areas which though they may differ importantly in terms of social class or housing characteristics, are nevertheless relatively homogeneous in themselves. This is by no means the case, although some wards are far more heterogeneous than others. In the first place, there are variations in social class between adjacent streets, and within individual streets and from an ecological point of view there are very few wards which can be said to constitute "natural areas" in a cultural sense. East and Shirley are perhaps the only two *solidly* middle class areas, although even East has a council estate, and Shirley a Rest Centre for homeless families. At the other end of the scale the picture is more confusing. Broad Green and Whitehorse Manor are undoubtedly the poorest and most dilapidated areas of the town, and to see the children romping over the car-wrecks dumped on the bomb sites and the women in turbans pushing their prams, one would imagine that here too is some degree of cultural uniformity. Closer acquaintance tends to dispel this idea. Alongside the families of the unskilled labourers who at election times are herded rather unwillingly into cars to be

---

[1] The cost of obtaining material from the Census to obtain Polling District statistics on housing was quite prohibitive.

taken to cast their Labour votes, are the costermongers and the junk men who are as staunch in their Conservatism as the backwoodsmen of the House of Lords. In dress, and speech and their methods of child rearing they share common values, but in their levels and sources of income which may have an important influence upon their other values, they have less in common.

The zonal theory of urban development has little relevance for Croydon except perhaps for the earliest period of its expansion in the 19th century, nor does an analysis of land use tell us very much that is meaningful because so much of it is residential. Broadly speaking one may say that to the east of the main north-south road and the railway line through East Croydon station land use is predominantly residential and the area has been developed fairly recently. West of this axis development is much older. In the oldest areas surrounding the central business district there are many small factories, laundries and so on, and slightly further out are located larger industrial enterprises, the power stations and refuse tips. There is a complete absence of the classic "interstital" area which is characteristic of the great city, and the ecological changes which have taken place have been gradual rather than dramatic, accelerated perhaps only by the war and the bombing which destroyed or damaged some 54,000 houses. Contrary to the findings of the Chicago School, patterns of land use have little real relationship to the distribution of delinquent residence although they have considerable relationship to the distribution of offences. The table on the opposite page is an attempt to summarise the main social and economic characteristics of the 16 wards.[1]

There is perhaps only one context in which the dominant social characteristics of the wards are clearly demonstrated, the field of local politics. It may be an overstatement to say with Park that the spatial pattern of human living is the basis of a moral order, but it is evident that the spatial distribution of the various social classes in the community is the basis of a political order. Political behaviour is very largely determined by social

[1] This material is based upon field observations in the Summer of 1954 and upon the 1951 Census Reports. At the time of writing (1956) some changes have already taken place and a Private Bill is being promoted which if successful will change the whole centre of the town. For a full description of the town in 1954 see the author's thesis, "The Concept of Social Ecology in Criminological Research", University of London, 1955, pp. 179-207.

TABLE 11
SOCIAL AND ECONOMIC CHARACTERISTICS OF CROYDON

	Class Characteristics	Main types of land use	Period of Development	Condition of Property	Political Complexion	Persons per acre	Rateable Value to nearest £ thousand[1]
r Norwood	M & LM	Residential	1880-1914	Well maintained	Ratepayer	18.3	189
ury*	M & LM	,,	1910-1940	,,	,,	28.5	183
Thornton	M & LM	Residential some industry	1910-1930	,,	,,	35.5	144
ham Manor	M & LM	Residential	1900-1920	,,	,,	46.9	136
nton Heath	LM & W	Residential small industrial units	1890-1920	Deteriorating since 1940	Marginal	42.2	125
n Norwood	M, LM & W	Residential small industrial units	1880-1914	Generally well maintained but some deterioration	Ratepayer	28.9	146
dside	LM & W	Residential with large industrial units	1870-1914	Deterioration since 1940	Labour	34.1	109
	UM & M	Residential	1920-1940	Well maintained	Ratepayer	15.2	187
scombe	LM & W	Residential small industrial units	1880-1914	Some deterioration since 1940	Marginal	45.4	135
ngton*	UM & W	Residential	1930- to date	Well maintained	Labour†	4.9	129
ey	UM & M	Residential	1930-1950	,,	Ratepayer	8.1	161
ehorse or	W	Residential small indus-units	1870-1900	Badly bombed deteriorating	Labour	41.1	103
d Green*		Residential with large industrial units	1870-1930	Deteriorating	Labour	42.6	112
ral	W & LM	Commercial with some residential	Roman times to date	Commercial well maintained residential deteriorating	Marginal	28.5	354
don*	LM & W	Residential with largest industrial units	1920-1930	Well maintained	Labour	22.0	170
h	LM & W	Residential, small industrial units	1870-1914	,,	Ratepayer	12.1	222

= Upper Middle   M = Middle   LM = Lower Middle   W = Working Class

ards with large council estates

ue to population of housing estates at New Addington and Monks Hill

April 1st, 1953.

class[1] and political representation in both national and local government is on a territorial basis. In Croydon it is possible to trace a connection between the spatial distribution of the social classes and such end products of local government as the level of the rates and the character and scope of the services and amenities provided by the local authority. It will have been noticed that the controlling political group is the Ratepayers Association and not the Conservative Party as such. This fact is of some importance for although electorally the people who vote Ratepayer vote Conservative at Parliamentary elections, the "Party bosses" are not entirely the same people. The orientation of Ratepayer policy is by and large to the Right of the Conservative Party nationally, particularly in respect of the provision of social services. In 1953 the then Chairman of the Health Committee announced with some pleasure the closing of certain day nurseries and in 1952 drastic cuts in the Libraries service were made to help minimise the rate increase. It was even suggested by one councillor that children should clean their own schools to reduce the expenditure of the Education Committee. On occasion, certain of the younger Conservatives have actually run in opposition to Ratepayer candidates and expressed profound disagreement with such extreme policies.

It is a commonplace that in local elections the proportion of electors exercising their right to vote is lower than at Parliamentary elections, but apart from this there seem to be considerable differences between wards. In East and Shirley the poll falls from about 85% to about 60%, but in Broad Green and Whitehorse Manor it may fall from about 80% to below 30%. Political apathy equally with other forms of political behaviour is a concomitant of social class.

THE DESIGN OF THE RESEARCH

Broadly speaking, the aim of the inquiry was to survey the crime position in Croydon and to discover whether there was any significant relationship between the crime pattern and the ecological characteristics of the town. Thus far it was an attempt to test out some of the hypotheses of Shaw and McKay in an

---

[1] cf., Benny, M. and Geiss, H. "social class in one or other of its protean manifestations is the chief determinant of political behaviour", 'Social Class and Politics in Greenwich', *British Journal of Sociology*, Vol. 1, No. 4, 1950, p. 326.

urban community markedly different from those studied in the United States and reported in *Juvenile Delinquency and Urban Areas*. Further than this it was hoped to investigate the statement that Croydons' delinquents were not "slum" children but those of the middle classes, and the provisions made for the prevention and treatment of delinquency and crime.

The difficulties inherent in the single handed study of crime in a town of a quarter of a million inhabitants need scarcely to be elaborated. The major problem of research design was to define those few avenues of inquiry which could be pursued in some detail and which were likely to provide meaningful data. It was decided at the outset to concentrate on a single year, 1952, during which the Craig and Bentley affair took place. In many ways a synchronic study would have been more fruitful in that it might have shown important trends in the distribution of both crime and criminals, but the task of handling the statistics for three years, let alone five or ten, would have proved well-nigh insuperable in the two years available for the research. In addition to the statistical material it was decided to collect a number of individual case studies in view of the fact that case studies play a valuable complementary role to statistics in understanding the dynamics of individual delinquencies. The data were collected therefore under three main headings:

Series I: A complete list of all indictable offences, and certain non-indictable offences of a "criminal" character, known to the police and committed in the Borough during 1952, classified by type and geographical location.

Series II: A list of all persons aged 8 years and over, charged in 1952 with offences committed in the Borough and classified by offence, age, sex and residence.

Series III: The Case Histories of all Juvenile offenders placed on Probation, under Supervision, or committed to Approved Schools in the period January 1st - December 31st, 1952, by the Borough Juvenile Court, or (in the case of certain Probationers) dealt with by other Courts which immediately transferred the order to the offender's home town.

Series I: THE DISTRIBUTION OF OFFENCES

The majority of offences in this Series were indictable, that is to say crimes of a fairly grave nature as far as the community is

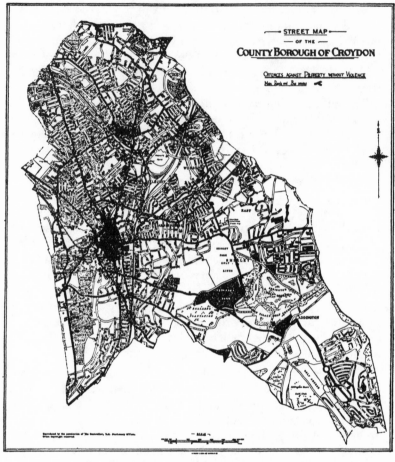

Croydon: Offences against Property without violence.
Each spot represents one offence.

concerned. Certain types of non-indictable offence had never-theless to be included on the grounds that they are actions which are strongly deprecated by the community, such as dangerous and drunken driving, unlawful possession, being found upon enclos-ed premises, indecent exposure, and immoral soliciting by males, and are closely akin in character to many indictable offences.

The figures of "Crimes cleared up" is to some degree an index of police efficiency, and it was fortunate that in 1952 at least the percentage of crimes cleared up was actually higher in the "Z"

Division than it was for the Metropolitan Police District as a whole, being 35.41 % compared with 31.9 %.[1] The efficiency of the police determines in no small degree the reliability of the data in Series I, and also that of Series II in that the more efficient the police, the less likely are offenders to slip through the net and not be charged with their crimes.

It is difficult to make valid comparisons between Croydon and other towns on the basis of Crimes Known to the Police because there are few towns of the same approximate size and even fewer of the same size with similar ecological characteristics.

TABLE 12

COMPARATIVE INCIDENCE OF INDICTABLE URBAN CRIME

Source: *Home Office*. Supplementary Criminal Statistics for 1952.

	Pop. Nearest '000	Variation in size by '000	Indictable crimes per 10,000 pop.	% Crimes cleared up
Portsmouth	243	—7	130	48
Cardiff	245	—5	138	43
Croydon	250	—	82(86†)	35‡
Coventry	261	+11	158	48
Stoke-on-Trent	272	+22	73	66
Leicester	286	+36	102	54
Bradford	288	+38	115	44
Newcastle	290	+40	153	55
Kingston-upon-Hull	298	+48	133	50
England and Wales	43,940*	—	117	48

* Based on an estimate of the Registrar-General before the availability of the 1951 Census material.
† Based upon Series I and therefore inclusive of certain non-indictable offences akin to indictable crime.
‡ Based on figure for "Z" Division which is not co-extensive with the County Borough.

In terms of size Croydon compares very favourably with Cardiff and Portsmouth which is perhaps hardly surprising since docks and a transitory seafaring population are likely to increase the crime rate. Coventry, on the other hand, which is similar in size has a rate over 70 % higher, while Stoke-on-Trent which is both larger and more industrialised has a rate which is appreciably lower.

[1] Report of the Commissioner of Police for the Metropolis for 1952. Cmd. 8944, H.M.S.O., 1953. 'Z' Division covers the whole of Croydon and parts of the surrounding area.

TABLE 13
TYPES OF OFFENCE: CROYDON C.B. 1952
Source: Series I

	No.		% of total	
a. Offences against the person (excluding sex offences)	15	⎞ 123	0·70	⎞ 5·70
b. Sex offences	108	⎠	5·00	⎠
c. Larcenies without violence (excluding receiving)	1456	⎞ 1847	67·72	⎞ 85·92
d. Breakings including attempted breakings, burglary and unlawful entry	391	⎠	18·20	⎠
e. Receiving, unlawful possession, frauds and miscellaneous offences	179		8·38	8·38
TOTAL	2,149		100·00	

From this broad analysis of the types of crime committed it can be seen that there is nothing particularly unusual in the pattern of offences, crimes against property, (c) and (d), accounting for nearly 86% of all crime. The gravity of these offences varied considerably, but for the most part the bulk were petty crimes. Simple larcenies, for example, were 800 in number, larcenies from unattended motor vehicles 200, and the larceny of pedal cycles 172.

Offences, against the person, if one excludes sex offences, form a very small percentage of the total. Of the 15 crimes in question only 5, two murders and three felonious woundings were very grave offences. Although sex offences constituted 5% of all those in Series I, again, relatively few were really serious. For one case of rape and 11 indecent assaults, there were 63 cases of indecent exposure and 20 cases of male solicitation. With the exception of 2 cases of defilement of girls under 16 years of age, and one homosexual assault on a boy, all the rest were cases of homosexuality between consenting adults. As far as it was possible to discover, no female prostitutes had been prosecuted in the town since the war, and it is in fact virtually impossible to find a real prostitute in Croydon since the West End of London is so near, both for the local girls who wish to follow this occupation and the men who require their services.

Ward Distribution of Crime. Central Ward, comprising the central business district was the major blackspot, most of the total being made up of a very large number of larcenies of all

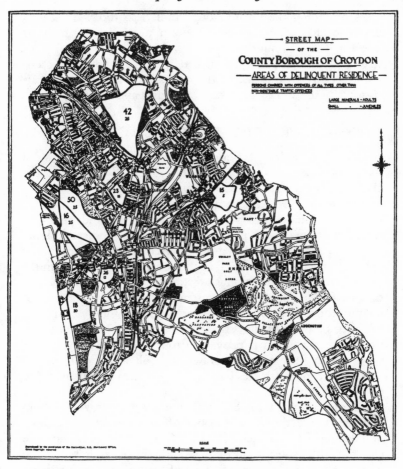

Croydon: Areas of Delinquent Residence

kinds. The average number of crimes for each of the remaining
15 wards was 109·14, or about 1/5th of the total.

After Central Ward the satellite shopping districts of London
Road (Norbury), High Street (Thornton Heath), High Street
and Portland Road (South Norwood), and Westow Street (Upper
Norwood) had the greatest concentrations of larceny. In addi-
tion the building sites at the new power station in Waddon Ward
(MC District) and on the New Addington housing estate (SG
District) reflected the opportunities afforded for crime.

Just as crimes against property were concentrated in those

areas providing the greatest opportunity, so too were sex offences located where opportunities for their commission were greatest. Thus although there was a wide scatter of such offences, streets which were poorly lit, shaded by trees or with few passers-by, especially to the east of the central business district, were commonly the scene of indecent exposures and assaults.

Series II: THE DISTRIBUTION OF OFFENDERS

The basic data for this Series were derived from en analysis of the charge books in the police stations in the "Z" Division. The choice of charge books as a source was made mainly because they represented a more systematic record than those of the Court. Records of Summonses were ignored on the grounds that they would relate mainly to petty offences of a non-indictable kind, mostly to do with the Road Traffic Acts. Broadly speaking, a "charge" means something fairly serious, except perhaps in the case of drunkenness or a minor disturbance of the peace. Nevertheless, if the object of a rate constructed from such a source is to identify those areas of a town which produce the bulk of what might be described as its "social problem group" then the inclusion of such charges is relevant. From a sociological point of view one might expect the brawlers, hooligans and drunks to originate from much the same ecological areas as many delinquents and criminals.

Information was assembled on some 997 persons, all of whom had been charged with at least one offence committed in Croydon during 1952. Of these, 758 were Croydon residents, and 139 either lived outside the Borough or had no fixed address. On the basis of the 758 Croydonians a set of *rates of delinquent residence* were calculated. It may be argued that such rates are subject to error on account of the unknown numbers of "expatriate" offenders; but on the other hand, it may be to some extent assumed that the error is evenly distributed over the 16 Wards.

Ward Distribution. The greatest concentrations of both adult and juvenile offenders occur in the same areas which may be approximately ranked as follows:

(1)   The deteriorating area which lies along the north east side of Mitcham Road, mainly in Broad Green and partly in West Thornton,

(2) The inter-war council estate situated south of the Mitcham Road, in Broad Green Ward,

(3) The deteriorating slum area of Whitehorse Manor, known as "Bang 'Ole",

(4) The Waddon Council estate, especially in its south west corner,

(5) The old area of Central Ward, with its small Council estate known as "Old Town",

(6) The old and declining area in Thornton Heath, north of the High Street,

(7) The Ashburton Council estate in East Ward.

Because ward boundaries do not exactly coincide with "natural areas" the ward statistics do not always reflect the criminogenic character of certain areas. Nevertheless, the total of crimes or the rate of delinquents in any ward is usually determined by their concentration in a natural area which happens to fall within its boundaries. Thus when Waddon Ward has a high rate of delinquent residence it is due almost entirely to a high rate on the Council estate; in the case of East Ward which has a low rate, the rate would be lower still but for the Ashburton estate.

The average number of offenders per ward was 47.39. Those wards which exceeded this, Thornton Heath, Whitehorse Manor, Broad Green, Central and Waddon were those which contain either extensive tracts of deteriorating housing or large Council estates.

TABLE 14

CROYDON RESIDENTS CHARGED WITH OFFENCES IN
CROYDON BY WARD AND AGE

	8 & under 14	14 & under 17	17 & under 21	21 & under 30	30 & under 40	40 & under 50	50 & under 60	60 & over	TOTAL
Upper Norwood	8	—	2	7	5	2	2	5	— 31
Norbury	1	4	3	8	1	2	3	1	— 23
West Thornton	2	4	9	7	10	2	3	2	— 39
Bensham Manor	3	17	—	1	4	5	2	—	— 32
Thornton Heath	18	11	5	12	10	9	5	6	+ 76
South Norwood	1	9	2	8	6	4	7	—	— 37
Woodside	4	10	6	9	5	4	2	1	— 41
East	7	2	1	8	5	—	1	4	— 28

(Continued)	8 & under 14	14 & under 17	17 & under 21	21 & under 30	30 & under 40	40 & under 50	50 & under 60	60 & over		TOTAL
Addiscombe	12	5	4	7	5	6	3	2	—	44
Addington	6	2	1	21	5	5	3	—	—	43
Shirley	1	2	3	—	5	2	—	1	—	14
Whitehorse Manor	3	10	16	14	12	11	8	—	+	74
Broad Green	20	16	11	22	15	7	7	5	+	103
Central	4	4	11	22	15	11	3	—	—	72
Waddon	21	21	13	12	12	6	—	1	+	67
South	2	2	3	7	8	6	1	2	—	34
Croydon CB.	113	113	90	165	123	82	50	30		758

+ indicates above Average
— ,, below ,,

In area (6) most of the juvenile offenders lived in a fairly homogeneous area and attended two particular schools. Over half of them were under 14 and most of their offences were highly localised larcenies. Supplementary information suggested that there was a loosely knit delinquent sub-culture, but one which excluded adults. This is an area which has in local parlance "gone down" very much in the last fifteen years and has experienced probably as much social and economic change as any in the town. The rather prosperous generation of artisans many of whom were the original tenants are fast disappearing; the once flourishing shopping districts of Beulah Road and High Street have junk shops where there were once furniture dealers, a dairy has become basket works, a garage a breakers yards, and so on.

Whereas Thornton Heath has become known for its delinquents since the war, the old area of Whitehorse Manor (3) has had a "delinquent reputation" for many years, and if it had not been for the devastation caused by the bombing and a consequent reduction in population density, its delinquents would probably have been as numerous as those of the adjacent Broad Green Ward with which it has many features in common. 'Bang 'Ole" is the home of a great many stallholders in the Surrey Street market and of many of the market workers. While by no means all of them are serious lawbreakers—indeed the majority are law abiding citizens, this area, with others is the home of not a few of the groups of young rowdies who disturb the bright light district of North End.

The Broad Green area (1) has perhaps fewer people associated with the market and rather more who make a living from the junk trade or the second-hand car business. Alongside them live the unskilled labourers from whom they differ virtually only in income and politics. The Mitcham Road (or Broad Green) Council estate (2) which adjoins, although not physically dilapidated has a population with similar characteristics. Both districts are depressing in that industry dominates both the skyline and the atmosphere with a rain of grit and smoke.

The Waddon Council estate (4) produced in 1952 about as many offenders as the Mitcham Road estate. They were, however, concentrated in one part of the estate, which may be due to the fact that in contrast to Mitcham Road, the Waddon estate is much less socially homogeneous. What is perhaps interesting here is that there are large open spaces to the north and south, indicating that at least where juveniles are concerned the provision of play space is less relevant to delinquency than is sometimes supposed.

The Ashburton estate in East Ward (7) is much smaller than those at Waddon or Broad Green, but in terms of residential or social status is similar to Waddon. It lies partly in East Ward and partly in Woodside forming a working class enclave in a predominantly middle class area.

Old Town (5) is a mixed area of Central Ward containing both old cottage properties and a small Council estate in what was once an Italian immigrant quarter. Ecologically the area extends up the hill into what is politically Waddon Ward. If anything, adult offenders were more numerous than juveniles in this area, but they were individuals who began street quarrels or who unlawfully received stolen goods rather than "professional" criminals.

The gross distribution of offenders is, however, only a general indication of where delinquents live, and to translate the data into more meaningful terms a series of rates of delinquent residence were calculated. These rates are subject to a further error than that previously mentioned, insofar as the denominators of each fraction (of which they are expressions in percentages) were derived from the 1% Sample Data of the 1951 Census. The "blown up" size of the various age categories was therefore subject to a measurable sampling error. In order to minimise this, the age categories used in the preceding table were combined to form three new categories namely,

1   Juveniles (under 17)
2   Young Adults (17-39)
3   Older Adults (40 and over).

The rates for each ward were then classified as "high" or "low" in relation to the Borough rate for each category.

TABLE 15

RATES OF DELINQUENT RESIDENCE

i.e. Distribution of Offenders expressed as a percentage of Population at Risk

	Under 17	Rank Order	17-30	Rank Order	40+	Rank Order	All ages ward rate	Rank Order
Upper Norwood	—0·19	12	—0·23	14	0·14	7	—0·18	12
Norbury	—0·20	11	—0·25	13	—0·08	12	—0·15	15
West Thornton	—0·12	15	—0·28	12	—0·12	9	—0·25	9
Bensham Manor	+0·42	7	—0·08	16	—0·99	11	—0·17	13
Thornton Heath	+0·97	4	+0·53	6	+0·26	3	+0·48	4
South Norwood	—0·36	8	—0·32	10	—0·13	8	—0·23	10
Woodside	—0·33	9	—0·45	7	—0·10	10	—0·26	8
East	—0·24	10	—0·30	11	—0·06	13	—0·16	14
Addiscombe	+0·43	6	—0·34	9	+0·15	6	—0·27	7
Addington	—0·14	13	+0·59	5	+0·20	5	0·30	5
Shirley	—0·06	16	—0·17	15	—0·06	13	—0·09	16
Whitehorse Manor	+0·68	5	+1·24	1	+0·28	2	+0·61	3
Broad Green	+1·57	1	+0·87	3	+0·32	1	+0·75	1
Central	+1·00	3	+1·17	2	+0·24	4	+0·66	2
Waddon	+1·10	2	+0·60	4	—0·09	11	+0·33	5
South	—0·13	14	—0·42	8	0·14	7	—0·21	11
Croydon C.B.	0·39		0·48		0·14		0·30	

\+ indicates above Borough Rate
—   „   below   „   „

The four wards with the highest rates for all age groups, (all of which are well above the Borough rate) Broad Green, Central, Whitehorse Manor and Thornton Heath are those with the largest tracts of property in decline, and where the worst housing is situated. The four with the lowest rates, Shirley, Norbury, East and Bensham Manor are by no means as similar, East and Shirley being highly prosperous middle class areas of relatively recent development, Norbury being a rather less prosperous area, and Bensham Manor a much older and socially more heterogeneous district. The four high rate wards also have high rates in each of the separate age categories, confirming the view that high juvenile and high adult rates tend to occur together. The low rate wards conversely had rates which were uniformly low, with a few noticeable exceptions. Bensham Manor, Addiscombe and Addington each had one category in which the rate was high in contrast to the others, and Waddon one category, that of 40 and over, for which the rate was surprisingly low in comparison with the Ward rate.

The high Ward rate of Waddon is in effect the high rates for juveniles and young adults on the Waddon estate, just as the high adult rate of Addington is in reality the high adult rate of the New Addington estate. To some extent variations of rates within a ward may be explained in terms of the age structure; at New Addington, for example, there are many more children under the age of criminal responsibility than there are between say 8 and 17 years of age. Much of the difficulty of explaining such anomalous rates springs from the fact that they are calculated upon the basis of political and administrative boundaries rather than natural areas.

Bensham Manor and Addiscombe are interesting in that they are highly diversified in both land use and social class. The former tends to be middle class in its J. Index 0.5 above the Borough Index, and the latter working class with a J. Index 3.4 below it. The offenders in Bensham Manor were widely scattered but came almost invariably from those streets or parts of streets which were predominantly working class. The picture in Addiscombe was remarkably similar with the special feature that many of the adult offenders came from the area which was once an upper-middle class residential district in which the large old houses are being or have been converted into flats. West Thornton, South Norwood and Woodside, althoug having consistently low rates, must also be considered in this context. In West Thornton, for example, CE and CC districts are an extension of the natural area of Broad Green. If these districts were abstracted, the West Thornton Ward rate would be appreciably lower.

Croydon has not developed radially as so many American cities appear to have done and there are as a result no well defined zones to which variations in the rates can be meaningfully related, nevertheless, the three highest ward rates occur in those wards which make up and immediately surround the central business district. It is unlikely, however, that this is either relevant or indeed exactly true. Considering the precise areas of delinquent residence one finds them to be spatially separate from the central area and highly varied in their ecological characteristics. The suggestion implicit in so much of the work of Clifford Shaw and his collaborators is that the physical deterioration of a neighbourhood is somehow vitally related to the problem of delinquency and crime. The evidence, at least from Croydon, suggests that the physical characteristics of the area are of little relevance save as an indirect determinant of the social status of an area. Low status and low rentals are normally found together in urban areas and physical deterioration, where it helps to depress both status and rentals, can be said to be a feature likely to attract those individuals who may be loosely described as the core of the "social problem group". But where the provision of housing is not solely within the province of the market, and the local authority has stepped in to provide housing as a social amenity for a not inconsiderable proportion of the population, then the natural ecological processes of selection manifesting themselves in the cycle of "invasion-dominance-succession" are likely to be severely modified by social policy with strikingly different results. The ecological process may be modified yet there is still crime and delinquency, though this is not to suggest that the concept of a criminal or delinquent sub-culture resulting from the interplay of ecological influences is necessarily invalidated; far from it. It does suggest, however, that there must be a shift of interest from the natural area which has grown up of its own accord to the "planned" area which has resulted from conscious social and political deliberation. In particular, emphasis must be laid upon the individual cultural unit, the family, which remains essentially unaltered as a social institution for the transmission of cultural values and as an agency of social control. By analogy, plants are plants whether on the mountainside or in the window box, and the relationships they have to one another and to their habitat, though differing in character are no less real. So too the interaction of individuals resulting in the establishment of some kind of social order, however artificially defined, are its territorial limits or its social and demographic characteristics. It is the individual delinquent and his family whom we must now go on to consider.

VIII

SOME YOUNG DELINQUENTS:
AN ANALYSIS OF CASE MATERIAL

(a) *The purpose of the material and construction of the sample.*

FROM an analysis of rates of offenders living in different areas of the town, two things are apparent (a) the rates vary between wards, and indeed, between different parts of the same ward in some instances, and (b) nowhere are all the persons in a particular age category involved in crime or delinquency, even in those areas with the highest rates. It would seem important then to amplify the ecological analysis of the incidence of certain measurable and objective social indices by examining in more detail the processes whereby individuals interact with others in a common environment, and to inquire whether in the personal lives of those individuals there are any important factors which cannot be fully appreciated except by specific investigation.[1]

Ideally one might begin by constructing a random sample of the population of each ward, in which the delinquent and non-delinquent would have an equal chance of being selected, and by an analysis of the case material thus obtained produce a composite picture of the common social universe of which both were members in the fullest sense. Unfortunately, the limitations of time and finance did not permit such an inquiry, and indeed precluded the use of the familiar control group technique. With the only material readily available being that relating to persons who had in some way come to the notice of such official agen-

---

[1] This need was of course recognised by Shaw, Thrasher, Whyte, and most of the other important members of the Chicago School, as well as by Thomas and Znaniecki in *The Polish Peasant*.

cies as the Police, the Probation Service or the Children's Department, the problem became one of a different order, namely how to construct a representative sample of the group we may very loosely term "offenders".[1]

It was originally intended to stratify the whole group on the basis of age, using the categories employed in the Criminal Statistics on the grounds that the variations in criminality between different age groups are significant, and then to take random samples of males and females in each age group. In this way it was hoped to obtain a representative sample of Croydon's delinquents and criminals in 1952, taking into account the factors of age and sex which are generally recognised to be of some importance.

Although the construction of such a sample in itself involved no particular difficulties, a preliminary inquiry as to the availability of data on the individuals selected showed that the task of collecting material of a uniform quality would prove insuperable. Furthermore, the complete unavailability of data on so many individuals seemed likely to destroy the validity of the whole sample. For example, while information was available from the case records of Probationers, there were no similar records relating to persons fined or in many instances, to those imprisoned. Although those on Probation could be interviewed, given certain favourable conditions, this was considerably less of a practical possibility where those in prison were concerned, and in the case of those not detained or restricted in any way, the chances of establishing sufficient rapport for a successful interview if the source of the interviewer's original information were known, were virtually nil. It was also felt that the use of confidential sources to construct a sample for interview which would include persons who had expurgated their offences by having paid fines or having served a prison sentence would be unethical.

In the last resort it became clear that the most uniform and most detailed information was likely to relate to juvenile offenders. It was decided to rely upon information already gathered by the social workers concerned, who in many instances had come to know offenders and their families extremely intimately, and which would almost certainly be fuller than anything obtained

---

[1] The inclusion in this group for instance of children in need of care, in moral danger, or beyond control is not intended to imply any degree of 'moral culpability' on their part.

by the maximum of two or three research interviews. By a process of elimination therefore, the children and young persons who were to form the basis of the sample were drawn from those on Probation or under Supervision Orders, or in Approved Schools.

In order to make the case material comparable with other data the 89 children who were committed to Approved Schools or against whom a Probation Order was made by the Croydon Juvenile Court between January 1st and December 31st, 1952, were separated from those on Probation or in Approved Schools during the year, but who had come before the Court earlier than January 1st, 1952. From the following table it will be seen that the Croydon Court was fairly discriminating in its use of these two methods of disposal,[1] and the probability was that they were used only in the more serious cases in which the features which our inquiry sought to discover would be likely to be most pronounced. Because a Commital Order to an Approved School was seldom made for a single first offence, information contemporaneous with previous offences dealt with less severely would also appear on the files.

TABLE 16

CROYDON JUVENILE COURT: METHODS OF DISPOSAL 1952 *

	Abso-lute disch.	Cond. Disch.	Fine	Re-mand H.	A/ School	Prob-ation	Fit Per-son Order	TOTALS
BOYS								
Under 14	9	46	9	2	14	28	2	110
14 - 17	3	19	13	1	11	26	1	74
TOTALS	12	65	22	3	25	54	3	184
GIRLS								
Under 14	1	1	—	—	—	6	1	9
14 - 17	—	—	—	—	2	6	—	8
TOTALS	1	1	—	—	2	12	1	17
GRAND TOTAL	13	66	22	3	27	66	4	201

* Table compiled from information from Children's Dept. of the Home Office. Certain discrepancies between this table and the subsequent analysis of the cases may be noted. This is due to overlapping in the first table, e.g. if a Probation Order were discharged and an Approved School Order substituted in the same year, this would appear as if there were two separate individuals concerned.

[1] The writer attended a number of sittings of the Croydon Juvenile Court during the winter of 1952-3 and witnessed the adjudication of a variety of magistrates, all of whom appeared to be both well informed and considered in their judgements.

The Criminal Area

(b) *The method of collecting information.*

The names, addresses and charges of all juveniles brought before the Juvenile Court appear in a chronological register of the Court's business throughout the year. The name of each child for whom a Probation or Supervision Order was made or who was committed to an Approved School was abstracted and numbered in series 1 - 93. This number was subsequently reduced (a) by the fact that where a Probation or Supervision Order was cancelled and the child was committed to an Approved School before December 31st, 1952, the name appeared twice, and (b) because in a few cases no information (except details of age, address and offence) was available at all and in some others such reports as existed were so superficial as to be of scarcely any more value. There remained therefore, 79 cases,[1] from which data could be obtained. This naturally varied in both quality and quantity, depending to some extent on the social worker's skill in reporting, and partly on the length of time the individual or his family had been known to the agency concerned.

Where Probation or Supervision[2] cases were concerned, the case files contained two basic documents:

1 The report made to the Court by the Probation Officer
2 The record of supervision in the period following the Court's decision.

In some instances these were supplemented by special reports from the School, Children's Department, or the Child Guidance Clinic. For those committed to Approved Schools similar reports were available, most of them being statutorily required,[3] and when the child was already on Probation the supervision record naturally formed a useful adjunct.

In a few rare cases, a copy of the statement made by the offender to the Police was included, but by and large most of the information in the files dealt with the offender as a person rather

[1] This included all the 14 girls dealt with by the Court by Probation or Approved School committal.
[2] There were actually only 3 Supervision Orders made among the 79 cases, each of which was amended to Probation or Approved School during the year.
[3] Under the provisions of the Children and Young Persons Act, 1933, Sec. 72 (2), the 'Record of Information Regulations for Approved Schools' S.R. & O. 1933, No. 955, require (a) general information (b) School report (c) other relevant information (d) home surroundings report (e) medical report (f) comments of Court or social agencies. See Clarke-Hall & Morrison 4th ed. 1951. pp. 250-251.

than his offence. Most of the case files bulged with correspondence of every sort and description, some of which proved a very valuable source of information.

The most common period of Probation ordered in 1952 was 2 years so that in the late summer of 1954 the author not only had a living record of events in the probationers' lives in the interim, but was able to put specific questions to the Probation Officers concerned who were recently, or who were still in direct contact with them and their families. In this way inconsistencies in the records were removed, and perhaps, more important, many gaps in the data were able to be filled in.

(c) *The nature of the information.*

Information was collected with two aims in view, firstly to attempt to build up a meaningful picture of the individual, as a person, and in relation to his social world, which included his family, the school, the neighbourhood, and any other organised groups to which he might belong. Secondly, it was hoped to establish the presence or absence of 23 factors having a known association with delinquency, including data on social class and educational level.

The purpose of recording data in this way was an attempt to make them comparable with other facts by eliminating the qualitative assessments which might lead to a good deal of methodological hairsplitting. For example, in assessing the relationship between emotional disturbance and delinquency it seems important first to establish that the former exists, before going on to consider the precise extent of the disturbance. In this part of the study, it was facts rather than opinions which mattered most, and they all had to be reduced to some common level at which quantification was possible.

It is of course true, that treatment of factors which are essentially qualitative, and which seldom appear identical in the lives of different individuals in this way must be severely limited. The difficulty in quantifying such factors while at the same time taking full account of qualitative variations seems to be that of establishing thoroughly adequate criteria for the construction of sub-categories of data. The simple criteria of "presence" or "absence" seem to be the most objective available, and except in the matters of social class and parental discipline, these were used throughout.

It might be argued that in some of the subsequent analysis, lack of evidence for a certain factor, for example parental disharmony, has been automatically assumed to imply its non-existence. This danger was foreseen, and every effort was made to establish the non-existence of such factors by other means when an error or omission in the records seemed a possibility.

The 23 factors were not derived from any one source, but seemed to be a fair selection of variables from the literature of social and psychological studies in the field which have at various times been found to be associated with delinquency. These factors could, of course, have been multiplied, but only at the expense of increasing the numbers of instances in which information was not available. Those selected bear a close relationship to the kind of questions social workers tend to ask, and the final selection was not made until the case material had been initially surveyed.

Although some of the case material relates to the period following the initial 1952 offence, the only factors noted in the analysis are those which were in evidence at the time of the offence or preceding it. For example, if parental disharmony developed after the offence, it is not noted as a positive, factor although it appears in the case history.

(1) *Sibling Offenders.* In a number of cases siblings were concerned together in offences. Where siblings had committed offences separately, the information was always available, either on the home surroundings report of the Probation Officer to the Court, or in the master index of all persons who had come before the Court.[1]

(2) *Parent Offenders.* An offence of any kind, by one or both parents, excluding traffic offences, was recorded, though lack of information here could not allow one to be certain that no offence had been committed. The reliability of evidence relating to their adulthood was naturally greater than that concerning their childhood, as adult offenders with delinquent children are invariably known to the Probation Service through the close liaison which exists between them and the Police.

(3) *I.Q. below 95.* Intelligence quotients were available in a

---

[1] These sources were very reliable. For example, in the case of one boy, details of an offence committed by his elder brother in 1935 were available.

surprisingly large number of instances in view of the fact that not every child was remanded for a psychological report. When the I.Q. did not come from such a report it came from the School. The Stanford-Binet Test was used in Croydon in all but a very few cases in which the Moray House Test was used. The reports derived from this test were discarded on the grounds of their incomparibility with the Stanford-Binet results. 95 was chosen so as to include all children who were dull, yet who were by no means Educationally Sub-normal, and whose dullness might not be clearly apparent from the School report. Appreciating the limitations of the concept of I.Q. that the tests have perhaps an undue verbal bias, that results may be affected by conditions immediately surrounding the child at the time of testing and that variations may be discerned by subsequent retests, it is intended here to be complementary to the data on educational attainment, that is the factor designated "below average educational attainment."

(4) *Physical disability or epilepsy.* It may be questioned whether physical disability and epilepsy may be validly included under a single head. In the category of physical disability are included such things as physical deformities which would result in some handicap, together with asthma, tuberculosis, heart disease and very poor physique. Although epilepsy may be regarded as a psycho-pathological state and a behaviour disorder the fact that it is a disease of the central nervous system which may be due to a variety of causes from congenital syphilis to head injury at birth[1] would seem to indicate that it is better described as a physical disability than an emotional disorder. The same argument seemed relevant to cover the single case of Huntingdon's chorea.

(5) *Maladjustment, emotional disturbance and enuresis.* When a child was clearly unable to exist in relative harmony with his parents, siblings, or school fellows, and demonstrated this inability either by rebellious or defiant conduct at school or at home, or by shunning or being hostile to his siblings, he was designated as maladjusted. Emotional disturbance, which to some extent overlaps with maladjustment, was deduced from evidence of behaviour rather more abnormal than that associated with maladjust-

---

[1] See Henderson D. and Gillespie R.D. '*A Text-Book of Psychiatry*', 7th ed. Oxford, 1950, p. 547 et. seq.

ment, for example, stealing of a symbolic nature, from mother's purse rather than anyone else, of sweet and sickly food, or jewelry, or wandering away from home. In the majority of instances the child coud be described as both maladjusted and emotionally disturbed, and attendance at the Child Guidance Clinic was regarded as confirmation of this description.

Enuresis, in contrast, is a somatic sympton of a psycho-neurotic state. In view of the now overwhelming body of evidence which shows that with the exception of a very few cases of organic defect, enuresis is related to emotional disturbance, it was included in this category rather than (4).

(6) *Maternal deprivation.* This factor was derived directly from the work of Bowlby,[1] and is used in a specific sense. Where a child had been deprived of its mother between birth and 5 years for a period of six months or more, it was regarded as having been "deprived" in this sense. Where a mother substitute had been available during this period, the child was not considered deprived unless there had been a succession of substitutes.

(7) *Traumatic experience in childhood.* The concept of trauma is used here fairly widely to cover a variety of social experiences which may be regarded as having been likely to result in a severe emotional shock. A sudden and serious illness which isolated the child from its mother by the need for hospital treatment, the death of a member of the family or the desertion of a parent, experience of aerial bombardment or the revelation of illegitimacy, are all events which by reason of their dramatic and sometimes horrifying character, may have had some important effect upon the emotional stability and personality of the child concerned.

Childhood is regarded as the period between birth and puberty that is to say, roughly up to the age of 14. Although it might be argued that a similar shock might have very different effects upon a child of 3 and a child of 13, in view of their being at different levels of maturation, it remains that the delinquent sample was not conspicuous for its emotional maturity. Although, too, the shock might have different effects, it is likely that even at 14, particularly in view of the emotional disturbance created by puberty, the individual would probably respond in a way more characteristic of a child than an adult.

[1] See Bowlby J. 'Child Care and the Growth of Lowe', London. 1950.

(8) *Rejection by parent or parents*. Whether the child was actually rejected by one or both parents, or whether this rejection was a supposition on the part of the child, the child's attitude towards them and the general tenor of the relationship seemed eventually to blur into something between mistrust and hostility. In deciding whether rejection could be reasonably said to exist, the material was sifted as carefully as possible, and only direct evidence accepted. When, for example, a father openly called his son a bastard and refused to visit him, even when seriously ill in hospital, or when a mother grossly deprived her child of affection and turned her out of the house at 7.45 a.m. to go to school, the child was regarded as rejected.

As a term it perhaps ought to be used carefully to distinguish it from mere indifference or coldness on the part of parents which are essentially negative attitudes. In the cases of rejection noted in this analysis it will be seen that the parent—for it was invariably the mother *or* the father—adopted a distinctly positive attitude in trying to dissociate himself or herself from the child.

(9) *Behaviour problems among the immediate family*. The term "immediate family" is used to cover both parents as well as siblings. The purpose of this extension, for as may be imagined where behaviour problems did exist elsewhere in the family they were usually found to be among siblings, was to cover cases of behaviour in parents clearly related to anxiety or some other emotional disturbance, yet which did not seem serious enough to warrant their inclusion in the category of serious mental disorder.

(10) *Serious mental disorder or epilepsy among immediate family*. "Immediate family" is again used to cover both parents and siblings. "Mental disorder" is employed in this instance to describe the more serious neuroses and the psychoses, states of mental health which, unlike the less severe forms of emotional disturbance, require intensive clinical treatment, possibly with hospitalisation. Epilepsy was included in this category in that as a disease of the central nervous system it had more in common with psychosis than mere emotional disturbance, and as in both instances the factor of heredity could not altogether be discounted.

(11) *Parental separation by death, divorce or desertion*. This factor was intended to describe the fact of parental separation which

resulted in a deviation from the established form of family structure. It was not used in the case of illegitimate children on the grounds that there had never been a family structure to be altered.[1] When this separation had come as a shock to the child, it was also noted as a traumatic experience under (7).

(12) *Both parents away from home during the day.* The effects of a mother being at work during the day are manifold. Among those relevant here would seem to be (a) the extra burden of keeping house which is put upon her leisure time and a fall in the standard of domestic hygiene and housewifery, (b) the additional responsibilities, often resented, which are placed upon the older children, particularly the oldest girl, in caring for the younger members of the family, (c) the absence of parental control over children during the day, especially during the crucial periods of the school lunch hour, and the period following afternoon school, and (d) the impression of disorganisation and insecurtiy which may be created as a result of there being no mother in a specific place around whom the emotional ties of the child may be fastened. This point may be summed up in terms of the difference between a "home" and the house where a family sleeps.

(13) *Parental disharmony.* Occasional friction between parents was extremely difficult to identify in the material, and in any case did not concern us. Unambiguous disharmony which did concern us, was usually so evident to the caseworker that it appeared automatically in the case material. Examples which might be cited are continual nagging and violent quarrels, failure on the part of husbands to keep their wives adequately supplied with money, basic disagreements about family discipline or blatant infidelity.

The terms "parent" and "parental" are incidentally used throughout the analysis to describe step-parents or parent substitutes. The co-incidence of factors (11) and (13) therefore, would not only appear in the case of a child who had experienced first parental disharmony and then parental separation, but in that of a child whose natural parents had separated, and whose "new" pair of parents, after a subsequent remarriage or cohabitation were also at loggerheads.

[1] If there had been evidence of cohabitation, followed by subsequent desertion or death, then this factor would have been regarded as operative, but there were in fact no cases of this kind.

(14) *Low standard of hygiene and comfort in the home*. The difficulty of establishing this factor from the evidence was due to the unconscious tendency on the part of social workers to apply middle class criteria to working class homes, Those homes which were furnished in lower middle class style, with three piece suites and highly polished sideboards were described as "very comfortable", and those which were not, conversely, as "with a minimum of comfort". In assessing the evidence, an attempt was made to distinguish between a style of life which differed from the middle class norm, and a style of life which differed from the normative standards of working class families.

Very poor sleeping arrangements, inadequate bedding or lack of essential furniture were included under this heading, besides inadequate clothing and diet. For example, a child eating bread and jam on the front doorstep was not regarded as indicative of a low standard of comfort and hygiene; on the other hand, if the children went hungry to school on Monday morning because there was no food in the house the description was applied.

In fact, the families which it was desired to isolate were those in extreme poverty, or those which by their improvidence came close to or within the classical "problem category.

(15) *Child in institution or foster home*. This category included all children who were in care at the time of their offence, either with the Local Authority, or with a foster mother. Illegitimate children who had been adopted early in infancy were not regarded as being in foster homes—though strictly this was the case—as it was felt that if the child had never known any other home than his foster home it was to all practical purposes his real home, certainly in psychological terms. On the other hand, a foster home, to which the child had come much later, possibly after a succession of homes, might reasonably be expected to possess a distinctly different emotional climate.

(16) *School types*: *Primary, Secondary Modern, Technical, Grammar and Special*. Because our data related only to fairly serious offenders, analysis of school types could not show with any certainty the distribution of delinquency among the various categories of school children. Even if the proportions of delinquents were equal in each type of school, the Primary and Secondary Modern schools would have the worst numerical showing because their

numbers are so much greater. It is much more likely, however, that the proportions are not equal, and that the disproportionate distribution of delinquency unfavourable towards the Primary and Secondary Modern schools reflects a similar distribution derived from an analysis of the social class of offenders.

School type was based, in the case of offenders still at school, on the school they were attending at the time of the offence, and in that of the young wage earner (15-17 years) upon the school last attended. The Grammar and Technical school children in the sample were few in number, but tended to be among the most difficult cases of emotional disturbance. The numbers of Special school children are in fact lower than they ought to be, because a number of offenders in ordinary schools would have been in Special schools but for the grave shortage of places in them.

(17) *Below average educational attainment.* Although below average attainment might be expected to do little besides coincide with poor intelligence and ability, it was included in order to isolate those individuals who though endowed with good intelligence failed to make adequate use of it. Burt[1] thirty years ago showed that the majority of delinquents failed to do themselves justice in this respect, while Stott[2] has indicated how often poor attainment is connected with inability to concentrate with stems primarily from anxiety and insecurity. This factor then, although it will often coincide with low intelligence (3), may also be expected to coincide on occasions with emotional disturbance (5).

(18) *Bad conduct in school.* Evidence of this factor had to be very carefully considered in view of the fact that "good" and "bad" conduct are not always easy to define. Some teachers, in writing their reports showed an open hostility to the offender which led one to suppose them to be unduly prejudiced.[3] Accordingly, only direct evidence of misconduct was accepted, for example, stealing and lying, or bullying other children.

(19) *Poor attendance (less than 80% of possible attendances).* School attendance was based upon the school reports which related to the last complete term, and a 20% margin was allowed for

[1] Burt, C. *The Young Delinquent,* London, 1924.
[2] Stott, D. H. *Delinquency and Human Nature,* Dunfermline, 1950.
[3] One Headmaster actually ruined much of the work of a Probation Officer, by sending a report to the boy's employer which cost him his job. It was the job into which the boy had finally settled after months of upheaval.

illness. Beyond this margin poor attendance was regarded as indicative of one or both of two things, (i) truancy, (ii) parental irresponsibility in sending their children to school.

(i) The relationship between truancy and delinquency is well-known, and scarcely needs elaboration here save to say that not only may they both stem from a common source, emotional disturbance, but that truancy may stimulate such offences as larceny in a very practical sense.

(ii) When parents were careless about school attendance, or as was more often the case, when children were kept away in order to do household chores, they exhibited a lack of responsibility which was invariably related to their inefficiency in controlling their children.

(20) *Membership of a Youth Group*. This factor attempted to isolate the offenders who possessed some organised leisure activity. Needless to say, the numbers were small, but the smallness of the numbers for the whole group must be considered in the light of the fact that the whole group included an age group in which organised leisure is perhaps neither so important nor so frequent, i.e. the 8 to 10 year olds.

(21) *Above average intelligence or ability*. This factor was intended to combine both intelligence and aptitude. Those with an I.Q. of 115 or more were included, besides those who showed ability in other ways, for example, by manual dexterity[1] which could not altogether be divorced from intelligence. The more able and intelligent offenders also seemed to be among the most emotionally disturbed.

(22) *Social class*. The occupations of the head of the offender's household were classified according to the Registrar General's five basic categories. Children in institutions or foster homes were regarded as belonging to Class V.

(23) *Parental discipline*. This factor alone was subdivided on a qualitative basis. "Inconsistent" was used to describe a situation in which *either* the disciplinary attitudes of the parents were at variance, for example, an overprotective mother and a bullying father, *or* the attitudes of both parents oscillated between indulgence and severity. "Severe" and "lax" were used to describe the

---

[1] e.g. one boy, Secondary Modern School, while of average general attainment, was nevertheless a 'natural' engineer in the metal-work shop.

overall characteristics of home discipline in situations in which only one parent exerted any discernible discipline, as well as those in which the attitudes of both parents were more or less identical.

TABLE 17

CHILDREN PLACED ON PROBATION OR COMMITTED TO APPROVED SCHOOLS (Series III)

	Boys No.	Boys % Total	Girls No.	Girls % Total	Factor No.
Sibling offender(s)	16	25·0	2	13·34	1
Parent offender(s)	4	6·25	1	6·67	2
I.Q. below 95	8	12·50	4	26·67	3
Physical disability or epilepsy	6	9·37	2	13·34	4
Maladjustment/emotional dist./enuresis	29	45·31	6	40·00	5
Maternal deprivation	7	10·93	1	6·67	6
Traumatic experience in childhood	15	23·43	3	20·00	7
Parental rejection	15	23·43	1	6·67	8
Behaviour problems among immediate family	5	7·81	—	—	9
Mental disorder/epilepsy among immediate family	14	21·86	4	26·67	10
Parental separation by death/divorce etc.	15	23·43	6	40·00	11
Both parents away from home during day	14	21·86	—	—	12
Parental disharmony	16	25·00	1	6·67	13
Low standard of hygiene in the home	12	18·74	4	26·67	14
Child in institution or Foster Home	4	6·25	—	—	15
School Type Primary	8	12·50	3	20·60	16
School Type Sec. Modern	47	73·44	10	75·00	16
School Type Technical	1	1·56	—	—	16
School Type Grammar	3	4·68	1	6·67	16
School Type Special	2	3·12	1	6·67	16
Below average educational attainment	35	54·68	8	53·34	17
Bad conduct in school	18	28·80	5	33·34	18
Poor attendance (less than 80% possible)	15	23·43	3	20·00	19
Member of Youth Group	17	26·52	1	6·67	20
Above average I.Q. or ability	9	14·40	2	13·34	21
Social Class Class I	—	—	—	—	22
Social Class Class II	—	—	—	—	22
Social Class Class III	11	17·16	5	33·34	22
Social Class Class IV	18	28·16	1	6·67	22
Social Class Class V	35	54·68	9	60·00	22
Parental Discipline Inconsistent	14	21·86	5	33·34	23
Parental Discipline Severe	9	14·40	2	13·34	23
Parental Discipline Lax	22	34·41	2	13·34	23

TABLE 18

PROSECUTION DETAILS OF PROBATION APPROVED SCHOOL
CASES (Series III)

	Boys		Girls	
	No.	% Total	No.	% Total
First offenders in 1952	40	62·5	11	73·34
Subsequent offence(s) up to Aug. 1954	44	68·75	7	46·67
Offences with others in at least 1 instance	40	62·5	8	53·34
Committed to Approved School for original offence in 1952	14	21·86	1	6·67
Committed for subsequent offence(s) up to Aug. 1954	16	25·0	2	13·34
Prosecuted for larceny	59	92·18	12	80·00
Prosecuted for other offences	17	26·56	1	6·67
Beyond control	10	15·62	5	33·34
Prosecuted for larceny and other offences	15	23·43	—	—
Prosecuted for larceny and beyond control	7	10·93	2	13·34

TABLE 19

AGE DISTRIBUTION OF PROBATION AND APPROVED SCHOOL
CASES (Series III)

Ages at First Prosecution in 1952

		8	9	10	11	12	13	14	15	16	17
Boys	No.	1	2	5	7	10	7	13	9	10	—
	% Total	1·56	3·12	7·81	10·93	15·62	10·93	20·3	14·4	15·62	—
Girls	No.	—	1	1	1	1	3	4	1	3	—
	% Total	—	6·67	6·67	6·67	6·67	20·0	26·67	6·67	20·0	—
Total Nos.		1	3	6	8	11	10	17	10	13	—

Delinquent activity among boys

Of a total of 64, 14 were committed to Approved Schools for
the first offence for which they were brought to Court in 1952.
By August 31st 1954 a further 16 of them had been committed
either for subsequent offences or for breaches of Probation
bringing the proportion of the boy's group which finally grav-
itated to Approved Schools to nearly 50%. In 1952 over 60% of
the boys had been first offenders, but of these 40 boys nearly
half (18) committed subsequent offences, increasing the percentage of male recidivists from 37·5 in 1952 to 68·75 in 1954. In
joint delinquent enterprises, partners in crime were almost
invariably members of highly localised street play groups. Over
the period 1952-54 62·5% committed offences with other boys
in at least one instance, usually in groups of two or three.

The grounds for Court appearance were headed as might be expected by prosecutions for larceny. Between Jan. 1952 and August 1954, 59 (92.18 %) were charged with larceny, 17 (26.56 %) with other offences, mostly breaking and entering and 10 (15.62 %) with being beyond control or in need of care and protection.[1] Of those prosecuted for larceny about a quarter were also proceeded against on other charges, mostly breaking or attempted breaking, and about one eighth were deemed to be "beyond control". The circumstances of stealing varied widely from thefts at home and spontaneous housebreaking to planned raids on the department stores downtown and premeditated cycle thefts.

Delinquent activity among girls.

Only one girl in the first instance was committed to an Approved School, though subsequently she was joined by two others. Of the 11 first offenders in 1952, 3 had reappeared before the Court by August 31st 1954, one for a technical breach of Probation, one for being "beyond control", and one being "in need of care and protection". Gang organisation or joint delinquent enterprises are usually characteristic only of boys but 8 out of the 15 girls committed offences in association with others; there were two pairs, one girl who stole with her brother, and one group of three. The locality factor appeared to be as important as in the case of the boys. Their criminal offences were restricted to larcenies, mostly from the department stores in the centre of the town.

School Type.

In Croydon the majority of children attend the Primary Schools run by the Local Authority, and most of them will pass on into Secondary Modern Schools to leave at 15. Some will pass on to the two Technical Schools and leave slightly later while a fortunate few will go on to the Grammar Schools. There are 41 Primary Schools feeding 5 Direct Grant Grammar Schools so that competition is keen. To supplement its own Grammar Schools the Education Committee has an option on a few places in the 9 private Grammar Schools in the area.

[1] 'Beyond control' relates to the Court's function as a Court of Chancery and not a Criminal Court. The inclusion of Chancery cases in a group loosely described as 'offenders' was not intended to castigate them as 'law breakers', but rather followed from the view that the overt differences between the two groups are largely a matter of chance or legislative accident.

The analysis of school type for the delinquent sample tended to suggest that delinquency and low attainment go together, but because the Primary Schools include many potential Grammar and Technical Schools pupils, comparisons are only valid between the groups attending different schools after the age of 11. The Secondary Modern Schools provided three-quarters of the boys and two thirds of the girls, the Special Schools providing rather fewer than one might have imagined partly because a number of children who should have been at a Special School were still in ordinary schools owing to the shortage of places. The main difference between the Grammar School delinquents and the rest seemed to be in the field of emotional disturbance. Two of the three Grammar School boys were severely disturbed as was the one Grammar School girl, while the remaining boy was having difficulties in keeping up with his school work and was temporarily led astray by a thoroughly delinquent Secondary Modern boy.

School Record and Intelligence.

Out of a total of 79 children only 12, or just over 15% were of low intelligence and 11, approximately 14%, of above average intelligence. The remaining 56 were of "average" intelligence, between 95 and 115 I.Q. Those rated as "below average" in educational attainment numbered 43, or 54% of the total. From this 43 however must be subtracted 8 children of low intelligence in ordinary schools and who were therefore somewhat unfairly judged.

Of the 56 endowed with average intelligence only 23 had managed to achieve a standard of educational attainment consistent with their intellectual ability, suggesting that as Burt[1] established three decades ago, delinquents with poor school records are not so much dull, as failing to make the best use of their mental endowment. The extent to which this discrepancy between ability and attainment can be associated with anxiety and inability to concentrate is difficult to measure but very evident in certain instances. Comparing the intelligence of the boys with that of the girls, a much larger proportion of the girls were of low intelligence, 4 out of 15 compared with 8 out of 64, while the proportions with above average intelligence were roughly the same. A possible explanation of this might be that resistances to delinquency are greater amongst girls; not only

[1] See *The Young Delinquent*, pp. 294-5 (4th Ed.) London, 1944.

are they more strictly brought up but they tend to approach social maturity much more quickly. It may be therefore, that the kind of girl most prone to delinquency is the dull or backward type who has failed to internalise any social norms and who tends to be immature and impulsive in her behaviour.

TABLE 20

INTELLIGENCE AND EDUCATIONAL ATTAINMENT

(Series III)

	Attainment*			
	Below Average		Normal	
	Boys	Girls	Boys	Girls
Low Intelligence	—	1	3	—
Average Intelligence	29	4	18	5
Above average	1	—	9	2

* Consistent with the child's level of intelligence. Table excludes 5 boys and 3 girls of low intelligence in ordinary schools.

Although a child may exhibit signs of open rebellion against authority in the home, it is not so likely that the same overt behaviour will always manifest itself at school. The child may run out of the house away from an angry parent but the irate teacher cannot be avoided in this way, except through truancy which is avoidance in anticipation rather than a flight from immediate punishment. The general impression one gathers is that notwithstanding legal safeguards, corporal punishment figures rather prominently in the Primary and Secondary Modern Schools from which most of our delinquents came, and that there was a tradition among certain teachers concerning the necessity of "treating them tough".[1] The children who were prepared to run the gauntlet of swift physical punishment for bad behaviour in school must be regarded as either wholly insensitive to punishment or so defiant of authority as to give the impression of challenging authority to "do its worst". The following table illustrates some of the characteristics of this group.

Rebellion against authority in school and disregarding the norms of the larger world by stealing and other delinquencies seem to be related, and it is noteworthy that of this group of unusually recalcitrant children nearly two thirds, 14 out of 23, exhibited some form of emotional disturbance or maladjustment.

[1] c.f. Mays' comments in *Growing up in the City* on corporal punishment in Liverpool schools.

TABLE 21

CHILDREN WITH BAD CONDUCT SCHOOL REPORTS

	Boys	Girls	Total
Prosecuted once	3	1	4
Prosecuted more than once	15	4	19
Poor attendance at school	7	2	9
Below average educational attainment	9	3	12
Maladjusted or emotionally disturbed	13	1	14
Below 95 I.Q.	2	3	5
Above 115 I.Q.	5	1	6
Total no. of children with Bad Reports	18	5	22

From the survey of the delinquent sample a number of features stand out. In the first place the delinquent is by no means always maladjusted in a way which is unmistakeable to both his family and the world at large. Secondly his family seems more often to be one characterised by low social aspirations rather than high ones, and to be resident in an area where other families of a similar kind are to be found in close proximity, often a Council housing estate. Thirdly his partners in crime are almost invariably the members of his local street play group or children who attend the same school. Perhaps most striking of all is the gross distribution of these serious delinquents between the social classes. In spite of the middle class characteristics of Croydon which might be expected to influence the situation, it is the unskilled and semi-skilled manual worker's family which seems to throw up more delinquents than the other socio-economic groups. The children from Class V especially, experienced more parental disharmony, rejection and maternal separation, had more upsetting experiences in early childhood and were more emotionally disturbed. They came from families with a greater incidence of mental disorder and epilepsy and were subjected to more irregular discipline than the others. The evidence would seem to suggest that the psychology of family relations is one critical area in which the genesis of anti-social behaviour may be observed, for by no means every delinquent came from a delinquency area or grew up in close proximity to those with anti-social values. The fact remains nevertheless that there are certain sociological variables which are nearly constants—the occupation of the head of the household and educational level of the child. Both these factors are highly correlated with social class, indeed occupation may be said to be its principal determinant, and by and large the most important characteristics of any residential area can be viewed in terms of social class. Because of the operation of the market or local authority housing policy, families of a given type have a strong tendency to be highly localised, the net effect of which is to create neighbourhood groups of children in which the proportion prone to delinquency by reason of their defective family environment is often unusually high.

IX

SOME CASE HISTORIES

THE stereotype is invariably misleading, and among
delinquents and criminals it is in some ways harder to
establish the basis of such a generalisation when the
characteristic they have in common, the fact of having broken
the law, is often no more than a facade behind which lies
an infinite variety of motivation, personality and circumstance.
Much of the justification for the sociological study of anti-social
or deviant behaviour lies in the fact that the actions of individuals
go to make up trends which can be studied as objectively as
natural phenomena, quite independently of specific motivations.
In this way it can be demonstrated that delinquency is related to
the facts of social class, to age, to sex, to the extent of urbanisation and so on. But it remains that the delinquent is nevertheless
an individual whose behaviour is a response to a complex set of
stimuli from both without and within himself, whose personality
has unique elements which separate him out from his fellows. It
is surely due to the unique quality of the individual human
personality that some break the law while others do not, in
circumstances which press equally heavily upon every member
of a family or social group.

Clifford Shaw has written of the need for what he calls a
"situational analysis" of delinquency, and in collecting the case
histories of the 79 children in the Probation and Approved
School sample it was hoped to discover precisely this kind of
material. The case histories which follow are only few in number
and have been selected in order to demonstrate some of the
arguments in this book. Needless to say they have been completely anonymised.

FAMILIES WITH EMOTIONAL DISTURBANCE:
OUTSIDE DELINQUENCY AREAS

3/21. *Charles* R. *Aged* 16. (Woodside Ward).

Court Record. April 1951. Larceny. 2yrs. Probation cond. of 1 yr. Child Guidance.

Feb. 1952. Amendment of Probation Order.

Feb. 1952. Larceny. Approved School.

Family F. aged 38. Commercial traveller.

Stepmother aged 32 (deserted by F.)

CHARLES aged 16.

Home: Terrace house in respectable working class street in GB district, Woodside. Fairly comfortably furnished.

Charles' early life was very unsettled. When he was 4 his mother began consorting with Canadian soldiers and father left home. One night in 1941 he returned to find Charles alone in the house during an air raid, mother being out with a soldier. He took the child to friends who looked after Charles for 18 months. Father then found a housekeeper and took the child back to a new home in South Croydon, though this arrangement lasted only for a year when Charles was sent to a boarding school at Barnstaple. In 1943 father divorced the mother and remarried, although Charles was not told of this until his return home to Croydon in 1945.

In 1948 Charles won a coveted place to a local Public school, though after one term as a boarder he was sent home for chronic enuresis. Finally in 1950 he was expelled for laziness and bad conduct and was transferred to one of the "toughest" Secondary Modern schools in the town. In the 3 months before his first appearance in Court Charles is known to have gone "joy riding" on at least 40 bicycles, subsequently abandoning them.

By this time father's second marriage had failed and in May 1951 he had left home and taken a mistress. Charles began to steal from the larder and indecently expose himself, and within a month had gone to live with his father. He took work in a grocer's shop but was fired for stealing marked coins. To his enuresis was now added incontinence. He took another job as an engineering apprentice and although he managed to keep it his behaviour deteriorated, stealing continually, staying out late and being involved in promiscuous sexual activities. In February 1952 there was a great row following a bout of incontinence and indecently exposing himself to the two young daughters of his father's mistress, to which Charles responded by staying out all night. For this he was brought to Court and his Probation Order amended; he responded by stealing a £1 note at home the same day for which he was charged with larceny and committed to an Approved School.

Charles' troubles seem to relate almost entirely to his grossly inadequate home background, and the Psychiatrist's report to the Court stated that he was in need of "intensive" treatment. None of his offences were committed in concert and there is no record of his having had contacts with other known delinquents.

3/13. *Violet D. Aged* 15. (Woodside Ward).
Court Record. Sep. 1951. Care & Protection. Stealing from mother and staying out all night. Supervision Order 1 year.

Jan. 1952. Care & Protection. Continued to be beyond parental control. Approved School.
Family.

    F. aged 43. Office Manager.
    M. ,, 41. Housewife.
    VIOLET 15. Schoolgirl.
    Br. Robert 13. Schoolboy.
    Sis. Rosemary 10. Schoolgirl.
Home. Well furnished semi-detached house being bought on mortgage in respectable lower middle class district.

Violet was a very intelligent girl. She was expelled from the local Girls Grammar School on account of her "bad influence" on other girls and transferred to a Secondary Modern School. She was a well developed girl and looked much older than her years. As a small child she had always been difficult to manage, but no help was ever sought by the family until she reached puberty when she became completely beyond her parents' control. At the time of her first appearance she was a psychiatric outpatient awaiting a mental hospital vacancy. She finally stole her M's handbag and stayed away two nights from home having had intercourse with several men.

In November 1951 she was admitted to a mental hospital where she began to deteriorate, scarcely noticing her parents when they visited. She absconded twice, being picked up successively in the West End and sleeping out in Park Hill recreation ground. The decision to commit her to an Approved School seemed dubious in that her need for psychiatric treatment was paramount. Violet's was a case where her actions brought her into conflict with the law on account of her age. Her delinquency was scarcely criminal. although her amateur prostitution finally brought her into contact with criminal groups.

SOCIALLY DEFECTIVE FAMILIES WITH EMOTIONAL DISTURBANCE
LIVING IN OR NEAR DELINQUENCY AREAS

3/35 and 3/36. *The 'F' Family.* (Bensham Manor Ward).
Court Records

(WILLIAM). April 1951. Larceny of a cycle with John. Probation 1 year.

March 1952. Larceny. Charged with John and two local boys. Probation 2 years.

(JOHN). April 1951. Housebreaking and larceny. Charged with boy next door. Cond. discharge.

April 1951. Larceny of cycle. Charged with br. Probation 1 year.

June 1951. Breach of Cond. Disch. (above offence). Fined £1.

March 1952. Larceny. Charged with br. and two local boys. Probation 2 years. Fined £2.

Sept. 1952. Larceny. Charged with local boy. Conditionally discharged.

Family.

F. aged c. 48. Milkman.
M. „ „ 48. Part time domestic worker.
Br. Jim aged 19. Engineering apprentice.
WILLIAM 17. Machine hand in timber works.
JOHN 15. Schoolboy.
Br. Peter 13. „
Br. Andrew 8. „

Home. 3 bedroomed flat in old working class district adjoining the "Bang 'Ole" area of Whitehorse Manor.

When William and John stole the bicycle they were remanded for medical reports; William was found to show no signs of emotional instability or neurosis. John on the other hand was "abnormally anxious", a chronic nailbiter and enuretic to age 11. Andrew was nevertheless the real problem. He had a habit of joy riding on trains and pilfering from shops from an early age, and stole a collecting box from the local fish shop. Child Guidance had been arranged but his attendance was so irregular that treatment was discontinued.

In the family can be observed a combination of delinquency, psycho-somatic and psychiatric disorder. At the age of 20 Jim developed intestinal mumps — Father refused even to go into the bedroom to see him. Subsequently he became unemployable and was given electro-convulsive therapy in a mental hospital. In June 1952 John went to hospital with a serious stomach ulcer and an internal haemorrage — Father again refused to visit him or even recognise his illness. Within a month of the operation he was suffering from facial skin eruptions, and a year later the Mass X-Ray discovered cysts in his neck and throat which had to be removed. John, however, did well on Probation, although he became a typical "Teddy" with a strong addiction to velvet collared suits and the South London Dance Halls.

Mother, continually anxious about becoming pregnant, suffered from cancer and had a breast amputated in 1951. Father was perhaps the most disturbed of all the members of the family, taking no interest in his sons except to refer to them as "bastards" and to attempt, unsuccessfully, to rule them with a cruel and unloving hand. Sexual relations were bad with his wife and he kept her perpetually short of money. Mother, a weak and inadequate woman did her best to cope with the family, but because of the atmosphere at home the boys spent most of their time loafing around the streets.

William finally enlisted in the RASC and settled down quite happily away from home; John became less delinquent and more ill. Andrew became more disturbed. As far as could be seen delinquency in this family was one of a series of alternative responses to a grossly inadequate family life, tempered by contacts with local delinquents in one area. The need for preventive family casework in this instance was largely unmet.

3/9, 3/60 and 3/80. *The 'W' Family. Thornton Heath Ward.*

Court Records
ROBIN June 1952. Larceny of binoculars. Charged with local boy. Probation 2 years.
ALBERT June 1950. Larceny of child's tricycle. Charged with Fred. Probation 2 years.
    Jan. 1952. Larceny of wristwatch. Probation 2 years.
    Sept. 1952. Larceny of £1 with Fred. Approved School.
FRED Sept. 1950. Larceny. Charged with Albert. Probation 2 years.
    Aug. 1952. Breach of Probation (with Albert).
    Probation 1 year.

Family.
    F. aged 47. 'General dealer' (junk man).
    M. ,, 47. Factory hand (irregular). Epileptic.
    Sis. Kathleen, aged 22. Factory hand (Irregular). Epileptic.
     ,, Evelyn   ,, 18. Laundry hand.
    Br Donald, aged 17. Factory hand.
     ,, William   ,, 16.   ,,   ,,
     ,, Reg.   ,, 15. Schoolboy.
     ,, ROBIN   ,, 13.   ,,
       ALBERT ,, 12.   ,,
       FRED   ,, 11.   ,,
       John   ,, 9.   ,,
       Eric   ,, 5.   ,,

Home. Requisitioned flat, badly overcrowded and poorly furnished, in a once prosperous working class shopping district which is now dingy and depressed.

Robin, Albert and Fred all had atrocious school reports; they were lazy, innattentive and untruthful, although it was Albert and Fred who were the most delinquent. They were well known for their shop-pilfering in the district, though they were never prosecuted. Father thrashed them repeatedly but without effect; mother "gave up all interest".

The family had a number of difficulties. The presence of epilepsy in three members meant that work was irregular. Kathleen had had several periods in mental hospitals. Father, a shiftless and unsettled man was an ineffective character who had long spells of idleness, not always involuntary — and a reputation for sharp and sometimes illicit dealing. Both parents had good intentions, but the size of the family and the extent of the physical overcrowding, there not being room for all the family even to sit down in one room, made control difficult. As a result discipline oscillated between thrashings and a policy of "peace at any price".

Although there was epilepsy and mental disorder in the family, none of the boys was ever remanded for a medical report, and there seems a good deal of evidence to suggest that Albert, the really black sheep of the family was quite seriously in need of psychiatric treatment. A sit was, the Probation Officer was able to offer a degree of support to the family, but this terminated with Robin's Probation Order. Forced to wander the streets because of the physical overcrowding it seems little wonder that these boys were in trouble.

3/86. *Annette H. Aged* 15. (Central Ward).

Court Record. July 1950. Beyond Control. Supervision Order 1 year.

October 1952. Larceny from gas meter. Probation 2 years. 1 year cond. of residence in Probation Hostel.

Family.

F. Regular soldier killed in N. Africa 1942.

M. aged c. 40. Seamstress.

Br Alan aged 19. Regular soldier.

ANNETTE aged 15. Factory hand.

Home. Top floor flat in large old house in "transitional" area.

During the war the family was in Egypt, returning to the U.K. in 1942. The double effect of F's death and the terrifying voyage home at the age of 5 did not improve Annette's already poor health. Up to the age of 2½ she had had ear trouble culminating in a serious mastoid After the removal of her tonsils she remained in hospital for 12 months. While still a little girl she broke her collar bone and developed a curvature of the spine. All her life she had been enuretic. A psychiatric report described her as "a passive, inadequate personality, emotionally immature". At school with an I.Q. of 71 she was well behind even in the 'C' stream and was described as "untruthful" and "boy crazy". She had been sexually mature since the age of 12.

After she left school her associates were of the worst type, most of her time being spent hanging around North End in search of boys. A great friend, one of the several she had who were well known as "problem" girls, was at the age of 16 already married, a mother, separated from her husband, producing an illegitimate child at 17. For a few months Annette worked as an assembler in a watch factory but was dismissed for perpetual absenteeism. After breaking open the gas meter at home she was sent to a Probation Home where her behaviour improved slightly. At first when she returned to Croydon she settled in a job, but the bright lights of North End were still an irresistible attraction. Relations with mother became much worse and when she became pregnant she answered mother's question as to the child's paternity by a petulant "How the hell should I know". In fact she may not have known, as by this time she had become quite promiscuous.

Annette seems likely to continue as a "problem" individual by reason of her low intelligence and emotional instability, though not necessarily as a "delinquent".

LARGE OR DULL, SOCIALLY INADEQUATE FAMILIES LIVING IN OR NEAR
DELINQUENCY AREAS

3/89. *Arthur E. Aged* 15. (South Norwood Ward).

Court Record. Aug. 1952. Larceny of £1 note from another child in street. Probation 2 years.

Family.
   F. aged C. 37. Builders labourer.
   M.   ,,   ,, 37. Housewife.
      ARTHUR aged 15. Schoolboy.
   Br. Alan   ,,   14.   ,,   on Probation, 2 Court appear-
                                        ances.
   ,, Charles   ,,   13.   ,,   subsequently on Probation.
   Sis. Joan   ,,   10. Schoolgirl.
   ,,   Sylvia   ,,   9.   ,,
   Br. Keith   ,,   8. Schoolboy, subsequently on Probation
                             and to Approved School.
   Sis. Pauline   ,,   6. Schoolgirl.
   ,,   Marian   ,,   4.
   Br. Graham   ,,   3.
   ,,   Adrian   ,,   2.
   Another child born 1953.

Home. A five-roomed house in working class district, adjacent to Delinquency area of Thornton Heath. Very poor and squalid. "Full of dirt and confusion".

Arthur came from a problem family. His report from the local ESN school described his educational attainment as "fair for an I.Q. of 58", but noted that he was continually in trouble, very spiteful and aggressive to younger children, and spoke of him as a "difficult child who has made little progress".

In contrast to most "problem mothers" Mrs. E. had a great deal of energy and was always trying—without success—to keep her brood in hand. When Keith was sent to an Approved School she made a hysterical scene in the Court. None of the children had an adequate amount of care or control, and the parents were prone to violent rows, on one occasion the police having to be called to quell what was degenerating into a public breach of the peace. To escape from this background the boys were always on the streets, and every Saturday they worked on various stalls in the Surrey St. market.

3/32. *Ray M. Aged* 12. (East Ward).

Court Record. April 1952. Larceny of groceries from a doorstep. Had meant to run away because of trouble at school. Charged with another local boy, a member of a well known delinquent family. Probation 2 years.

Family.

F. aged 45. Coalman.

M. „ 38. Domestic work.

Br Alan aged 19. Coalman. Charged in 1948 with being on enclosed premises by night.

„ Roy „ 17. Labourer. Ex Approved School. Charged subsequently with insulting behaviour, later with housebreaking.

RAY „ 12. Schoolboy.

Sis. Diana aged 8. Schoolgirl. Lives with friends.

Br. Keith „ 5.

Home. 5 roomed Council house on small inter-war housing estate.

Ray's school report was poor and he was a suspected truant. Father and eldest brother used to leave home at 5.30 a.m. and mother was at work all day, hence none of the younger children were adequately cared for. Ray's pals were all delinquents living on this Council estate. Father left the discipline to mother who could not cope, feeling she had lost the respect of her children and the support of her husband. Trying to find happiness elsewhere she took a lover and on becoming pregnant went to live with her sister.

.Father then paid the next-door neighbour to look after the children and had an extra-marital affair himself. His wife would not come home because the neighbourhood was "so unfriendly". Finally she returned with her baby.

The social inadequacy and the amorality of these parents made a stable family life virtually impossible, and the prognosis seemed poor for the younger children.

3/65. *David B. Aged* 10. Waddon Ward.

Court Record. Dec. 1951. Breaking and Entering. 2 cases of larceny. Charged with a local boy. Probation 2 years.

July 1952. Larceny of growing trees. Charged with local boy. Further Probation Order 2 years.

Aug. 1952. Breaking and Entering and larceny. Charged with local boy. Approved School.

Family.
F. aged 40. Machine operator.
M. „ 38. Laundry hand.
Br. John aged 17. Hotel page boy. Ex Approved School. Subsequently Bound Over for pestering his exgirl friend in the street.
„ Charlie „ 14. Schoolboy. On Probation for larceny.
„ William „ 12. „
DAVID „ 10. „

Home. Council house in the heart of the Waddon delinquency area. Drab and poorly furnished.

The B's were moved from Broad Green under a slum clearance scheme, and all their existing furniture had to be destroyed as it was infested with vermin. As a classical problem family, well known to both the Health and Childrens' Committees their capacity to supervise their children was very limited indeed. Father took little interest in his family keeping his wife short of money and spending a good deal on drink. He himself had had a miserable childhood under a vindictive stepfather. In order to supplement the family budget mother took a full time job which left the younger children free to roam the streets.

David who was born in an air raid was emotionally and educationally backward and a confirmed truant. His two greatest friends were both on Probation and together they went on a number of delinquent escapades the last of which is vividly described in David's own words.

"One dinner time me and Dick went out to play up Purley Way. We saw a man unloading a lorry outside the Aerodrome Hotel. On the lorry was some bottles of lemonade. Dick took one and we drank it. Then we helped a man pump the tyres of his car up and he gave us sixpence. Then we went down to Waddon on the bus to the coal yard. We kicked in the wall of a shed and got inside. We found some paint and brushes and we started to paint the inside of the hut but we got tired of doing that. In the corner was a big box what we broke open with an iron bar and took five and six out of a tin inside.

Then we went up to . . . 's (a local chocolate factory) to try and get some chocolate. We went in through the main gate into a room where there was some coats. We went through the pockets of the coats and took some matches and cigarettes and fourpence and some chocolate. Then we left.

We wanted to break into a house and get some money to go to the pictures and on the boats. We knocked at the door of six houses but people came so we asked for a drink. At the last one there didn't seem to be anybody in so we went round to the back. The door wasn't locked so we went in and Dick took some money from a box on the sideboard. He gave me a quid and kept the rest himself. Then we left.

We went to the Park and bought some ice cream and went on the boats and played golf ("clock" golf). Then we went up Surrey St. and bought some chips. Then we went to the pictures at the Palladium. We stayed there till they closed. Then we got on a Green Line to a farm Dick knows (near Godstone). We knocked at the door but nobody came so we went round the back and found a coal shed and we went to sleep in a sack in there.

In the morning we tried to find a "caff" but we couldn't find one. Then when we were playing in a quarry I fell down the side of it and hurt my head and my nose. After that we thought we had better go home. We started to walk down the road but a lady stopped us and called the police. The money they found on us was the money we took from the house. I knew we was doing wrong when we took it".

The spontaneity of this escapade and its psychological implications seem to speak for themselves. In 1954 David was licensed, but there were no indications of any real change having taken place either in him or his family. The neighbourhood still provides a risk of further delinquencies.

3/10. *Eric I. Aged* 14. (Waddon Ward).

Court Record. Jan. 1952. Larceny of junk. Charged with another local boy. Conditionally discharged.

Jan. 1952. Larceny of a pram. Larceny of ammunition. Charged with two local boys. Approved School.

Family.
    F. died of cancer 1949.
    M. aged 34. Factory hand.
    Br. Jollyon aged 15. Factory hand.
        ERIC   ,,   14. Schoolboy.
    Br. William ,, 11.   ,,
    Sis. Sheila   ,,   7. Schoolgirl.
    Br. Brian   ,,   5. Schoolboy.
    ,, Charles ,,   2.

Home. Council house in the heart of the Waddon delinquency area.
    Very drab, dirty and poorly furnished.

This was another family so grossly inadequate in its social performance as to be categorised as a classic "problem" family. Mother was a
slovenly woman of low intelligence without the incentive after a day's
work to keep the home tidy and clean. Controlling the family seemed
quite beyond her.

Eric at the time of his Court appearance was spending a lot of time
truanting. During the morning he would collect wastepaper and
cardboard from Bowaters factory (on Purley Way nearby) which he
subsequently sold to the junk dealers in Duppas Hill Lane or South-
bridge Rd. In the afternoons he would go to the cinema on the
proceeds. He had no organised leisure and on Saturdays worked on a
stall in Surrey St. market. On the occasion which resulted in the
second charge Eric had truanted with two brothers from an equally
poor family up the road. (These two boys were expert junk collectors
and their father used to send them out every night to scavenge for
greenstuff for his innumerable rabbits. If they came home empty
handed it was to a thrashing). Together they stole a pram to sell as
junk and later broke into the premises of a Rifle Club. They stuffed
their pockets with ·22 ammunition and were arrested in the street
when a policeman saw cartridges falling through the lining of
Eric's pocket as he walked along.

In 1954 he was licensed, and it was then that he told the present
writer about the escapade; conditions at home however had if
anything deteriorated, and his chances of being "mixed up" in further
trouble in this district are quite substantial.

THE "AFFECTIONLESS" OR PSYCHOPATHIC DELINQUENT UNAFFECTED
BY LOCAL CONDITIONS.

3/22. *Hugh V. Aged* 15. (Bensham Manor Ward).

Court Record. December 1943. Beyond Control. Committed to L.C.C.
under a Fit Person Order.

September 1946. Larceny. Discharged.

December 1946. Beyond control. Approved School.

May 1952. Unlawful wounding and causing grievous bodily harm.
Approved School.

Family.

Illegitimate. Whereabouts of mother unknown. Lived with series
of working class foster parents.

Soon after his birth Hugh was placed in an orphanage, but when
in 1943 his mother married he returned to live with her. He persistent-
ly ran away from home and stole from her and she charged him as
being beyond control. His teacher described him (aet. 6) as "not a
naughty little boy, but profoundly uninterested in school. He has no
initiative, does not play with other children, refusing all approach and

just wanting to sit alone". Other contemporary reports describe the mother's state of mind as unfit to deal with him, divided in her loyalties between her husband and Hugh's father.

Hugh never saw his mother again for by 1944 she had disappeared without a trace. He was placed first in a foster home at Lewes and then in another at Chichester, where towards the end of 1946 he began to steal. He was again transferred, this time to Croydon, but he continued to lie, steal and have temper tantrums. He was sent to an Approved School and licensed in 1950.

Following a period of pilfering and truanting in February 1952 he broke into a house not far away and hit an old lady of 81 severely over the head. At 7.30 a.m. next day he attacked a young woman on her way to work and seized her by the throat. The psychiatric report for which he was remanded noted: "He has suffered lifelong maternal deprivation and has become jealous of other Approved School boys in his foster home. Because he felt rejected he withdrew from Sunday School and the Boys Brigade. Grossly emotionally immature with neurotic symptoms, and in conflict with his developing sexuality. Aware of his parents desertion of him which he feels deeply, tending to compensate through grandiose fantasy". Hugh had no known contacts with other delinquents and his offences seem clearly explicable in terms of his emotional experiences.

3/42. *Henry K. Aged* 16. (Shirley Ward).

Court Record. October 1951. Taking and driving away a motor cycle without licence or insurance. Fined 10s. Disqualified for 18 months.

May 1952. Taking and driving away a motor cycle without licence or insurance whilst disqualified. Fined £2. Probation 2 years.

December 1953. Robbery and taking and driving away a car. Bound over 2 years. (2 companions sentenced to 12 months imprisonment).

January 1954. Larceny of WD Property. (4 companions were all army delinquents). Breach of Probation. Borstal Training.

Family.

    F. aged 38. Shopkeeper.

    M.   „   36. Helps in shop.

        HENRY aged 16. No steady employment.

    Sis. Yvonne „   13. Schoolgirl.

    Br. Anthony „   4.

Home. Flat adjoining shop in middle class residential district. Very comfortably furnished.

Henry was a complete enigma in his family, none of the familiar patterns either of family disorganisation or of neighbourhood influences which relate so often to delinquency can be discerned in his case.

His school report noted that his educational attainment and ability were well below average and his attendance poor. He was an unsettled boy, alternating between working for his father and as a building labourer, with the cinema and dance hall providing his recreations. His one abiding passion was for motor vehicles; his father described him as "mad on them". The taking away of the motor cycles was an impulsive action reminiscent of Toad in *The Wind in the Willows*.

When conscripted he put down for the RASC and was drafted to the Army Catering Corps. It is hardly surprising that after 17 days as a soldier he allied himself with two other malcontents and embarked on an escapade which landed them in the dock at the Old Bailey. Within a month he was in trouble again, this time with four other delinquent soldiers, and he was committed to Borstal.

His Probation Officer described him as "very much the spiv type" who responded little on Probation being especially lax in reporting. Whether if he had been drafted to the RASC it would have satisfied his passion for motors remains conjecture, but the Catering Corps does seem to have been an unfortunate placing. The frequency of his offences and his apparent indifference to punishment seem to indicate some degree of psychopathy.

X

CRIME, DELINQUENCY,
AND SOCIAL CLASS

AS a people, we often foster the notion that social class differences are superficial, perpetuated largely by those who have a vested interest in social and economic inequality. It is over half a century since Kipling wrote

> 'The Colonel's lady and Judy O'Grady
> Are sisters under the skin.'

Indeed, such are the sentiments of almost every radical or egalitarian philosophy which sees equality of opportunity at the basis of an efficient society. The evidence of a great deal of social research, however, indicates that even in a welfare state the facts of social class continue to determine in an extraordinary degree the course of an individual's life from the cradle to the grave. The differences in health and infant mortality, for example, still persist, notwithstanding the rise in the standard of living of the lowest classes and the benefits of socialised medicine.[1] In a

---

[1] There are wide margins between the mortality rates of the classes, notwithstanding a decline in the general mortality rate. Indeed, the gap between Class I and Class V has actually widened in the last 40 years.
"Different sections of the population have been very differently affected by recent social changes ... full employment, higher real wages and expanding social services have led to relatively greater improvement in the situation of building and dock labourers of Class V ... for example than of clerks or professional people ... however this different experience is not reflected at all in the infant mortality rates, despite the fact that there was so much room for improvement in the worst rates." Heady, J. A. and Morris J. N., "Mortality in Relation to the Father's Occupation", *The Lancet*, March 12th, 1955.
See also, Hare, E., "Mental Illness and Social Conditions in Bristol", *Journal of Mental Science*, Vol. 142, No. 427, 1956. also Hare, "Mental Illness and Social Class in Bristol", *British Journal of Preventive Social Medicine*, Vol. 9, No. 4, 1956.

society where educational opportunity is the primary avenue to upward social mobility through the acquisition of jobs with higher status and pay, we known that the unskilled worker's children are likely to stay unskilled workers and the professional man's children professional men because of the entrenchment of inequality in our class system.

Although for our purpose we have talked of "social class" on the basis of data about occupation, it is clear that the notion of social class extends further. Occupation is a useful criterion of definition in that jobs carry not only status but also definitions of income which go far to establish a pattern of consumption and a way of life. However intangible arbitrary definitions of class may be, it is a fact that in the real world individuals are aware of class and class differences to a degree of unusual subtlety. Such awareness comes about very largely as a result of differences in the way of life between individuals with differential amounts of status and income, not merely in the pattern of consumption but in the organisation of attitudes and behaviour. Even in the United States where a hereditary class system such as our own is scarcely known and there is an almost standarised consumption pattern, class differences in status and achievement are still clearly discernible. For our purpose, however, the importance of social class is that it determines through the mechanism of a sub-culture the social norms, attitudes, and responses of the individual. Individuals grow up in families and families exist in a socio-economic matrix which we call the class system, and it is possible therefore to examine the behaviour of individuals in terms of their class membership. It may well be that for some purposes it represents the most meaningful frame of reference. We know for example, that fox-hunting is behaviour which relates to membership of a rural upper and upper middle class, and not specifically religious or political groupings. It is part of a way of life; it is sub-culturally determined behaviour. Our problem is whether crime and delinquency may be understood in similar terms.

The problem is posed quite simply because, however reluctant we may be to feel that the poor are less honest or the rich more law-abiding, the facts of the matter are that crime and delinquency are almost exclusively a proletarian phenomenon. Such is the experience of every Probation Officer, Approved School Teacher and Prison Governor. In the Croydon material, amongst the series of persons charged (Series II) "Labourer", "dealer" and "no gainful occupation" occurred with monotonous regularity. Amongst the Probation and Approved School cases (Series III) not one child came from Classes I or II although in the population of the town these two classes were larger than Classes IV and V. 35 boys came from the families of unskilled workers and the like, compared with 18 from those of the semi-skilled and 11 from those of skilled artisans and minor "white collar" workers. Taking both boys and girls together, and the Census estimate of the social classes (expressed in terms of the occupational distribution of employed and retired males), the distribution appears as follows: Class III, 1 case per 3,003, Class IV, 1 case per 380 and Class V, 1 case per 187.

Warner and Lunt in their analysis of arrest rates over a 7 year period in Yankee City[1] produce data pointing in the same direction.

TABLE 22
ARREST RATES IN 'YANKEE CITY'

Class	% of Population	% of Arrests
Upper	1.44	0.43
Lower-Upper	1.56	0.28
Upper-Middle	10.22	1.84
Lower-Middle	28.12	7.80
Upper-Lower	32.60	24.96
Lower-Lower	25.22	64.69

It has often been argued, of course, that differential arrest or charge rates merely reflect partiality on the part of the police or those responsible for prosecution.[2] Such a charge cannot really be sustained for several reasons. In Britain, certainly, partiality would make headline news, and in any case the average policeman on the beat has a good deal of kindly sympathy towards the socially under-privileged child if not always perhaps towards the adult.[3] In the United States where the police have a reputation for graft unparalleled by British standards, one supposes that the individual well connected in the powerful criminal underworld

[1] Warner, W. L. and Lunt, P. S., *The Social Life of a Modern Community,* New Haven, 1941, p. 376.

[2] e.g., Barnes and Teeters, *New Horizons in Criminology,* New York, 1951, p. 176, and Sutherland, *Principles of Criminology,* p. 179. Clifford Shaw on the other hand refutes the idea that differential arrest rates are a function of police activity, see *Delinquency Areas,* Chicago, 1929, p. 199.

[3] Evidence of this is provided by such things as the Liverpool Juvenile Liaison Scheme and the Sir Philip Game Boys Club in Croydon, run entirely by policemen in their off-duty hours.

has as much chance of evading arrest and prosecution as the wealthy member of the social register.

The assumption that there is a valid class differential suggests that delinquency may be studied within a class frame of reference. This is not saying that morality varies inversely with social status, but merely that *legally defined* delinquency is a social characteristic of the working classes in general and the family of the unskilled worker in particular. The behaviour of individuals in other social classes is so organised that departure from established norms is far less likely to bring the non-conformist into collision with the criminal law.

TABLE 23

FAMILY RELATIONS AND MENTAL HEALTH BY SOCIAL CLASS
Source: Data from Series III

	Nos. of cases			
	Class III	Class IV	Class V	Factor No.
Parental disharmony	3	7	7	13
Parental rejection	2	6	9	8
Parental separation	5	3	13	11
Maternal deprivation	3	1	4	6
Low standard of hygiene	2	2	13	14
Both parents at work	3	6	6	12
Maladjustment/emotional disturbance	8	10	17	5
Behaviour problems in family	—	1	4	9
Mental disorder or epilepsy in family	3	3	12	10
Traumatic experience	2	6	10	7
Discipline { inconsistent	4	9	6 }	
severe	3	—	8 }	23
lax	4	2	18 }	
Total Nos. in each Class	16	19	44	

From this material it appears that the *proportional* distribution of those factors which characterise families with serious problems of social inadequacy or mental ill health are relatively similar for each of the three classes in question, with Class V taking a rather larger share of some of them. Parental separation, for example, occurs in about 1/3 of all the cases in each class, maladjustment or emotional disturbance in about half the cases. Other factors which have social or cultural rather than purely psychiatric connotations seem less evenly distributed. Traumatic experiences such as being left alone in an air raid or the sudden desertion of the mother occur in about 1/4 of the Class V cases but only in 1/8th of those in Class III.

In general terms the data from Series III suggest four things.

1 That serious delinquency occurs more frequently among the families of unskilled workers than amongst semi-skilled workers, white-collar workers or skilled artisans.

2 That in each occupational group there is a hard core of "psychiatric delinquency" related to serious emotional disturbance in the family, or mental ill health, which accounts for between 1/5th and 1/4 of all the cases.

3 That the residue may be regarded as "social delinquency" related to the cultural milieu of the delinquent.

4 That the uneven distribution of delinquency between the social classes is indicative of the uneven distribution of the factors making for both "psychiatric delinquency" and "social delinquency".

The efficiency of the family as an effective agency of social control must inevitably be impared when relationships within it are subjected to stress. These stresses may arise from personality problems, from the failure of parents to live in equanimity together, or from factors which are predominantly economic. Undoubtedly among the most important of these is housing. By and large, inadequate housing is a concomitant of low social class, for those with a strong position in the market are able to secure adequate housing for themselves even in a time of housing shortage. Those whose position is weakest must be content with what they can get. Legislation concerning housing (in Britain) is primarily concerned with the problem of public health. It defines minimum standards of accommodation and sanitation which are designed to minimise the unhealthful effects of overcrowding and inadequate sanitation. But the demands of public health legislation seldom extend to the social consequences of inadequate housing, and it is precisely these factors which contribute to the stress placed upon families in unsuitable accommodation. The relationship between overcrowding, social class and delinquency is demonstrated from correlations between rates of delinquent residence and social class and overcrowding.

TABLE 24

OVERCROWDING AND SOCIAL CLASS CORRELATED
WITH RATES OF DELINQUENT RESIDENCE

	With Overcrowding	With % middle class households
Under 17	+ 0.71	— 0.69
17 - 39	+ 0.69	— 0.65
40 and over	+ 0.71	— 0.65
All ages	+ 0.74	— 0.76

For the purpose of this calculation an overcrowding index was based upon the percentage of households in each ward living at a density of 2 persons per room or more, the average density in the whole Borough being 0.69 persons per room. The percentage of middle class households was based upon the Juror's Index.

In each case the correlation was significant at the 1% level, meaning that the element of chance in the association of the variables was small. Correlations, however, do not provide *proof,* through this may not be the crucial issue. Rather, it is important to demonstrate that factors which relate to an objective class situation provide the *possibility* of certain stressful experiences occurring which, by complex interaction with other more specific and unique factors may result in delinquency.

Why are some classes more delinquent than others?

This is a question which must inevitably be posed. There are some people who would reject its validity altogether, on the grounds that "delinquent" means not only "legally delinquent", but "legally delinquent *and apprehended*". Such is the view of distinguished criminologists like Barnes and Teeters and the late Edwin Sutherland. There are naughty boys in Public Schools and naughty boys in Secondary Modern Schools, but in the main Public schoolboys do not commit actions which are likely to result in their transfer to an Approved School. Sutherland suggested that the allegedly conforming middle classes contain in reality a large number of criminals, but of the "white collar" variety. On this basis one might argue that the problem of the class differential was largely one of academic definition, but it remains nevertheless that the vast majority of crimes consist of the straightforward stealing of property and their numbers are by no means balanced by elaborately contrived frauds and deceit on the part of business men and large corporations. The "dark number" theory may substantiate Sutherland's claim that in the United States the dimensions of white collar crime would be enormous if only they could be exposed, but in Britain Her Majesty's Commissioners of Inland Revenue exercise a vigilant eye and have no price. It seems much more reasonable to say that the class differential in legal delinquency results from the cultural differences between the social classes, in that anti-social behaviour may be expressed in a variety of ways depending upon the forms of expression made available to an individual by his class membership.

Differences in a way of life

The task of identifying social classes on the basis of a way of life alone is becoming increasingly difficult. The redistribution of income has made the middle classes somewhat poorer, and the working classes undoubtedly richer though some of the benefits of social security have gone as much to the former as to the latter. Differences in consumption patterns have become blurred; the ownership of cars and TV sets, for example, is a most unreliable indication of class membership. Amongst the skilled workers there is movement upwards on the social scale, their attitudes beliefs and whole way of life are exposed to a tremendous blast of influences in the popular press, from radio, television, advertisement hoardings and glossy magazines directing them towards the attainment of a middle class way of life. A century or less ago a proletarian or working class culture could be clearly distinguished from that of the middle classes; there was no mistaking the lady of the house for her cook or the clerk for the factory worker. Today no such distinctions may be confidently made; the man in the Underground with a homburg hat may be an office doorkeeper or a chartered accountant. Working class culture as a distinctive way of life is receding further and further with the passage of time. When we speak of "working class", we mean a culture increasingly confined to the mass of unskilled workers whose chances of upward social mobility are negligible, in contrast to "middle class", a culture parodied in the sterotype of the three person household living in a semi-detached suburban house and riding in a small family car. "Middle class" in most cases must be equated with "white collar" occupations, but it is essential to bear in mind that when the skilled manual worker is able to command an equivalent or greater income and has social aspirations, his style of life will approximate very closely to his white collar neighbour.

The most fundamental differences relate to the socialisation of the child. It is in childhood that the foundations of a way of life are laid, for the child constantly inquiring and experimenting with behaviour is quick and eager to learn the most satisfactory means of exploiting his environment and satisfying his own needs and desires. There have been in the United States a number of important studies of the problem of child rearing in different class situations,[1] and although the American material indicates what may ultimately happen in Western Europe, it is complicated by special American factors such as ethnic and national cultural differences. Undoubtedly the best study in Britain to date has been Betty Spinley's *The Deprived and the Privileged*,[2] and although her middle class group of controls is undoubedtly upper middle class and rather atypical for the mass of the population, her analysis of socialisation in a London slum area is extremely valuable. The picture it presents confirms that drawn by Jephcott and Carter in their study of Radby, of life overshadowed by economic insecurity and dominated by the demands of the moment.

The middle class child is brought up in an atmosphere of controlled care. As a baby his feeds are regulated, his periods of sleep and play carefully ordered. An early bedtime becomes an institutional ritual. Toilet training and table manners are enforced by patient and persistent exhortation; sanctions against bad behaviour consist of the threat to withdraw mother love rather than physical violence. The child may grow up without siblings, or in a family in which births are deliberately planned at convenient intervals. Play is confined to the house or garden; the street play group scarcely exists because other chidren are "brought home" to play. The family itself tends to act as a corporate unit, and although father and mother may have their own individual interests, the joint family holiday or outing is as important as the joint entertainment of friends at home.

In contrast, the working class child grows up in an atmosphere

[1] see, for example, Allison Davis, 'Socialisation and Adolescent Personality' in *Readings in Social Psychology*, ed. Newcomb and Hartley, New York, 1952. Davis and Havighurst, 'Social Class and Color Differences in Child Rearing', *American Sociological Review*, Vol. 53, 1946.
[2] London, 1954.

in which restraint is often conspicuous for its absence. The baby is quietened by the dummy or crust dipped into mother's tea. He may be carried hither and thither, to the cinema or the fish and chip shop in the evening regardless of the hour. His diet soon becomes that of the adult members of the family; he is seldom dry. Punishment and indulgence may follow in swift succession; other babies will arrive inconveniently and displace him as the family pet. His play will be largely in the street in which he will form an autonomous social group with boys of his own age. As a social unit his family will only be united on relatively rare ritual occasions such as weddings and funerals, the rest of the time father and mother will spend their leisure separately.

Cohen has summed up the differences in the sentence " . . . middle class socialisation, in comparison with working class socialisation is conscious, rational, deliberate and demanding".[1] The middle class child is conditioned to control and restraint from his earliest years; the immediate gratification of desires is discouraged and the virtues of thrift and abstinence emphasised. In almost every sphere of life he is made aware of the desirability of restraint and order. He does not urinate in the gutter or take food out into the street; mealtimes and bedtime are as fixed as the amount of his weekly pocket money. The working class child in contrast is allowed to develop in relative freedom. Because he is cast at an early age, maybe three or four, into street play-group society, the process of his social maturation is accelerated in some aspects and retarded in others. It is accelerated in that he is exposed to the influences of the outside world much earlier than the middle class child; at five or six, for example, he goes shopping regularly and travels alone or with his pals on public transport. At the same time, the fact of being so much in the company of his peers and left free to do as he pleases with his leisure time, means that the opportunity of learning about a wider system of adult values—which may indeed conflict with those of his own parents—will be severely limited to contacts with the school and perhaps the social worker or Probation Officer.

Emotional sophistication does not necessarily proceed at an equal rate with social and sexual sophistication. From the age of eleven or twelve the sexes begin to interact. On winter evenings

[1] Cohen, A. K., *Delinquent Boys, The Culture of the Gang,* London, 1956.

the girls will sit on a low wall or seat by the park entrance and hold court for a group of boys on bicycles which are never ridden further than a few blocks. It is essentially group interaction one suspects because the group is able to provide the emotional security which is not possessed individually. At fifteen they cease to be children and become wage-earners. This dramatic precipitation into the adult world tends to accentuate the difficulties which arise out of what might be termed "uneven maturation". Sexuality assumes an enormous importance, and with it sexual experimentation. By sixteen or seventeen a girl considers herself lacking if she does not have a steady boyfriend, by eighteen or nineteen she is contemplating marriage and motherhood. By such thinking she tends to become emotionally mature more rapidly than her boy friend, for whom at seventeen or eighteen boyish pursuits are still current. He will ride his motorcycle endlessly round and round the block to impress an audience with his new toy, and when he is conscripted at eighteen his train journeys to and from camp will still be enlivened by the *Hotspur* as well as by *Blighty* and *Reveille*.

Cohen has written of the activities of the delinquent gang as characterised by "short run hedonism"[1] but in fact this description may be regarded as a fundamental attribute of working class culture. The child seeks immediate gratification and is seldom denied; in the autonomous play group activities are organised only on a short run basis to secure an immediate end without thought of the consequences. Sexual behaviour ultimately follows the same pattern, and the resistances of working class adults to middle class birth control propaganda become more meaningful when considered in this light. The norms of behaviour which the child acquires for himself tend to be of the most rudimentary kind and their observance related as much to the effectiveness of external social pressures as to the degree of self-control which has become internalised. By contrast with the middle class child, the working class child is more likely to react to stressful situations in flagrantly anti-social terms because he has not been conditioned to restraint from his earliest years. Whereas the middle class way of life tends to inhibit spontaneity, working class culture tends to encourage it. In particular, aggression is seldom the subject of social disapproval.

The working class child is not only less able to cope with

[1] Cohen, *op. cit.*, p. 30.

stressful situations but more likely to encounter them. The task of bringing up a family on a limited budget, particularly when the husband keeps her "short" seldom fails to leave its mark on the working class mother. Because husbands allot their wives a fixed rather than proportional amount of their wages, the mother must frequently work as well as run a home. The tensions and discords which result from disagreements over money are augmented by sexual difficulties. The woman's interest in sex rapidly becomes a pre-occupation with avoiding unwanted pregnancies; "good" husbands are those that make no sexual demands. Parental discord is undoubtedly one of the most disturbing experiences any child has to face because it strikes at the very foundations of his emotional security. But because no premium is put on restraint, husbands and wives may fight like tigers or simply desert the home. It is not intended to suggest that marital discord and "broken homes" are to be found only amongst working class families, but that in contrast with the middle class situation there are fewer mechanisms of control.

The working class child cannot escape from the bad or unhappy home except into the street and until he goes to work his activities out of school are likely to be severely limited by the amount of money he can get hold of. Stealing therefore pays dividends, whether it be cash from mother's purse or junk which can be sold for cash. Not for him is the boarding school where he can seek out parent substitutes more satisfactory than his own, except if he should commit an offence and be sent to one by order of the Juvenile Court. The middle class child by reason of his superior economic position has more outlets for his feelings. He does not need to roam the streets when he can create a world of fantasy with his toys or lose himself in a world of books.

Why are not all working class children delinquent?

The reader may feel that the picture of working class life which has been drawn is unduly pessimistic, but the picture of life in the delinquency areas of Croydon's older housing estates is very much of this order. Lest it be suggested that this in an argument from the particular to the general, the evidence of Jephcott and Carter and Spinley seems to indicate that the pattern is "normative" at least in a statistical sense. If all working class children grow up in a culture which exerts few social controls on the one hand and produces stressful situations on the other, how is it that not all of them succumb and appear in the Juvenile Court?

Mays' answer would probably be that most of them *do* in fact succumb but only a few are unlucky enough to get caught. There can of course, be no absolute refutation of this view, but it seems likely nevertheless that if the majority of delinquent acts are impulsive and seldom efficiently planned, then the chances of detection and prosecution are fairly high. On the other hand, amongst working class adults at least, larceny must run at a fantastic level. "Whipping" or "knocking off" are universally legitimate activities. Electric light bulbs, scrap metal or wood, towels, paper, food, almost any commodity which can be utilised is stolen from the employer without a qualm. It is attitude of mind encouraged by army experience where the theft of kit penalises the victim and not the thief, resulting in an almost Hobbesian situation of a war of all against all.

The question can be answered by analogy. In the 19th century conditions of housing and sanitation in urban areas were such that mortality rates especially from contagious diseases such as cholera were extremely high. But even in a time of epidemic not everyone was stricken down, nor indeed did all those who were necessarily die. In other words, although everyone was exposed to virtually the same risks of contagion, some managed to escape the worst effects of the disease and some to escape infection altogether. The reason for this was simply the differential resistance offered by different individuals. A similar situation may be observed with regard to the stressful experiences which may engender delinquency. While socio-economic factors such as housing and income may make life difficult for the unskilled labourer and his family, the degree of stress which they create within the family depends very much upon the adaptability of the individuals concerned in the situation. Cultural norms are frequently "tailored" to fit the needs and capacities of individual personality, and if husband and wife are relatively well adjusted to each other they are less likely to come into violent conflict over money, the control of children or their sexual life. What we have earlier termed "psychiatric" delinquency is unlikely to be a feature of the behaviour of children who grow up in families which are well adjusted, even though they may nevertheless grow up in the cultural milieu of the street play group and its hedonistic philosophy. Their delinquency is more likely to be if anything "social", that is to say anti-social behaviour which is well integrated within the confines of the play group.

Those who come into marked conflict with the criminal law, who progress from Probation to Approved School, from Approved School to Borstal, from Borstal to Prison and ultimately to Preventive Detention, are those who have as it were, succumbed "mortally" in that their lives are firmly fixed on the path of crime. They are "outside" society almost as the dead are beyond life in their complete and utter rejection of societal norms. For them the sanctions of punishment have but little effect and then only in the short run. Ultimately they become a-social as well as anti-social. Such individuals are few in number and are drawn almost exclusively from the hard core of "psychiatric" delinquents. The "social delinquents" in contrast are those who get into trouble, sometimes seriously, but who nevertheless pass through the delinquent phase. They are like the individuals who sicken but do not die, and who recover with varying degrees of success. Some will, as it were, carry the marks of delinquency all their lives; they will "whip" and "knock off" when the opportunity presents itself. Others when they grow up will put dishonesty behind them forever.

The stressful situations which result in "psychiatric" delinquency cannot be classified as wholly economic or wholly cultural in origin but as an admixture of both aggravated by personality factors in the individual family. "Psychiatric" delinquency as a consequence occurs in all social classes, and in the Croydon material with only slight differences in its proportional frequency among the cases in each class. "Social" delinquency on the other hand flourishes in working class neighbourhoods because of the support it finds in working class culture. The older teenagers and adults are still like "carriers" of disease, because although they do not actively come into conflict with the law their attitudes and behaviour represent a logical continuity with the delinquent phase of their earlier years. Attitudes to property remain egoistic and unaltered, irresponsible lateness and absenteeism replaces truancy; the boss takes the place of the schoolmaster as the unreasonable over-demanding figure of alien authority whom to deceive or defy is a mark of cleverness and success.

The reasons for not all working class children becoming delinquent may be listed then as follows.

1 The degree of stress resulting in "psychiatric" delinquency tends to vary with the circumstances of individual families and personalities.
2 Not all delinquents whether "psychiatric" or "social" will necessarily commit delinquent acts which are specifically *illegal*.
3 By no means all those who commit illegal acts will be detected and prosecuted and identified as delinquents within the definition of law.

Social control in the working class neighbourhood

Park described the process of social control in the ecological community as characterised by restraints which are internal and moral, and based on some kind of consensus. The stability of the social order is seen as dependent upon the stability of relationships which have a spatial base. The absence of such a stable order has been equated by Clifford Shaw and others with "social disorganisation".

On the surface it would seem indeed that the working class neighbourhood which was also a delinquency area was "socially disorganised" in this sense. But anyone who has worked or lived in such a neighbourhood soon realises that this is by no means so. On the contrary, one is confronted with a sub-culture unambiguously defined and in some aspects blatantly at variance with widely accepted middle class norms. Because the working class way of life rejects so many of the norms of middle class society it has been erroneously equated on occasion with social disorganisation. The problem of consensus and a normative system of behaviour was examined by Durkheim in *Suicide* and his statement of it is usefully paraphrased by Parsons in *The Structure of Social Action*:

'. . . not merely contractual relations but social relations in general, and even the personal equilibrium of members of a social group are seen to be dependent on the existence of a normative structure in relation to conduct, generally accepted as having moral authority by members of the community, and upon their effective subordination to these norms. They do not merely regulate the individual's choice of means to his ends, but his very needs and desires are determined in part by them. When this controlling normative structure is upset and disorganised, individual conduct is equally disorganised and chaotic—the individual loses himself in a void of meaningless activities.'

Such disorganisation is infrequent in human society, and as Sainsbury has shown, is characteristic of areas of high suicide rates and not of delinquency areas, neither of which incidentally coincide.[2] The normative structure of conduct may appear to be an inversion of that of the world at large but it is by no means disorganised. Nor indeed is a neighbourhood "disorganised" if there is no perceptible structure at all which is dependent upon a local consensus. If it were, then many middle class suburban neighbourhoods where social contacts over the garden fence may take years to establish, would be areas of social disorganisation. The maintenance of normative structures of action in an urban population with a high degree of physical mobility depends as much upon the existence of reference groups as upon local groups for their legitimation. These may be work groups, religious denominations, professional organisations or even the concept of membership of a social class. The effectiveness of social pressures within the neighbourhood as a means of achieving social control must depend in considerable degree upon the amount of time the individual actually spends within its confines and the extent to which he interacts with his neighbours.

The differences which exist between systems of social control in middle class and working class neighbourhoods relate largely to the content of the cultural norms themselves. Middle class culture stresses the importance of the family as a social unit and the family therefore tends to accept collective responsibility for the behaviour of its members. If little Charles falls foul of the law, the whole family suffers in the disgrace; if father goes to prison, although he may actually have spent little of his time in the neighbourhood every family member must expect to face ostracism and social disgrace. In the working class neighbourhood because the family is much less of an identifiable social unit it is the actions of individuals which are judged rather than whole families.

The family as a whole has, therefore, less interest in controlling the activities of its members, and because of this tends to be

---

[1] Parsons, T., *The Structure of Social Action*, p. 377.
[2] Sainsbury, P., *Suicide in London*, London, 1955.

much less effective than its middle class counterpart as an agency of social control. The experience of every Juvenile Court must endorse this fact when, for example, fathers are not only unaware of the doings of their children but usually express extreme reluctance to appear in Court when they are in trouble. When out of sight they are also out of mind. To walk down a street in any typical delinquency area, one might wonder how it was that other people did not exert some control over the children swarming everywhere, but any such interference by outsiders tends to evoke the most primitive feelings of familial solidarity. In one instance noted by the writer, a group of boys were beseiging another group in a house where both mother and father were out at work. The doors and windows were barred and so the attackers seized a pickaxe and began to belabour the front door. The woman next door seeing this, took action and dispersed the group, that evening going round to see the father of the boy who had wielded the pickaxe, only to be met with a stream of angry resentment for her pains. The next night her own front door was bombarded with cabbage stalks and garbage.

The virtual impossibility of any single community member being able to exert authority on behalf of the neighbourhood in enforcement of conduct norms, would suggest that no such norms exist. Paradoxically this is not so, for neighbours are continually evaluating behaviour, but always the behaviour of third parties not present. A woman who is pregnant by her lover or who has had her children taken into care, is a "no-good" or a "lazy bitch". The women castigating her immorality may nevertheless have all been pregnant out of wedlock or have sons who have been fined or put on probation. In contrast to a middle class situation where families keep up a front of conformity for fear of social ostracism, social controls have not been internalised in the process of socialisation. Ostracism and hostility on the part of neighbours are less effective because there is scarcely any guilt upon which they may operate. Judgments of behaviour by neighbours are seen not so much as evaluations of behaviour on the basis of normative criteria but as an expression of hostility to be met characteristically with hostility. The mother of the Approved School boy does not therefore hang her head in shame but ensures that any detractors feel the sharp end of her tongue.

Against this background of acrimonious moral judgement must be seen the street play group. The group is in effect one of a series of groups recruited on the basis of age and territory which grows up together in the neighbourhood. So much has already been written on the subject of the juvenile gang that it would be superfluous to summarise it here. Among the most important points which have emerged, however, is that the street play group is essentially autonomous in that it establishes and enforces its own norms independently of adult or other external interference. It has in addition to satisfy the emotional needs of its members for security, feelings of competence, or being wanted, when they cannot be supplied in a socially inadequate or grossly unhappy home. When the activities of the group become seriously anti-social and illegal it can only be restrained by the formal agencies of law enforcement which belong to society at large, the Police and the Courts. Because of the social gulf which exists between the group and most of the personnel of such agencies, their function is seen as hostile, aggressive and negative rather than positive and helpful in safeguarding the rights of individuals and the community.

Effective social controls then, are largely external and formal and stem from outside the local community. As a result the only kinds of anti-social behaviour which can be successfully limited are almost always illegal. Those delinquencies which are not illegal, and which would be kept in check by the informal pressure of public opinion in a middle class neighbourhood are integrated within a normative cultural pattern, the only control being exerted by an adaptation of the *lex talionis*. Feuds and reprisals, however, are essentially group activities and are confined therefore to those sections of the population which are organised on a group basis, the children and adolescents. For the rest, the principle of "giving as good as you take" operates, so that abuse over the garden fence must be met by further abuse, slanders by counter-slanders and so on. Such a way of life is essentially unsatisfying and frequently mentally unhealthy. It is not surprising that almost all those individuals who can, seek to abandon it and adopt the norms of the middle class. The fulfilment of middle class norms necessitates far reaching changes in style of life and expenditure, but those who have benefitted by full employment and the redistribution of income are able, generally for the first time in their lives, to realise their social aspirations. They therefore send their children to Secretarial Schools if they fail at 11 +, and place a premium on "respectability". But sooner or later they come up against the fact that to make their new status position secure they must move away, and herein lies a major difficulty. The situation in the housing market is such that there is little accommodation at medium rentals, and because their resources will not stretch always to the highest rentals or home ownership, they are compelled to stay in Council housing or other comparatively low cost accommodation. Some of the problems which arise out of this are discussed in our next chapter.

XI

DELINQUENCY, HOUSING AND SOCIAL POLICY

Housing

IN discussing the ecological concept of the natural area the point was made that "cultural differentiation" between urban neighbourhoods for the most part resulted from the fact that the social classes tended to be residentially segregated through the operations of the housing market and through individual choices made with reference to class determined systems of cultural values. In the preceding chapter it has been suggested that anti-social behaviour in general and delinquency in particular may be meaningfully studied in terms of the sub-cultural differences between the social classes. It would seem at first sight then, that the study of the delinquency *area* was not only a procedure whose usefulness might be called into question but whose validity might also be doubted. Now while it is true that instances of "psychiatric" delinquency may crop up anywhere in the city, "social" delinquency tends to be much more highly localised. The Croydon evidence confirms that whilst the former is more evenly distributed over the middle and working class areas of the town "social" delinquency predominates in old working class areas and on the inter-war housing estates.

We must at this stage return to the concept of the "area of delinquent residence" in which a constellation of factors may be identified which can be said to constitute a "delinquency potential". They can be summarised by the following propositions:

1 *Delinquent or criminally anti-social behaviour of a "social" kind tends to be characteristic of working class culture and to be perpetuated by it.*

2 *Factors engendering "psychiatric" delinquency are likely to be aggravated in working class situations by poor housing and cognate socio-
economic factors.*

3 *Working class families and therefore working class culture predominates on housing estates.*

Because it is the inter-war housing estates in Croydon which
present the major delinquency problem, most of the discussion
will turn about them. At the same time almost everything which
applies to them applies to the older and relatively homogeneous
working class areas of the town. The main difference lies in the
fact that the Housing Authority in the former instance exercises
many of the controls which are exercised in the latter by private
landlords or by the forces of the market. In some ways the
dichotomy of the "Council" and the "Private Landlord" is a
false one for in terms of many of their day to day activities there
is no real difference between them. It is only when it comes to the
question of *policy*, in the selection and placement of tenants that
there is a real divergence. For the private landlord housing
ownership is a form of investment from which a profitable return
is expected—though this hope is often sadly disappointed. For
the Local Authority, however, the provision of housing is much
more than that; it is a fundamentally important social service
which exists for the benefit of the community in which the
element of profitability must be a secondary consideration. There
are, of course, those who argue that housing is not a social
service in this sense, but an amenity provided for the benefit of
certain sections of the community at the expense of a subsidy
from the rest. Carried to its logical conclusion such an argument
could be applied to any of the services provided in the community. If those whose social needs are not matched by power
effectively to make demands in the housing market must do as
best they can, then, by the same token, those who cannot afford
to employ a refuse contractor or to make up the road outside
their own front door should be content to have their garbage
accumulate and their streets remain with ruts. We live in a time
in which the unrealism of total *laissez-faire* is still not without
advocates, though they seem to be found in local government
more often than elsewhere. Such individuals with ultramontane
views represent only a minority, but it may happen that their
presence in council chambers may not be without its effect upon

those with more liberal views. When it is a question of a social service being financed out of the rates there is not unnaturally a reluctance to spend money except where it is statutorily required or clearly necessary. Where statutory obligation is absent the definition of necessity becomes inevitably a matter of political philosophy.

It is perhaps significant that the recognition of the need for the provision of low cost housing adequately constructed and efficiently maintained, occurred more than half a century ago. It was a recognition of the fact that there are some things the provision of which is too important to be left to the vagaries of the market whose principal criterion is profitability. But it was not until after the First World War that Local Authorities began to assume in appreciable numbers the mantle which had been borne by the pioneer Housing Trusts.

Croydon's first housing estates were built approximately between the years 1924 and 1932. They were built partly to provide for the needs of a growing working class population and partly to improve the housing conditions of those who were living in insanitary or overcrowded conditions. Accordingly, the accommodation provided was designed to provide a maximum improvement in housing standards at a minimum cost to the ratepayers. The most common design was a three bedroomed semi-detached house with a single living room downstairs running from back to front, kitchen and bathroom. By contemporary standards these houses seem very spartan. Original equipment, for example, consisted of a kitchen range in the living room and a rather primitive boiler for heating bathwater. The only place for personal washing other than the bath was the kitchen sink. Two out of the three bedrooms were without fireplaces and no electric plug points were provided. Immediately prior to the war the Council began to install gas heaters over the kitchen sinks and many tenants have replaced the old iron ranges by open fireplaces at their own expense.

In an endeavour to maintain houses in a reasonably clean condition and good repair, the Council in common with most other Local Authorities imposed stringent conditions of tenancy. Consent had to be obtained in writing before a tenant could keep any animal or bird or affix any telephonic or telegraphic apparatus to the structure; lino or other floor covering might not be laid within one foot of any wall "which space might however be suitably stained". One suspects that many of these provisions were more honoured in the breach than in the observance and in recent years some regulations, like that concerning floor covering, have quietly disappeared from the back of the rent book.

Council housing then, was intended to alleviate bad housing conditions and to provide a minimum standard of accommodation for the individual working class family. By careful control the Housing Department has been able to ensure the maintenance of such standards and in some cases raise them by the installation of hot water appliances, electrical power points and so on. But the basic design of the majority of dwellings does not necessarily assist in the development of tension-free family living. To take the case of the three-bedroomed semi-detached house. Its occupation is limited to $6\frac{1}{2}$ persons (infants under 12 months not counted). This means that $6+$ persons—more in fact if there are children counted as half-persons—must wash in the kitchen sink as there is no wash hand basin, or have a full bath, the water for which may take three-quarters of an hour to heat. Mother will not encourage them to hang about in her small kitchen so the single back-to-front living room is the only place where the whole family can assemble for meals and relaxation. In summer the children can at a pinch play in their bedrooms but in the winter these are likely to be cold. If the whole family wants to indulge in the same activity the living room is adequate, but if one member wants the radio on, another to play the piano, another to read the paper, and so on, conflicts are likely to arise. Theoretically the maximum density of occupation may be 1·3 persons per room while in terms of effective living space the maximum density may be 6·5 persons per room.

Conditions such as these are not of course confined to Council properties, indeed those of private landlords are sometimes far worse. It remains nevertheless housing of this kind tended to reproduce a pattern of physical living not substantially different from that experienced by families before they became tenants of the Local Authority. The natural result of such a pattern is to encourage individual family members to seek their recreation outside the home, the children in the street and fathers in the "local" or Men's Club. Post-war housing especially on the New-Addington estate is of a radically different standard, and the observer cannot fail to be impressed by overt social differences between life on the old and on the new estates.

Perhaps the most important fact about areas of delinquent residence is that they tend to be small and highly localised. On the Waddon estate, for example, both juvenile and adult offenders in 1952 were exclusively concentrated in the back streets on the south-west corner of the estate. The main road through the centre, and the streets to the north were in contrast entirely without individuals who had been charged and brought before the Courts. Bearing in mind the differences between these latter streets with their rows of parked cars and neatly trimmed hedges and the former with cycle tyres hanging from trees and neglected gardens, it seemed reasonable to assume that on the housing estate itself some ecological segregation had taken place, and if this were so, then it was probable that it had been the outcome of housing policy.

It was not an easy task to gain information about housing policy some 25 years ago when the estates were first settled, but from evidence culled from a variety of sources including the fact that there were many families still living in the houses they had occupied in 1928 and 1930, it seems almost certain that some segregation took place. Those whose previous accommodation had on inspection shown them to be houseproud were given the houses on the frontage roads, whilst those who were former slum dwellers or who were undoubtedly "rough" by comparison were placed in the back roads and crescents. It so happened that the rents of the houses on the frontage roads were appreciably higher, being four bedroomed parlour type houses. Over time, however, this broad differentiation based in the main on the economic factor of rents became modified by cultural factors. If rent were simply the criterion one might expect families with both high and low standards to be randomly distributed in properties of the same rental, but this is by no means the case. Families with higher standards and aspirations who found themselves in "rough" areas either moved out of their own accord or applied for a transfer; similarly families who found themselves with "stuck up" or "toffy-nosed" neighbours applied to be transferred to streets where they would be more at home. No-one was allowed a direct choice of street, but other things being equal, no-one was forced unreasonably into one street if they preferred a house available in another. What appears to have happened then is that families have exerted a degree of choice in accepting or rejecting particular neighbourhoods, the pattern of choice has followed broad ecological and economic lines, and the policy of the Housing Department has attempted as far as possible to accord with what is clearly a desire for segregation on the part of both "rough' 'and "respectable".

"Segregation" was undoubtedly a burning issue in the earlier days of housing estates and it is worthy of note that the policy of the Central Housing Advisory Committee has consistently opposed it since the first report of its Housing Management Sub-Committee.[1] In a recent publication the view is stated explicitly

'Segregation has two main disadvantages. In the first place it is difficult, if not impossible to prevent a group of houses occupied by tenants of poor standards from getting a bad name, and hence some stigma falls upon those who live in them. To make families feel that they are set apart from the normal community in this way only increases the difficulty of helping them to achieve ordinary standards. Secondly to group such families together is to expose them to a continual demonstration of those habits which it is desired to cure. It is much easier to persist in such habits if supported by the example of others doing the same thing.'[2]

This, of course, relates to what are known as "unsatisfactory tenants", who are known in other contexts as "problem families" or the core of the "social problem group". By getting hopelessly into rent arrears, by maltreating the property and by living generally in an atmosphere of squalor they come to the prominent notice of social agencies. But while they are essentially the core of the problem there is nevertheless a penumbra of families around them whose standards and values are only slightly higher and it is largely they who perpetuate the sub-culture we have already discussed.

Croydon has not been alone in pursuing a segregation policy and indeed the view of the Central Housing Advisory Committee is in some respects naive in that it appears to neglect the fact that segregation is desired by both groups. Post-war housing management has been compelled to allocate housing in accordance with need as evidenced by tenants totals of "points" in a priority scheme, and this has undoubtedly led to a great of social mixing.

[1] *The Management of Municipal Housing Estates,* H.M.S.O., 1939, p. 20.
[2] *Unsatisfactory Tenants,* 6th Report, Housing Management Sub-Committee of the Central Housing Advisory Committee, H.M.S.O., 1955, p. 14.

The Criminal Area

The consequences of such mixing has been studied in a number of parts of Britain since the war[1] and although researches in this field have been described as "Neighbouring, or Storm in the Teacup"[2], it remains that the problems of neighbourhood relationships have often been neglected or overlooked by planners who have been concerned with the more formal aspects of new urban development. Those families who have middle class aspirations to respectability may be subjected to considerable strain by having to live in proximity to those whose standards are lower and whose values are totally different. Whatever arguments might be put forward for social mixing it remains a very difficult objective to achieve. As it was expressed by one man to a research worker, "It's easy to let yourself go, but harder to pull yourself up."[3]

The net effect of segregation is to create enclaves covering a relatively small area, but which contain a disproportionately large number of families belonging to the social problem group. As a consequence, the street play groups in such areas are likely to contain an unduly high proportion of children who by virtue of their cultural inheritance are prone to social delinquency. The conditions of family life are also such that their proneness to "psychiatric" delinquency is not inconsiderable. The "delinquency area" which is an ecological feature of the urban scene when development follows the trend of the market is thus perpetuated by an aspect of administrative policy.

It would be unfair, however, to suggest that Housing Authorities, in general, or indeed the Housing Authority in Croydon, *deliberately seeks to perpetuate* the delinquency area; on the contrary they try to satisfy the wishes of the majority of tenants and are concerned no less about the social problem group and those families lying about its fringe. Their dilemma is an unenviable one, for while segregation undoubtedly perpetuates a subculture which has little to recommend it from either the aesthetic

---

[1] See Kuper, L., *et al*, *Living in Towns*, London, 1953, Mitchell, G., Lupton, T., Hodges, M and Smith, C., *Neighbourhood and Community. An Enquiry into Social Relationships on Housing Estates in Liverpool and Sheffield*, Liverpool, 1954, Mogey, J., *Family and Community. Two Studies in Oxford*, Oxford, 1956.

[2] *Current Sociology*, Vol. IV, No. 4. Urban Sociology Trend Report, UNESCO Paris, 1955, p. 64.

[3] This was during a research into mobility on housing estates conducted for the Bristol Social Project in 1954. In this survey inability to get on with neighbours was a major cause of removal from certain 'bad' estates.

or practical point of view, the alternative is likely to be unpopular with all concerned.

"Mixture", though it might create no more than irritating tensions between neighbours tends to have more serious effects upon the children. It is in the nature of things that children are more plastic and more responsive to new cultural influences than are their parents. On a "mixed "housing estate the children of all families will tend to go to the same school with the result that while contacts between the adult population may be severely limited, the children of both social aspirants and the social problem group will be thrown together for a great deal of the time. It is here that Sutherland's theory of "differential association" is useful in explaining a certain amount of social delinquency, for when the influences towards non-conformity are stronger than those operating in the reverse direction, a certain amount of anti-social behaviour may occur among children from otherwise highly respectable and law abiding families. Such influences are naturally only effective in particular situations in this case in the relationships which arise through school contacts. The amount of social delinquency among families who aspire to membership of the middle class would seem to be a function of the efficiency of the family in inculcating middle class norms, especially those which relate to constraint and "respectability" in overt behaviour.

The chances are that among such families who are socially upward mobile many of the old norms remain; the taboo on street play, for example, may not yet be established, with the result that the children are still exposed to the influences of the play group, which may well contain a high proportion of children from the problem group. It is possible too, that the experience of upward mobility may set up strains and tensions within the family itself. The assimilation and acceptance of new norms may proceed at a differential rate between husband and wife, resulting in marital conflict; it is by no means uncommon to find that a woman may become highly neurotic as a result of the hostility and derision she experiences at the hands of neighbours who not only reject her aspirations but express their open contempt of them. If the woman goes to great lengths to protect her children from "contamination" she may set up conflicts of loyalties for them, between the family on the one hand and the child's contemporaries in the street with whom he goes to school.

Social Policy

So far we have been concerned with the identification of those areas of social living in which the causal processes that may result in delinquency can be observed. The discussion has also revolved in the main around the problem of *juvenile* offenders, but this has been for two important reasons. In the first place, when we examine the dimensions of the problem we find that in both relative and absolute terms the most criminal age groups in the population are aged between 8 and 21. In the second, persistent adult criminality is almost invariably the successor to a history of juvenile crime. In juvenile offenders then, we observe not only the bulk of those who transgress against the law, but the hard core of those who will persist in their anti-social behaviour into adult life. It follows that the constellation of influences which predispose the individual towards crime can be best observed in their youthful setting.

The problem remains of what can be done. Although there are no reliable statistics in Britain relating to crime in the 19th century which could form the basis of a valid comparison with the present day, it is likely that the volume of crime which was a concomitant of poverty and destitution has considerably diminished. One may nevertheless draw comparisons between say the evidence given before the Select Committee on Criminal and Destitute Juveniles in 1852 and the Seventh Report of the work of the Childrens Department of the Home Office. On the other hand, it is impossible to deny that since 1938, indeed since 1930, there has been a disquieting rise in the volume of crime and persons prosecuted for indictable offences, and of juvenile crime in particular.

It is difficult to assess how much of this rise, especially in the wartime and post-war period represents a real rise in juvenile criminality and how far it is a result of a changing attitude towards prosecution on the part of both the police and the general public. It is a commonplace to hear the view expressed (among policemen and Probation Officers) that "in the old days" young Willie would have got a "clip round the ear" whereas now he is brought to the Juvenile Court. On the other hand, the peak of juvenile crime was reached somewhere in 1951, and the subsequent trend has been a downward one notwithstanding the persistence of the new attitude towards prosecution.

In 1949 the Ministry of Education and the Home Office sent a joint Memorandum to the Chairmen of County Councils, Lord Mayors and Mayors of County Boroughs in England and Wales on the subject of juvenile delinquency. In Croydon a year earlier the then Mayor had already taken the initiative in calling a meeting of all sections of the community to discuss this very problem. This meeting foreshadowed the Memorandum when the latter stated

'... Among what might be described as long term causes stand out unsatisfactory home conditions (bad and over-crowded housing, family conflicts, neglect, lack of affection and parental interest); the failure to recognise and treat early enough children who are of sub-normal intelligence or who develop unstable anti-social characters; and the widespread influence of changing moral standards. Another main cause ... is lack of opportunity for and encouragement or guidance in the proper use of leisure.'

In many ways the concept of cause is illusory, but necessary at a practical level if anything is to be done about treating crime, and, more important perhaps, preventing it. Our treatment measures tend to be haphazard, and are so infused with moral judgments about punishment and responsibility that it is difficult to assess their effectiveness on a completely practical plane. Preventive measures tend to be equally haphazard and although not so crude as those employed, for example, in vetinerary hygiene where to prevent foot and mouth disease everything associated with the outbreak is destroyed, the scarce resources of the community are not always as effectively deployed as they might be if we understood more about the dynamics of the problem.

The Memorandum suggested that meetings be called to discuss the problem and that these might be transformed into standing committees. It further posed a number of questions relating to the scope and efficiency of the existing preventive services which could provide a basis for inquiry and discussion. In Croydon, the Chief Probation Officer, the Chief School Inquiry Officer and the Children's Officer drew up a report which stated that although the local problem was far from serious in comparison with other urban areas, at the root of the problem were a hard core of

'... a few hundred ... families who are known to most of the social agencies for one reason or another. The distinguishing marks of these families are two-fold; firstly a bad marital relationship which produces emotionally insecure children who in turn grow up to be bad parents; secondly a low degree of intelligence which is handed on from generation to generation.'[1]

Waddon, Old Town, and Broad Green were noted as especially bad areas of delinquent concentration, and the Report feared that on the new estates there is a proportion of "third-rate quarrelling parents who are bringing up broods of potential delinquents". The authors made six recommendations:

1 The establishment of a Family Service Unit to supplement the work done by Health Visitors and the N.S.P.C.C.
2 The establishment of a residential school for ESN children.
3 The strengthening of the Home Help Service to keep children at home under supervision during the illness of hospitalisation of the mother.
4 The strengthening of voluntary agencies associated with the Guild of Social Service.
5 The development of Child Guidance to obviate delays in diagnosis and treatment, to be followed by more widespread publicity of the service available.
6 The establishment of a residential hostel for Child Guidance

The designation of an officer to act in a co-ordinating capacity between the various services, particularly in relation to children in unsatisfactory homes was suggested by the Memorandum, was rejected by the Croydon Report on the grounds that the Probation Service was already in a unique position to do this work. Following a further Joint Circular in July 1950, a committee was set up for dealing with children neglected in their own homes and this, it has been admitted, has resulted in a better service.

The 1949 Report made important recommendations, but by 1952 none of these had been acted upon. Indeed in 1952 as a consequence of the financial pressures felt by all local authorities in that year there was some drastic pruning of existing social welfare estimates in order to minimise the amount of the rate increase which could not be avoided. The Family Service Unit

[1] Report of the Probation Committee, County Borough of Croydon, 1949, Appendix.

and an additional ESN school were still pressing needs. In the case of ESN children, for example, of the 12 who appeared before the Juvenile Court in 1952, no fewer than 10 were in attendence at ordinary schools. As late as 1955 there was still no single agency concerned with family casework, the burden being shared by a number of voluntary agencies, the Children's Department and the Probation Service. An analysis of the work done by the Probation Service in 1952 shows that it was in fact as much a general social welfare bureau as a specialised service. In addition to the 542 Probation Cases supervised in that year there were 75 cases of After-Care Supervision of ex-Approbed School Cases, Borstal trainees and ex-prisoners, notwithstanding the fact of two Approved School Welfare Officers to share the work. The volume of kindred social work was even greater as the generalised summary shows.

TABLE 25

KINDRED SOCIAL WORK BY CROYDON PROBATION
SERVICE 1952

Voluntary supervision of children and advice regarding refractory children	136
Advice regarding custody of children, consent to marry, accommodation, employment, divorce and adoption enquiries	318
Financial Assistance	71
Home leave and Prison inquiries	77
Matters concerning family and neighbour disputes	169
Matrimonial conciliation	743
Total of cases of kindred social work	1514

Not all of this necessitated casework over a period of time, but it seems fairly evident none the less that the Probation Service, in Croydon at any rate, plays a role in the community which extends far beyond the confines of the Court. Morever its provision of help has been preceded by a need, a case of supply arising out of demand.

It is evident from the thinking that lies behind, that much official policy is pre-occupied with the problem of "psychiatric" delinquency; almost all the factors enumerated in the Circulars and the Croydon Report relate to its genesis. It has been emphasised perhaps because it represents the intractable core of the problem against which so much social effort appears fruitlessly to founder and at the expense of consideration of what we have called "social" delinquency. It has been our argument that "social" delinquency arises not so much out of emotional maladjustment but out of the cultural system which we have broadly designated as "working class". Indeed as Shaw, Mays, and several other writers have pointed out, there are social situations in which participation in the delinquent activities of the gang is indicative of social *adjustment*, for in one sense adjustment means little more than that the individual responds favourably to the majority of influences bearing upon him and accepts the normative structure of values and action which exists in the most important reference group of which he is a member.

To speak of the "widespread influence of changing moral standards" as a long term factor in delinquency is to misunderstand the nature of working class culture. It is implied that standards are being lowered and that the change is for the worse. This is an "old men's view" of the contemporary world, indeed social anthropologists have found that in primitive societies untouched by Western civilisation where changes are unlikely to have occurred for a thousand years or more, the old men still look backwards to the Golden Age which is forever in the past. It is a subjective point of view cherished frequently by those who have lost rather than gained in the social changes which have accompanied the redistribution of income in the last generation. If we look at facts rather than feelings, a case to the contrary may be made out. Drunkenness, one of the major social evils of the era before 1914, is but a shadow of its former self. Imprisonment for cruelty to children has halved since 1914, and although divorce is more common, the institution of marriage has never been more popular.

The changes in moral standards among the group from which the majority of delinquents and criminals come have been, if anything, directed towards the attainment of a middle class ideal as a result of the increasing possibility of upward social mobility. There has been no decline in the standards of those whom the American literature sometimes calls the "bottom of the heap". Their standards have been, from the viewpoint of a middle class society, uniformly low for generations. The opportunism, the egocentricity and rejection of authority which this cultural system perpetuates, give these families socio-pathic if not psycho-pathic characteristics. Poor control over the bladder, inability to budget expenditure, and spontaneous pilfering from the employer are all facets of the same culture.

Such standards have become more apparent in the last ten years because the rising tide of prosperity and income redistribution has lifted up all those who were able to benefit from it. Whereas it was formerly difficult to distinguish between say the long term unemployed and the unemployable, now the social problem group are prominent. On the housing estate the "unsatisfactory tenant" is often illuminated by the reflections from the material prosperity of his neighbours. Indeed, it is in attitudes towards property that some of the clearest cultural distinctions are apparent. In a middle class society property rights are sacrosanct and the flagrant violation of them, especially in industry, is seen as especially immoral. When it comes to the provision of social benefits in the Welfare State it may seem that this group is prepared to get as much as possible for as little effort. One may have moral views about this, but in sociological terms it is reasonable behaviour seen in the context of a particular sub-culture. It must be recognised that "social" delinquency presents an important problem.

Can any effective measures really be taken? Undoubtedly in respect of "psychiatric" delinquency much more can be done than at present. If mental hygiene had developed at the same rate as physical hygiene, mental illness and disorder would not be of their present proportions. Marital conflict and maladjusted children are problems with dimensions scarcely less than those of "work neuroses", peptic ulcers and other psychosomatic disorders. They are problems more widely distributed in the community than crime and delinquency.

The extension of the Child Guidance Service by itself is unlikely to do more than reduce waiting lists, for while it is one thing to provide a service it is another to get people to use it. Those most in need are frequently those least willing to accept help, or indeed to be able to recognise their own needs. The parents of disturbed children are invariably disturbed themselves, and without their willing co-operation treatment for the child must be severely limited. Although successful treatment of the disturbed child may reduce the risk of delinquency, the real problem frequently lies in the family itself. Family casework where it is needed ought therefore to augment the work done by the Child Guidance Clinic, and though those most in need of such assistance are the core of the social problem group, there are nevertheless many others that could be more stable and satisfactory in providing for the needs of their members. In the absence of a Family Casework Service the role of the Health Visitors might be extended providing both the training and professional status of the Health Visitor were improved, say to the standard of the Psychiatric Social Worker. At the same time the School Medical Service as a whole might be better integrated with the Child Guidance Service. It is sometimes a criticism that the periodic medical examinations of children at school are perfunctory, but at least they are an institution established by the usage of 50 years. There seems little reason why the examination could not be extended to include some form of psyciatric interview with the child and the mother in order to diagnose trouble as early as possible. Nervous disorders in children cannot be less important than flat feet or carious teeth.

But none of this can do very much about the problem of "social" delinquency, the outcome of attitudes and behaviour patterns transmitted from generation to generation at what sometimes seems to be an instinctual level. Here both the problem and the challenge are greater. It is undoubtedly true of man's life that control from *within* is immeasurably more effective in the long run than control from without. If a man can only be honest when someone is watching then the security of property is tenuous indeed. In fact it is one of the distinguishing features of civilised life that rules are obeyed and rights respected by habit, rather than the result of a process of deliberation on the "pros and cons" of individual situations.

The problem is how to bring about changes in a culture which tends to perpetuate what are essentially a-social tendencies in individuals. It is not a middle class value judgment but a fact, that the culture of the unskilled worker is negativistic in that it works against the formation of wholesome personalities and a satisfying way of life; the evidence of research into mental disorders and social class for example, indicates that the severest disorders are concentrated at the bottom of the occupational ladder.[1] The culture must be changed in such a way that the first line of defence against the development of anti-social behaviour is *within the family*, and the second *within the local community*. The

[1] Hollingshead and Redlich found schizophrenia, for example, 11 times more frequent in the lowest than the highest of their 5 social classes. "Social Stratification and Psychiatric Disorders", *American Sociological Review*, Vol. 18, No. 2, 1953. See also Edward Hare, "Mental Illness and Social Class in Bristol", *British Journal of Preventive Social Medicine*, Vol. 9, No. 4, 1955.

Chicago Area Project of Clifford Shaw attempted to do precisely this, through the mobilisation of the community's own indigenous resources. Area projects have been criticised on the grounds that they afford only temporary relief and that they require the active participation of outside workers, or alternatively that they consitute an unwarranted and patronising intrusion into the lives of those who should be free to determine their own lives.

There seems however, to be a close analogy between the persistence of a delinquent and a-social sub-culture on a housing estate, and the persistence of a pitiably low standard of living in a village of some under-developed area of the world. The team of experts who arrive from UNESCO find the people underfed and undernourished. Their homes are squalid and dirty because they have not thought of whitewash or windows or modifying their cooking stoves. Their system of agriculture results in overgrazing, poor cattle and poor crops. Their technology is at a primitive level and a system of land tenure entrenched in local custom perpetuates low productivity. Against innovation there is a deeply embedded prejucide which arises from an innate conservatism. Gradually these resistances can be overcome and the people can be shown that new methods can make their labours more fruitful and their lives less arduous. They can come to be a happier people with lives less overshadowed by the threat of famine and disease.

Similarly with our own social problem group, there is a need for re-education and a re-shaping of traditional values. The rigid division of labour and leisure between husband and wife tends to weaken the in fluence of the family as an agency of social control; ignorance of the wider implications of sexuality leads to marital tensions which could be avoided. In the local community itself there are on certain occasions indications that indigenous leadership can be effective in organising and mobilising activity for a common aim. Probably the most striking example of this occurred at the recent Coronation when house to house collections were made for street parties. In one particular instance known to the present writer street parties at the Coronation in 1953 and on VE Day in 1945 were organised by a man with a long prison record (which was admittedly behind him, though his son is at present serving Preventive Detention!). Much clearly depends upon the attractiveness of the cause, and it is one thing to stimulate enthusiasm for a street party and quite another to encourage people to try to prevent their children from getting into trouble by keeping stricter control over them. In any case the problems of organising a local community for a specific object, and bringing about fundamental changes in a way of life are radically different. It remains nevertheless, that given such changes there is still a leadership potential to be tapped.

The means of re-education must of necessity be diffuse and of a long term character. The schools have an important part to play and education for citizenship must include education for marriage and parenthood. Youth organisations tend to preach to the already nor near converted, and there remains much to be done in utilising the spontaneous youth group. Largely un-recognised by the Local Authority, it may nevertheless fulfill an important role in the lives of its members.[1] The gang can be a force for good as well as for destructiveness.

Crime and delinquency are indicative of a social malaise and whether there is a fall in the crime figures or whether a local problem is scarcely serious by national standards—as in the case of Croydon—there are no grounds for complacency. During the last war the campaign against Venereal Diseases was sufficiently energetic that there was scarcely an adolescent or adult in the population who in the end was unaware of the symptoms of gonorrhoea and syphillis. A corresponding awareness of the symptoms of pre-delinquency would be of immense value in the work of prevention. While the precise aetiology of delinquency and crime must vary with each individual case, the broad condi-tions which generate and stimulate them are well known. It is the final eradication of such conditions which can alone provide the only sure guarantee against the continued presence of anti-social behaviour which involves the community in expense which is not limited to the financial sphere.

As with all social programmes, the expenditure of money is involved. The hard reality of the situation is that in spite of the emergence of a Welfare State, as a nation we spend surprisingly little in some of the areas where the need is greatest. It is in the nature of things that social welfare cannot take precedence over other items of national expenditure; it is imperative therefore that the resources of the community be deployed as effectively as possible, yet there are aspects of our penal policy for example

[1] See Morris, T. P., "The New Addington Rhythm Club" in *Spontaneous Youth Groups,* ed. Kuenstler, London, 1955.

which can scarcely be justified on practical grounds. The short prison sentence is a case in point where the expenditure of social effort and resources is inordinate when assessed by the results. The real issue may well be not "what can be afforded and how can resources be spent?" but "what do we *wish* to afford and how do we wish our efforts to be spent?" The cost of the social waste which results from crime is spread very widely over the community, and it is easy to ignore it except in the headlines of the newspapers. But denial does not make the problem any less real.

INDEX

Greg, W. R., 52
Guerry, André Michel, 42, 44-52 *passim,* 55, 61, 71
Guerry de Champneuf, 44

HAECKEL, Ernst, 1
Hall-Williams, J. E., 108n
Hare, Edward, 164n, 196n
Hawaii, crime in, 92-94
Heady, J. A., 164n
Healey, William, 40n
Hill, Matthew Davenport, 56
Hodges, M., 188n
Hollingshead, A.B., 196n
Home Office, Joint Memoranda on Juvenile Delinquency,
    of 1949, 190
    of 1950, 192
Hooton, Earnest A., 41
House of Commons, Select Committee on Criminal and Destitute Juveniles, 1852, 57, 190
Hull House, *see* Chicago, Juvenile Court
Hurd, R.N., 8

INDIANAPOLIS, crime in, 94-95
Iowa, crime in, 96-97

JEBB, Col. Joshua, 62
Jephcott, Pearl, 104
Jevons, William S., 51
Jonassen, C.T., 88-91

KU KLUX KLAN, 97n
Kuper, Leo, 188n

LACASSAGNE, A., 65
Lander, Bernard, 24, 29, 97-100
Levin, Yale, 41
Lind, Andrew, 92-93
Lindesmith, Alfred, 41
Liverpool, crime in 21, 35, 53, 87n, 90n, 101, 102-105
    Juvenile liaison scheme, 35, 166
Lombroso, Cesare, 39, 41-42, 60, 64, 65
London, crime in, 19-23 *passim,* 53, 60-62, 63n
    development of, 16-18 *passim;*
    suicide in, 38

Lottier, Stuart, 95
Lowie, Robert, 3
Lupton, T., 188n
Lyon, 52

MALINOWSKI, Bronislaw, 3
Mannheim, Hermann, 34n, 63, 101, 107n
Marseilles, 49, 52
Mayhew, Henry, 19, 42-43, 60-63, 71
Mayo Smith, R., 51
Mays, John B., 87n, 90n, 102-105, 148n, 175
Mental illness, social class differentials in, 164n, 196
Merton, Robert K., 105n
Mill, John Stuart, 41, 44
Ministry of Education, Joint Memoranda on Juvenile Delinquency, *of 1949,* 190; *of 1950,* 192
Minneapolis and St. Paul, 96
Mitchell, G., 188n
Mogey, John, 188n
Montesquieu, (Albert de Secondat) Baron de, 51
Montgomery-Hyde, H., 108n
Montpellier, 49
Morris, J. N., 164n
Morris, T. P., 116n, 198n
Mortality, social class differences in, 164n

McIVER, Robert, 33
McKay, Henry D., 42, 68n, 71-84, 92
McKenzie, R. D., 3, 73n, 92; on ecological theory 6-9 *passim,* 13

NANTES, 49
National Commission on Law Observance and Enforcement, (The 'Wickersham Commission'), 71, 78
Natural areas, 9-10, 17, 23-25, 115
New York State Crime Commission-75, 87
Niceforo, A., 53

Nimes, 49

OMAHA, 80

201